PLATO'S
Apology of Socrates

PLATO'S
Apology of Socrates

AN INTERPRETATION, WITH
A NEW TRANSLATION

THOMAS G. WEST

CORNELL UNIVERSITY PRESS

ITHACA AND LONDON

Cornell University Press gratefully acknowledges a grant
from the Andrew W. Mellon Foundation that aided in
bringing this book to publication.

First published 1979 by Cornell University Press.
Published in the United Kingdom by Cornell University
Press Ltd., 2-4 Brook Street, London W1Y 1AA.

International Standard Book Number 0-8014-1127-0
Library of Congress Catalog Card Number 78-11532
Printed in the United States of America
*Librarians: Library of Congress cataloging information
appears on the last page of the book.*

184
W

TO HARRY V. JAFFA

1

Around the hero everything becomes a tragedy;
around the demigod, a satyr-play; and around
God everything becomes—what? perhaps a "world"?—

—Nietzsche,
Beyond Good and Evil

Contents

Preface

This book is a translation and interpretation of Plato's *Apology of Socrates*. Following the structure of the dialogue section by section, I discuss each part both by itself and as it contributes to the argument of the whole work. Wherever appropriate in the course of the commentary, the broader questions of Plato's political philosophy are also addressed. The translation, with its accompanying notes, has been included as an aid for the reader who does not know Greek. Currently available renditions of the *Apology* lack the requisite precision for a close scrutiny of the text. The notes to the translation elucidate the important Greek terms and identify the references that Socrates makes to Athenian political events and contemporary personages.

My reading of the *Apology of Socrates* relies principally upon the text itself. I have not entered into the question of what happened at the trial of the "historical" Socrates because that question is unanswerable and, I believe, not very important. What matters for us is Plato's portrayal of the event, for it is Plato's Socrates who has truly made history. The *Apology of Socrates* is above all a philosophic document. Writing with extreme care, Plato supplies us through his words alone with most of the information needed to understand the work. Its parts are bound to one another with the same rigorous necessity as are the parts of a living being. Every sentence, every word, seems endowed with significance in the elaborately fashioned whole. Hence an account of the *Apology*, as of any Platonic dialogue, resembles the exegesis of a finely crafted poem. To do justice to its depth and subtlety, the interpreter must discover and expound the articulation of the work's parts: he must bring forth its *logos*, the reasoned thought or plan that animates and bestows unity upon the whole. Such is the aim of the present commentary.

The *Apology of Socrates* is the most often read dialogue of Plato, and for good reason: it occupies a central position in the body of his works. Socrates' future trial and death are alluded to frequently in other dialogues, and the conflict between the philosopher and his city, here vividly dramatized, is an explicit subject of conversation in the *Republic,* the *Gorgias,* and elsewhere. The questions at stake in that conflict lead, as the *Apology* shows, to other major themes of Plato's writings: education, justice and punishment, politics and the laws, rhetorical and truthful speech, the nature of being, opinion and ignorance, self-knowledge, soul and body, virtue and vice, and the worth of the philosophic life. The *Apology of Socrates* affords an appropriate introduction to Platonic thought generally and is indispensable to anyone who wishes to understand the principles of classical political philosophy.

My chief complaint against the writings of contemporary scholars on the dialogue concerns their general assumption that Socrates was right and Athens wrong. This assumption can be traced to the faith inherited from the eighteenth century that science and thought are the highest authority for the conduct of life. Matters were different in the time before the popularization of philosophy. It was then observed that the deracinated human understanding is evidently better equipped to debunk ancestral customs than to instruct men in their proper duties. The case of Socrates, who openly proclaimed his ignorance of life's purpose, posed the problem with particular clarity. Accordingly, Plato's *Apology of Socrates* approaches philosophy less as a self-evident good than as something questionable that calls for justification.

 The structure and argument of the dialogue convey a comprehensive teaching about the nature of political life, particularly about who rules and who ought to rule. Socrates' implicit analysis reveals the hidden but potent hierarchy of governors and governed: the politicians elected by the people are themselves unknowing followers of those poets who have formed the opinions of the Athenians. Socrates' philosophic questioning, which disputes the canons that the city holds sacred, weakens the cohesion of the political order by undermining those opinions. In the course of his analysis Socrates tentatively proposes a means of resolving this tension between philosophy and politics: the philosopher, rather than the poet, must undertake the education of his political community. If successful, he would establish a fundament of shared beliefs sympathetic to philosophy upon which new political modes and orders could be constructed. Socrates' solution, however, cannot be executed so long as the philosopher has not transformed his love of wisdom into knowledge. For if the philosopher who "knows that he knows nothing" cannot answer the greatest questions—those concerning the best way of life for a human being—how could he responsibly educate others?

The drama of Socrates' trial and death illustrates this dilemma, in which the philosopher can neither accept the way of life prescribed by his tradition nor discover an unquestionable alternative to it. Socrates defies his jury, insisting that he will never stop philosophizing, no matter what they threaten him with or do to him. Although he appears to put himself forward boldly as the only man in Athens who knows how to educate the young, the same Socrates submits to the sentence decreed by that jury and proceeds calmly to his death. Plato's brilliant defense of philosophy in the *Apology* must not blind us to the necessity of the conflict between the claims of the philosophic life and the conditions of decent politics.

I wish to acknowledge the guidance and aid I have received from teachers, friends, and acquaintances. I am grateful above all to Leo Strauss, who first made me aware of the leading themes of the *Apology of Socrates* during a course he taught at Claremont in 1969. I regard Strauss as our century's best teacher of how to read the great authors of the Western tradition. His writings on classical political philosophy in particular provide a standard of excellence for the interpretation of the ancients.

I thank Harry V. Jaffa for his generous encouragement of my work. His thoughtful exposition of the great issues of philosophy and politics has been a valuable spur to my own understanding. I am grateful for the time I have spent with Harry Neumann, especially for his insistent questioning of the possibility and value of philosophy itself. I also thank Allan Bloom, who first gave me an inkling of the breadth and beauty of political philosophy.

John Alvis deserves particular gratitude for his careful, conscientious editorial and critical help with the book. The Press's two anonymous readers raised objections that were, I think, almost always right; I have adopted most of their recommendations, and I thank them for their comments. James M. Nichols, Thomas Silver, Ken Masugi, and Patrick Coby also read the manuscript, and each of them provided detailed remarks and suggestions that have been consulted throughout my revisions. Likewise, George Anastaplo proposed useful alterations in the translation and notes. I especially thank Father Placid Csizmazia and Thomas L. Pangle for the time they devoted to a critical comparison of the translation with the Greek text. My wife, Grace Starry West, helped extensively with the translation and the proofreading; she listened patiently and responded with sympathetic criticism while I was thinking out the argument of the book.

Finally, I express my appreciation to the Deutscher Akademischer Austauschdienst (German Academic Exchange Service) for a research grant, and particularly to the Earhart Foundation for the grant that supported my revision of the original manuscript and the preparation of the translation.

THOMAS G. WEST

University of Dallas

PART ONE

Apology of Socrates

TRANSLATION

Introduction to
the Translation

The Setting

In 399 B.C. Socrates was charged with the crimes of impiety against the gods of Athens and corruption of the young.[1] In the Athenian democracy of the time, prosecutions could be initiated by any citizen or group of citizens; there was no public prosecutor. Cases of Socrates' sort were tried in a law court before a jury of five hundred citizens, selected by lot. The jury members were called "judges." There was no presiding judge in the American or English sense, although there were officials to conduct the trial and to take care of documents.

A trial proceeded in two stages: determination of innocence or guilt, and determination of penalty in case of guilt. In the first stage the prosecutors or accusers (in this trial there were three) presented their arguments in separate speeches, after which the accused gave his defense speech (*apologia* in Greek). Socrates' defense speech, which makes up the bulk of the *Apology of Socrates*, concludes at 35d. The jury then voted on the defendant's innocence or guilt; Socrates was voted guilty by a small majority.[2]

1. See *Apology of Socrates* 24b–c and n. 59 for the text of the indictment. On Athenian trial procedure, see *Oxford Classical Dictionary*, s.v. *Dikasterion*. My page references to the *Apology* and other works of Plato are those of the edition of Stephanus, which are used today as standard pagination in most editions and translations of Plato's works.
2. See 36a–b and n. 106.

15

There was no fixed penalty in Athenian law for Socrates' crimes. In such cases each party had to propose a penalty for the jury to vote upon. Socrates' accuser proposed the death penalty. Socrates gives his counterproposal in the second speech of the *Apology* (35e–38b). The jury voted to condemn him to death.

While the trial officials were still busy with matters pertaining to the trial, Socrates had time to make a short third speech to the jurymen and bystanders, after which he was taken away to jail to await execution (38c–end).

The *Apology of Socrates* is far from a rote transcription of Socrates' courtroom speeches. Plato aspired to more than being a court reporter—even for a Socrates. The work is a "fabrication" (cf. 17c5) whose intention becomes fully apparent only through careful study. I have tried to explain the argument and intention of the *Apology* in the chapters that follow the translation.

Political Events in Athens before the Trial

For readers unfamiliar with the political situation in 399 B.C., it may be helpful to relate some of the events that preceded the trial. Athens and Sparta, the two leading cities of the Greek world, fought an exhausting twenty-seven-year-long war which ended with a decisive Athenian defeat in 404, five years before Socrates' trial. Late in the war, on the night before the Athenian naval expedition departed on its disastrous attempt to conquer Sicily, many of the statues of Hermes in Athens were mutilated. The popular reaction was intense. As the investigation of this incident proceeded, a further scandal was revealed, in which certain wealthy and educated men were said to have made mockery of the Mysteries, an old, sacred Athenian rite concerned with the worship of the gods of the earth. The people of Athens feared that these incidents portended a conspiracy against the democracy and evil for the Sicilian expedition. Among those implicated in the profanation was Alcibiades, a brilliant young man who was a former associate of Socrates. Alcibiades departed for Sicily as one of the commanders who had been chosen by the Athenians for their expedition. As soon as he left Athens, his political enemies arranged for him to be tried *in absentia* for impiety, whereupon he was sentenced to death. Alcibiades fled to Sparta, where he successfully aided the Spartans in their war efforts against Athens. He was permitted to return to Athens for a short period later in the war, after he had changed sides again and won some naval victories for the Athenians. Soon thereafter, however, suspected of antidemocratic intrigue, he was exiled for the last time.[3]

After Athens' defeat in 404, the Spartans installed an oligarchy in Athens, afterwards called by some the "Thirty Tyrants." One of the most violent of the oligarchs was Critias, another former associate of Socrates. Also involved in this government was Charmides, an uncle of Plato; he too was a former associate of Socrates. The Thirty executed many supporters of the democracy. As they grew stronger, they also began to arrest and execute the wealthier citizens and foreign residents, in order to confiscate their wealth and to make their government more secure. Many of the citizens sympathetic to the democracy left Athens and went into exile. Led by Anytus (later one of Socrates' accusers) and others, the exiles overthrew the oligarchy after it had ruled less than one year. This was in 403. Only in 401—two years before Socrates' trial—did the partisans of the democracy finally overcome and kill the oligarchs themselves, who had withdrawn to a small town outside Athens. The democrats declared an amnesty for those implicated in the deeds of the Thirty; although there were abuses, Plato says the democrats acted with "much decency" toward their former enemies.[4]

Athens' humiliating defeat by Sparta, and the fierce civil strife between the democratic and oligarchic parties, were the turbulent events preceding the prosecution of Socrates on a charge of impiety and corruption of the young. While one should resist the temptation to interpret Socrates' trial solely in light of these political events, their importance for the trial cannot be denied. Socrates himself mentions the exile of the democrats and the reign of the Thirty in his defense speech (21a, 32c–d), and he

3. Thucydides VI–VIII, esp. VI.17–29, 53, 60–61; Xenophon *Hellenica* I–II.2; Andocides *On the Mysteries.*

4. Xenophon *Hellenica* II.3–4; Aristotle *Athenian Constitution* 34–40; Lysias *Against Eratosthenes, Against Agoratus* 78; Isocrates *Against Callimachus* 23; Plato *Seventh Letter* 324b–325c.

alludes to "those who my slanderers declare to be my students," Critias and Alcibiades (33a).

Socrates was the first native Athenian philosopher to be tried for impiety, although there had been previous indictments directed against foreign philosophers in Athens. During his defense speech, Socrates alludes to the accusation of Anaxagoras (see 26d and note 67), which occurred over thirty years earlier. More recent was the indictment of Diagoras of Melos, a notoriously atheistic philosopher or poet, about 415 B.C. He fled Athens to avoid the penalty.[5]

The Translation

I have translated the *Apology of Socrates* into English with a view to the reader who wishes to understand the work as much as is possible without knowing Greek. The translations currently available are too loose to permit a close study of the text. On first reading the translation may seem somewhat strange in tone, and occasionally awkward. The simplicity and vigor of Socrates' (or Plato's) language reveals itself best when the style of the rendition is not compelled to conform to the narrow conventions of modern scholarly prose. This "standard style," with its smooth flow of ordinary words and phrases, reduces the uncommon, lively idiom of an outstanding thinker to the common, homogeneous diction of the scholar. The reader may thereby easily be lulled into a false complacency toward the work. Such a soft style easily tempts the reader to skim quickly over the surface, without paying much attention to detail. Yet one who wishes to understand must think carefully about every step in Socrates' argument in order to grasp the purpose of the work. The reader must dwell on the words themselves, and not merely yield to the impressions conveyed by a cursory reading.

A perfectly "literal" translation from the Greek is impossible. The Greek words have depths of significance whose resonances cannot often be caught with lexicon equivalents. Moreover, an

5. Aristophanes *Birds* 1072; *Clouds* 830; [Lysias] *Against Andocides* 17; Diodorus Siculus XIII.6. An exhaustive historical treatment of impiety trials at Athens is given by Eudore Derenne, *Les procès d'impiété intentés aux philosophes à Athènes* (1930; repr. New York, 1976).

author of Plato's stature frequently uses traditional terms in novel ways. If the translator tries to capture the particular shade of meaning intended on each occasion a given word appears, the reader remains ignorant that the word recurs at all. But if the word is rendered by a consistent English expression, distortions and awkwardness invariably mar the translation. In the reading of Plato it is essential that repetitions of important terms be noted, because the arguments and plots of the dialogues are conveyed in large measure through the intentionally shifting meanings of these terms. My inelegant and incomplete (but I think helpful) solution has been to use, wherever possible, consistent translations of the important words and phrases supplemented by explanatory notes.

A second, more serious obstacle poses greater difficulties which even a thorough acquaintance with the Greek language might not be able to overcome. A philosophic and linguistic tradition over two thousand years old has changed our habitual way of speaking and thinking. A literal translation from Greek into any modern language, no matter how accurate, can conceal as much as it reveals. The work of Martin Heidegger has shown how hard it is, yet how indispensable, to recover the prephilosophic sense of Greek as exhibited in the outstanding poets and thinkers. A few of my notes refer to Heidegger's thoughts on some of the expressions found in the *Apology*.

I have been helped, in making the translation, by the examples of Allan Bloom's translation of Plato's *Republic*[6] and of Carnes Lord's translation of Xenophon's *Oeconomicus*,[7] as well as by some suggestions of Leo Strauss.[8]

The Text

I have used John Burnet's Greek text,[9] except for a few instances where I have retained the manuscript readings against

6. *The Republic of Plato* (New York, 1968).
7. In Leo Strauss, *Xenophon's Socratic Discourse* (Ithaca, N.Y., 1970).
8. "On Plato's *Apology of Socrates* and *Crito*," in *Essays in Honor of Jacob Klein* (Annapolis, Md., 1976), pp. 155–170.
9. In Plato, *Opera Omnia*, I (Oxford, 1900), by permission of the Oxford University Press. This text of the *Apology* is reprinted in John Burnet's annotated edition of *Plato's Euthyphro, Apology of Socrates, and Crito* (Oxford, 1924).

Burnet's emendations. The two occasions where my reading makes a significant difference are noted (nn. 54 and 87). I have introduced the paragraph divisions in the translation according to my own understanding of the structure of the work. (The Appendix contains my analytical outline of the dialogue.) There were no such divisions in the original Greek text, as far as we know. I have also added the quotation marks, the names indicating the speakers during the interrogation of Meletus (24d–28a), and the brief explanatory remarks at the end of Socrates' first and second speeches (35d and 38b). Long sentences have sometimes been broken up for the sake of clarity.

Translation

How you, men of Athens, have been affected by my accusers, 17a
I do not know. For my part, I nearly forgot myself because of
them, so persuasively did they speak. And yet they have said,
so to speak, nothing true. I was most amazed by one of the
many falsehoods they told, when they said that you should
beware that you are not deceived by me, since I am a clever[1]
speaker. They are not ashamed that they will immediately be b
refuted by me in deed, as soon as it becomes apparent that I am
not a clever speaker at all; this seemed[2] to me to be most shameless of them, unless perhaps they call a clever speaker the one
who speaks the truth. If this is what they are saying, then I too
would agree that I am an orator—but not of their sort. These
men, then, as I say, have said little or nothing true, while from
me you will hear the whole truth—but by Zeus, men of Athens,
not beautifully spoken speeches[3] like theirs, ordered and
adorned[4] with phrases and words; rather, what you hear will be c
spoken at random[5] in the words that I happen upon—for I trust
that the things I say are just—and let none of you expect otherwise. For surely it would not be becoming, men, for someone
of my age to come before you fabricating[6] speeches like a youth.
And, men of Athens, I do beg and beseech this of you: if you
hear me speaking in my defense[7] with the same speeches I am
accustomed to speak both in the market at the money-tables,[8]
where many of you have heard me, and elsewhere, do not be
amazed nor make a disturbance[9] because of this. For this is how d

17d   it is: now is the first time I have come before a law court, at the age of seventy; hence I am simply[10] foreign to the manner of speech here. So just as, if I really[11] did happen to be a foreigner, you would surely sympathize with me if I spoke in that dialect[12]

18a   and way in which I was raised, so I do beg this of you now (and it is just, as it seems to me): disregard the manner of my speech—for perhaps it may be worse, but perhaps better—and instead consider this very thing and apply your mind to this: whether the things I say are just or not. For this is the virtue[13] of a judge, while that of an orator is to speak the truth.

    So first, men of Athens, it is just for me to speak in defense against the first false charges against me and the first accusers, and afterwards against the later charges and the later accusers.

b   For many have accused me to you, many years ago now, saying nothing true; and I fear them more than Anytus[14] and those with him, although they too are dangerous. But the others are more dangerous, men. They got hold of many of you from childhood, and they accused me and persuaded you—although it is no more true than the present charge—that there is a certain Socrates, a wise man,[15] a thinker[16] on the things aloft, who has investigated all things under the earth, and who makes the

c   weaker speech the stronger.[17] Those, men of Athens, who have scattered this report about, are my dangerous accusers. For their listeners hold that investigators of these things also do not believe in[18] gods. Besides, there are many of these accusers, and they have been accusing for a long time now. Moreover, they spoke to you at that age when you were most trusting, when some of you were children and youths, and they accused me in a case which simply went by default, for no one spoke in my defense. And the most unreasonable thing of all is that it is not

d   even possible to know and to say their names, unless one of them happens to be a comic poet.[19] Those who persuaded you by using envy and slander[20]—and those who persuaded others, after being convinced themselves—all of these are most difficult to get at. For it is also not possible to have any one of them come forward here and to refute him, but it is a necessity for me simply to speak in my defense as though fighting with shadows and refuting with no one to answer. So you, too, must deem it to be as I say: that there have been two groups of accusers, the

22

ones accusing me now, and the others long ago of whom I 18e
speak; and you must also suppose that I should first speak in
defense against the latter, for you heard them accusing me earlier and much more than these later ones here.

Well, then. A defense speech must be made, men of Athens,
and an attempt must be made in this short time to take away 19a
your prejudice, which you got during a long time. I would wish
it to turn out like this, if it were in any way better both for you
and for me, and I would rather wish to accomplish something
through my defense speech. But I suppose this is difficult, and I
am not at all unaware of what sort of thing it is. Nevertheless, let
this proceed in whatever way is dear to the god, but the law
must be obeyed and a defense speech must be made.

So let us take up from the beginning what the accusation is,
from which has arisen the slander against me—which, in fact, is b
what Meletus[21] trusted in when he wrote this indictment against
me. Well, then. What did the slanderers say to slander me?
Their sworn statement, just as though they were accusers, must
be read: "Socrates does injustice[22] and is meddlesome, by investigating the things under the earth and the heavenly things, and
by making the weaker speech the stronger, and by teaching
others these same things." It is something like this. For you c
yourselves also saw these things in the comedy of Aristophanes:
a certain Socrates was borne about there, asserting that he was
treading on air, and spouting much other drivel about which I
comprehend nothing, either much or little.[23] And I do not say
this to dishonor this sort of understanding,[24] if anyone is wise in
such things (may I never be prosecuted with such indictments[25]
by Meletus!); but I, men of Athens, have no share in these matters. Again, I offer the many[26] of you as witnesses, and I main- d
tain that you should teach and tell each other, as many of you as
have ever heard me conversing—and there are many such
among you—tell each other, then, if any of you ever heard me
conversing about such things, either much or little, and from
this you will know that the same holds for the other things
which the many say about me.

But in fact none of these things is so; and if you have heard
from anyone that I try to educate human beings[27] and that I
charge money for it, that is not true either. Although this also e

19e seems to me to be noble,[28] if one is able to educate human beings, like Gorgias of Leontini, and Prodicus of Ceos, and Hippias of Elis.[29] For each of them, men, is able to go into each of the cities and persuade the young—who can associate with whomever of their own citizens they wish for free—they per-
20a suade these young men to leave off associating with the latter, and to associate with themselves instead, and to give them money and owe them thanks besides.

And for that matter, there is another man here, from Paros, a wise man, who I heard was in town; for I happened to go to a man who has paid more money to sophists than all the others, Callias, the son of Hipponicus.[30] So I questioned him (for he has two sons):

"Callias," I said, "If your two sons had been born colts or calves, we would have been able to get and pay a master for
b them who could make the two of them noble and good[31] in their appropriate virtue, and this man would have been from among those either skilled with horses or skilled in farming. But now, since they are two human beings, whom do you have in mind to get as a master[32] for the two of them? Who understands such virtue, that of human being and citizen? For I suppose you have considered it, since you possess sons. Is there someone," I said, "or not?"

"Certainly," he said.

"Who," I said, "and where is he from, and for how much does he teach?"

"Evenus," he said, "Socrates, from Paros: five minae."[33]

And I looked on Evenus as blessed if he should truly have this
c art[34] and teaches at such a modest rate. As for myself, I would plume[35] and pride myself on it, if I understood these things. But I do not understand them, men of Athens.

Perhaps, then, one of you might retort, "But, Socrates, what is it that you do?[36] Where have these slanders against you come from? For surely if you were practicing nothing more uncommon than others, such a report and account would not have arisen, unless you were doing something different from the
d many. Tell us what it is, then, so that we do not deal rashly with you."

In this, it seems to me, what the speaker says is just, and I will

24

try to demonstrate to you what it is that has brought me this 20d
name[37] and slander. So listen. And perhaps I will seem to some
of you to be joking. Know well, however, that I will tell you the
whole truth. For I, men of Athens, have gotten this name
through nothing but a certain wisdom. What sort of wisdom,
then, is this? Just what is perhaps human wisdom; for I am
really likely to be wise in this. But those of whom I just spoke
might perhaps be wise in some wisdom greater than human, or e
else I cannot say what it is. For I, at least, do not understand it,
but whoever declares that I do lies and speaks in order to slander me.

Do not, men of Athens, make a disturbance against me, not
even if I seem to you somehow to boast. For not mine is the
story that I will tell,[38] but I will refer it to a speaker trustworthy
to you. Of my wisdom, if indeed it is anything, and what sort of
thing it is, I will offer for you as witness the god in Delphi. Now
you know Chaerephon,[39] no doubt. He was my comrade from
youth as well as a comrade of your multitude, and he shared in 21a
the recent exile[40] and returned with you. You do know what sort
of man Chaerephon was, how vehement he was in whatever he
would set out to do. Once he even went to Delphi and dared to
consult the oracle about this—as I say, do not make a disturbance, men—he asked whether there is anyone wiser than I.
The Pythia[41] replied that no one is wiser. Of these things his
brother here will be a witness for you, since he himself has died.

Now consider why I say these things; for I am going to teach b
you where the slander against me has come from. When I heard
these things, I pondered them like this: "What ever is the god
saying, and what riddle is he uttering? For I am aware that I am
not at all wise, either much or little. So what is he saying when
he asserts that I am wisest? Surely he is not saying something
false; for that is not lawful[42] for him." And for a long time I was
at a loss about what ever he was saying, but then very reluctantly I turned to something like the following investigation of
it.

I went to one of those reputed[43] to be wise, supposing that
there, if anywhere, I would refute the divination[44] and show the c
oracle, "This man is wiser than I, but you declared that I was."
So I considered this man thoroughly—I need not speak of him

21c by name, but he was one of the politicians⁴⁵—and when I considered him and conversed with him, men of Athens, I was affected something like this: it seemed to me that this man seemed to be wise, both to many other human beings and most of all to himself, but that he was not. And then I tried to show him that he supposed he was wise, but was not. So from this I

d became hateful both to him and to many of those present.

At any rate, as I went away, I reckoned with myself: "I am wiser than this human being. For neither of us is likely to know anything noble and good, but he supposes he knows something when he does not know, while I, just as I do not know, do not suppose I do. I *am* likely to be wiser than he in just this little something: that what I do not know, I do not suppose I know."

From there I went to someone else, one of those reputed to be

e wiser than that man, and these things seemed to me to be the same. And there I became hateful both to that man and to many others.

After this, then, I kept going to one after another, all the while perceiving with pain and fear that I was becoming hateful. Nevertheless, it seemed to be necessary to regard the matter of the god as most important. So I had to go, in seeking what the oracle was saying, to all those reputed to know something. And

22a by the dog,⁴⁶ men of Athens—for it is necessary to speak the truth before you—I was affected something like this: those with the best reputations seemed to me nearly the most deficient, in my investigation in accordance with the god, while others with more paltry reputations seemed to be men more fit in regard to prudence.⁴⁷

Indeed, I must display to you how I wandered, as if performing certain labors,⁴⁸ so that the divination would become irrefutable for me. After the politicians I went to the poets of tragedies and dithyrambs, and the others, so that there I would catch

b myself in the act of being more ignorant than they. So I would take up those poems of theirs which it seemed to me they had worked on the most, and I would ask them thoroughly what they meant,⁴⁹ so that I might also learn something from them at the same time. I am ashamed to tell you the truth, men; nevertheless, it must be said. Almost all of those present, so to speak, would have spoken better than they did, about the poetry which

26

they themselves had made. So again, also concerning the poets, 22b
I quickly recognized that they did not make[50] what they made
by wisdom, but by a certain nature[51] and while inspired,[52] like c
the diviners and those who deliver oracles. For they also speak
many beautiful things, but they know nothing of what they
speak. It was apparent to me that the poets are also affected in
the same sort of way. At the same time, I perceived that they
supposed, on account of their poetry, that they were the wisest
of human beings also in the other things, in which they were
not. So I went away from there too supposing that I excelled
them in the very same thing in which I did the politicians.

Finally, then, I went to the manual artisans. For I was aware
that I understood nothing, so to speak, but I knew that I would d
discover that they understood many beautiful things. And I was
not wrong about this: they did understand things which I did
not understand, and in this way they were wiser than I. But,
men of Athens, the good craftsmen also seemed to me to make
the same mistake as the poets: because he performed his art
beautifully, each one deemed himself wisest also in the other
things, the greatest things—and this mistake of theirs seemed to
hide that wisdom. So I questioned myself on behalf of the ora- e
cle, whether I would prefer to be as I am, being in no way wise
in their wisdom nor ignorant in their ignorance, or to have both
things which they have. I answered myself and the oracle that it
profits me to remain just as I am.

Out of this examination, men of Athens, many hatreds have
arisen against me, and the kind which are harshest and gravest; 23a
as a result, many slanders have arisen from them, and I got this
name of being "wise." For those present on each occasion suppose that I myself am wise in the things about which I refute
someone else. But it is likely, men, that really the god is wise,
and that in this oracle he is saying that human wisdom is worth
little or nothing. And he appears to say this of Socrates, and to
use my name, in order to make me an example, as if he would b
say, "That one of you, O human beings, is wisest, who, like
Socrates, knows that in truth he is worth nothing with respect to
wisdom."

So even now I still go around seeking these things and investigating in accordance with the god whomever among the

27

23b townsmen and foreigners I suppose to be wise. And whenever someone does not seem so to me, I come to the god's aid and show that he is not wise. And because of this occupation, I have had no leisure worth speaking of, either to do any of the things of the city or any of my own things.[53] Instead, I am in ten-

c thousandfold poverty because of my service to the god.

In addition to these things, the young who follow me of their own accord—those who have the most leisure, the sons of the wealthiest—enjoy hearing human beings examined. And they themselves often imitate me, and in turn they try to examine others. And then, I suppose, they discover a great abundance of human beings who suppose they know something, but know little or nothing. Thereupon, those examined by them are angry

d at me, not at themselves, and they say that Socrates is someone most disgusting and that he corrupts the young. And whenever someone asks them, "By doing what and teaching what?" they have nothing to say, but are ignorant. So in order not to seem to be at a loss, they say the things that are ready at hand against all who philosophize: "the things aloft and under the earth" and "not believing in gods" and "making the weaker speech the stronger." For I do not suppose they would be willing to speak the truth, that it becomes manifest that they pretend to know, but know nothing. So since they are, I suppose, ambitious and

e vehement and many, and since they speak about me in a well-ordered[54] and persuasive way, they have beaten it into your ears, slandering me vehemently for a long time.

From among these men,[55] Meletus attacked me, and Anytus and Lycon.[56] Meletus being vexed on behalf of the poets, Anytus on behalf of the craftsmen and the politicians, and

24a Lycon on behalf of the orators. Therefore, as I said when I began, I would be amazed if I should be able to remove this prejudice of yours in such a short time, now that it has become so great. This is the truth for you, men of Athens; I am hiding nothing from you either great or small in my speech, nor am I holding anything back. And yet I all but know that I incur hatred by these very things; which is also a proof that I speak the truth, and that this is the prejudice against me, and that these are its

b causes. Whether you investigate these things now or later, you will discover that this is so.

So about the things which the first accusers accused me of, let   24b
this be a sufficient defense speech before you. But against
Meletus, the "good and patriotic,"[57] as he asserts, and the later
accusers, I will try to speak next in my defense. Now again, just
as though these are other accusers, let us take up their sworn
statement. It is something like this: it asserts that Socrates does
injustice by corrupting the young, and by not believing in the
gods in whom the city believes, but in other *daimonia*[58] that are   c
new. The charge is of this sort.[59] But let us examine each part of
this charge.

Now he asserts that I do injustice by corrupting the young.
But I, men of Athens, assert that Meletus does injustice, because
he jests in a serious matter, easily bringing human beings to
trial, pretending to be serious and concerned about things for
which he never cared[60] at all. That this is so, I will try to display
to you as well.

Now come here, Meletus, tell me: do you not regard it as a
matter of the highest importance, how the youth will be the best   d
possible?

[MELETUS]   I do.

[SOCRATES]   Then come now and tell these men: Who makes
them better? It is clear that you know, since you care, at least.
For since you have discovered the one who corrupts them, as
you assert, you are bringing me before these men and accusing
me. But come, tell them and inform them who it is who makes
them better.

Do you see, Meletus, that you are silent and have nothing to
say? And yet does it not seem shameful to you, and a sufficient
proof of what I say, that you have never cared? But say, my
good man, who makes them better?

[MELETUS]   The laws.

[SOCRATES]   But I am not asking this, best of men, but what   e
human being is it who knows first of all this very thing, the
laws?

[MELETUS]   These men, Socrates, the judges.

[SOCRATES]   What are you saying, Meletus? Are these men
here able to educate the young, and do they make them better?

[MELETUS]   Very much so.

[SOCRATES]   All of them, or some of them, and some not?

24e [MELETUS] All of them.

[SOCRATES] Well said, by Hera,[61] for you speak of a great abundance of helpers. What, then? Does the audience[62] here
25a make them better or not?

[MELETUS] These too.

[SOCRATES] And what about the Councilmen?[63]

[MELETUS] The Councilmen too.

[SOCRATES] But then, Meletus, surely those in the Assembly,[64] the Assemblymen, do not corrupt the youth? Or do all those too make them better?

[MELETUS] Those too.

[SOCRATES] Then all the Athenians, as it appears, make them noble and good except me, and I alone corrupt them. Is this what you are saying?

[MELETUS] I do say these things, most vehemently.

[SOCRATES] You have charged me with much misfortune. Now answer me. Does it seem to you to be so also concerning
b horses? Do all human beings make them better, while a certain one is the corrupter? Or is it wholly opposite to this, that a certain one is able to make them better—or very few, those skilled with horses—while the many, if they ever associate with horses and use them, corrupt them? Is this not so, Meletus, both concerning horses, and all the other animals?

Of course it is, in every way, whether you and Anytus deny or affirm it. For it would be a great happiness for the young if one alone corrupts them, while the others help them. But in fact,
c Meletus, you have sufficiently displayed that you never thought about the young. And your own lack of care is clearly apparent, in that you have cared nothing about the things for which you bring me in here.

But tell us next, Meletus, before Zeus, whether it is better to dwell among upright citizens or villainous ones?

Sir, answer. For surely I am asking nothing hard. Do not the villainous do something bad to whoever are nearest to them, while the good do something good?

[MELETUS] Certainly.

d [SOCRATES] Is there anyone, then, who wishes to be harmed by those he associates with, rather than to be helped?

Answer, my good man. For the law orders you to answer. Is   25d
there anyone who wishes to be harmed?

[MELETUS]   Of course not.

[SOCRATES]   Come then, do you bring me in here saying that I
voluntarily corrupt the young and make them more villainous,
or involuntarily?

[MELETUS]   Voluntarily, I say.

[SOCRATES]   What then, Meletus? Are you so much wiser at
your age than I at mine, that you know that the bad always do
something bad to those who are closest to them, and the good
do something good; whereas I have come into so much igno-   e
rance, that I do not even know that if I ever do something
wretched to one of my associates, I will risk getting back something bad from him? So that I do so much bad voluntarily, as
you assert? Of this I am not convinced by you, Meletus, nor, do I
suppose, is any other human being. But either I do not corrupt,
or if I do corrupt, I do it involuntarily, so in both cases what you   26a
say is false.

And if I corrupt involuntarily, the law is not that you bring me
in here for such involuntary mistakes, but that you take me
aside in private to teach and admonish me. For it is clear that if I
learn, I will stop doing what I do involuntarily. But you avoided
associating with me and teaching me, and you were not willing
to, but instead you brought me in here, where the law is to bring
in those in need of punishment, not learning.

But in fact, men of Athens, what I said is already clear, that
Meletus never cared about these things either much or little.   b
Nevertheless, speak to us, how do you assert that I corrupt the
youth, Meletus? Or is it clear, according to the indictment that
you wrote, that it is by teaching them not to believe in the gods
in whom the city believes, but in other *daimonia* that are new?
Do you not say that it is by teaching this that I corrupt them?

[MELETUS]   I certainly do say this, most vehemently.

[SOCRATES]   Then before these very gods, Meletus, about
whom our speech now is, speak to me and to these men yet
more clearly. For I am not able to understand[65] you: are you   c
saying that I teach them to believe that there are some gods—
and I myself, then, believe that there are gods, and I am not

26c completely godless, nor do I do injustice in this way—although I
do not believe in those in whom the city believes, but in others,
and this is what you charge me with, that I believe in others? Or
do you assert that I myself do not believe in gods at all, and that
I teach this to others?

[MELETUS] This is what I say, that you do not believe in gods
at all.

d [SOCRATES] Meletus, you amazing man, why do you say this?
Do I not even believe, then, that sun and moon are gods, as
other human beings do?

[MELETUS] No, by Zeus, judges,[66] since he declares that the
sun is stone and the moon is earth.

[SOCRATES] Do you suppose you are accusing Anaxagoras,[67]
my dear Meletus? And do you so much despise these men here
and suppose that they are so inexperienced in letters, that they
do not know that the books of Anaxagoras of Clazomenae are
full of these speeches? Moreover, do the young learn these
things from me, when it is sometimes possible for them to buy

e them in the orchestra for a drachma,[68] if the price is high, and to
laugh at Socrates if he pretends that they are his own, especially
since they are so strange? But before Zeus, is this how I seem to
you? Do I believe there is no god?

[MELETUS] You certainly do not, by Zeus, not in any way at
all.

[SOCRATES] You are unbelievable, Meletus, even, as you seem
to me, to yourself. This man seems to me, men of Athens, to be
very insolent and unrestrained, and simply to have written this
indictment with a certain insolence[69] and unrestraint and youth-

27a ful rashness. He is just like someone putting together a riddle
and testing me: "Will Socrates the 'wise' recognize that I am
joking and contradicting myself, or will I deceive him and the
rest of the listeners?" For this man appears to me to be contradicting himself in the indictment, as if he were saying, "Socrates does injustice by not believing in gods, but believing in
gods." And yet this is playfulness.

Now consider with me, men, how he appears to me to say
this. And you answer us, Meletus. But you others, as I begged

b of you from the beginning, remember not to make a disturbance
against me if I make the speeches in my accustomed way.

32

Is there any human being, Meletus, who believes that there ⟨ 27b are human matters,[70] but does not believe in human beings? ⟩

Let him answer, men, and let him not keep on making disturbances one after another. Is there anyone who does not believe
in horses, but believes in horse-matters? Or anyone who does
not believe in flute-players, but believes in flute-matters?

There is not, best of men. If you do not wish to answer, I say it
for you and for these others. But at least answer what comes
next. Is there anyone who believes that there are daimonic mat- c
ters, but does not believe in daimons?

[MELETUS] There is not.

[SOCRATES] How you gratify me by answering reluctantly
when compelled by these men! Now then, you assert that I
believe in and teach *daimonia*; and whether they are new or
ancient, at any rate I do believe in *daimonia* according to your
speech, and you also swore to this in the indictment. But if I
believe in *daimonia*, then surely there is also a great necessity
that I believe in daimons. Is this not so?

Of course it is. I set you down as agreeing, since you do not
answer. And do we not believe that daimons are either gods or d
children of gods? Do you affirm this or not?

[MELETUS] Certainly.

[SOCRATES] Therefore if I believe in daimons, as you assert,
and if, on the one hand, daimons are certain gods, then this
would be what I assert that you are riddling and joking about,
when you assert that I do not believe in gods, and again that I
believe in gods, since I do believe in daimons.

On the other hand, if daimons are certain bastard children
of gods, whether from nymphs or from certain others of whom
it is also said they are born,[71] then what human being would
believe that there are children of gods, but not gods? It would
be just as strange if someone believed in children of horses e
or asses—mules—but did not believe that there are horses
and asses.[72] But, Meletus, there is no way that you did not
write this indictment either to test us in these things, or else
because you were at a loss about what true injustice you might
charge me with. There is no device by which you could persuade any human being who is even slightly intelligent, that
the same man believes in both *daimonia* and divine things,

27e
28a but that this same man believes in neither daimons nor gods nor heroes.[73]

But in fact, men of Athens, that I do not do injustice according to Meletus' indictment, does not seem to me to need much of a defense speech, but even these things are sufficient. What I also said earlier—that much hatred has arisen, and among many men—know well that this is true. And this is what will convict me, if it does convict me: not Meletus or Anytus, but the prejudice and envy of the many. This has convicted many others, and b good men too, and I suppose it will also convict me. And there is no danger that it will stop with me.

Perhaps, then, someone might say, "Then are you not ashamed, Socrates, of having followed the sort of pursuit from which you now run the risk of dying?"

I would respond to him with a just speech:[74] "What you say is not noble, you human being,[75] if you suppose that a man who is of even slight worth should take into account the danger of living or dying, but not rather consider this alone whenever he acts: whether his actions are just or unjust, and the deeds of a c good man or a bad. For according to your speech, those of the demigods who died at Troy would be paltry, both the others and the son of Thetis.[76] Rather than endure anything shameful, he despised danger so much, that when his mother (a goddess) spoke to him as he was eager[77] to kill Hector, it was something like this, as I suppose: 'Son, if you avenge the murder of your comrade Patroclus and kill Hector, you yourself will die; for directly,' she declares, 'after Hector, your fate is ready at hand.' But when he heard this, he belittled death and danger, for he d feared much more to live as a bad man and not to avenge his friends. 'Directly,' he declares, 'may I die, after I inflict a penalty[78] on the one doing injustice, so that I do not remain here ridiculous beside the curved ships, a burden on the land.' Surely you do not suppose that he thought about death and danger?"[79]

This is the way it is, men of Athens, in truth. Wherever someone stations himself, holding that it is best, or wherever he is stationed by a ruler,[80] there he must remain and run the risk, as it seems to me, and not take into account death or anything else before what is shameful. So I would have done terrible e deeds, men of Athens, if, when the rulers whom you chose to

34

rule me stationed me in Potideia and Amphipolis and at De- lium,[81] I remained where they stationed me and ran the risk of dying like anyone else, but when the god stationed me, as I supposed and assumed, ordering me to live philosophizing and examining myself and others, I had left my station because I feared death or anything else whatever.

That would be terrible, and truly then someone might justly bring me into a law court; then he might say that I do not believe in gods, since I would be disobeying the divination, and fearing death, and supposing that I am wise when I am not. For to fear death, men, is nothing other than to seem to be wise, but not to be so. For it is to seem to know what one does not know: no one knows whether death does not happen to be the greatest of all goods for the human being; but they fear it[82] as though they knew well that it is the greatest of evils. How is this not that reproachable ignorance of supposing that one knows what one does not know? But, men, perhaps I am distinguished from the many human beings also here in this, and if I were to declare myself wiser than anyone in anything, it would be in this: that since I do not know sufficiently about the things in Hades,[83] so also I do not suppose I know. But I do know that it is bad and shameful to do injustice and to disobey one's better, whether god or human being. So rather than do the bad things which I know are bad, I will never fear nor flee the things about which I do not know whether they happen to be good.[84]

So if you let me go now, and if you disobey Anytus—who said that either I should not have been brought in here at the begin- ning, or, since I was brought in, that it is not possible not to kill[85] me (he asserted before you that if I am acquitted, soon your sons, pursuing what Socrates teaches, will all be completely corrupted)—if you would say to me with regard to this, "Soc- rates, for now we will not obey Anytus; we will let you go, but on this condition: that you no longer spend time in this investi- gation nor philosophize; and if you are caught still doing this, you will die"—if you would let me go, then, as I said, on these conditions, I would say to you, "I salute you and cherish you, men of Athens, but I will obey the god rather than you; and as long as I breathe and am able to, I will not stop philosophizing, and I will exhort you and explain this to whomever of you I

28e

29a

b

c

d

29d happen upon, and I will speak just the sorts of things I am accustomed to: 'Best of men, you who are an Athenian, from the city that is greatest and best reputed for wisdom and strength, are you not ashamed that you care for having as much money as

e possible, and reputation, and honor, but that you neither care nor think about prudence, and truth, and how your soul will be the best possible?' And if one of you disputes it and asserts that he does care, I will not immediately let him go, nor will I go away, but I will speak to him, and examine and test him. And if he does not seem to me to possess virtue, but only says that he

30a does, I will reproach him, saying that he regards the things worth the most as the least important, and the paltrier things as more important. I will do this to whomever, younger or older, I happen upon, both foreigner and townsman, but especially to the townsmen, since you are closer to me in kin.

"Know well, then, that the god orders this. And I suppose that until now no greater good has arisen for you in the city than my service to the god. For I go about and do nothing but per-

b suade you, both younger and older, not to care about bodies and money before you care just as vehemently about how your soul will be the best possible. I say: 'Not from money does virtue come, but from virtue comes money and all of the other good things for human beings in both private and public life.' If, then, I corrupt the young by saying these things, they may be harmful. But if someone asserts that what I say is other than this, he speaks nonsense. With a view to these things," I would declare, "men of Athens, either obey Anytus or not, and either let me go

c or not, since I would not do otherwise, not even if I were going to die many times."

Do not make a disturbance, men of Athens, but abide by what I begged of you, not to make a disturbance at the things I say, but to listen. For, as I suppose, you will be benefited by listening. I am going to tell you certain other things at which you will perhaps cry out; but do not do this. Know well that if you kill me, since I am the sort of man that I say I am, you will not harm me more than yourselves. For Meletus or Anytus would not harm me—he would not even be able to—since I do not suppose it is lawful[86] for a better man to be harmed by a worse. Perhaps,

d however, he might kill or banish or dishonor[87] me. But this

man, and someone else, no doubt, perhaps suppose that these 30d
are great evils. I do not suppose these are, but rather doing what
this man here is now doing—trying to kill a man unjustly.

So, men of Athens, I am now far from making a defense
speech on my own behalf, as someone might suppose. I do it
rather on your behalf, so that you do not make a mistake about
the gift of the god to you, by voting to condemn me. For if you e
kill me, you will not easily discover another like me, who—even
if it is rather ridiculous to say—has simply been set upon the city
by the god, as though upon a great and well-bred[88] horse who is
rather sluggish because of his size and needs to be awakened by
some gadfly. The god seems to me to have set me upon the city
as someone of this sort: I awaken and persuade and reproach
each one of you, and I do not stop settling down everywhere 31a
upon you the whole day. Someone else of this sort will not
easily arise for you, men. So if you obey me, you will spare me.
But perhaps you are vexed, like the drowsy when they are
awakened, and if you obey Anytus and slap me, you might
easily kill me. Then you would spend the rest of your lives
asleep, unless the god sends you someone else in his concern for
you.

That I do happen to be someone of this sort, given to the city
by the god, you might think about from this: it does not seem
human,[89] first, that I have been careless of all my own things b
and that for so many years now I have endured that the things
of my household[90] are uncared for; and next, that I always mind
your business, by going to each of you privately, as a father or
an older brother might do, and persuading you to care for
virtue. If I was getting something from this, and if I was receiv-
ing pay while I exhorted you to these things, it would be
somewhat reasonable. But now, even you yourselves see that
the accusers, who accused me so shamelessly in everything else,
have not been able in this to become so utterly shameless as to
offer a witness to assert that I ever took any pay or asked for it. c
For, I suppose, I offer a sufficient witness that I speak the
truth—my poverty.

Perhaps, then, it might seem to be strange that I go around
counseling these things and being a busybody in private, but
that in public I do not dare to go up before your multitude to

31c   counsel the city. The cause of this is what you have heard me speak of many times and in many places, that something divine

d   and daimonic[91] comes to me, a voice—which, in fact, is what Meletus wrote into the indictment, making a comedy over it. This is something which began for me in childhood; a certain voice comes, and whenever it comes, it always turns me away from whatever I am about to do, but never urges me forward.

This is what opposes my political activity, and its opposition seems to me altogether fine. For know well, men of Athens, if I had long ago tried to be politically active, I would long ago have perished, and I would have helped neither you nor myself. And

e   do not be vexed with me when I speak the truth. For no human being will preserve his life if he genuinely opposes either you or any other multitude and prevents many unjust and unlawful

32a   things from happening in the city. If the man really fighting for justice is going to preserve himself even for a short time, it is necessary for him to lead a private rather than a public life.

I will offer great proofs of these things for you—not speeches, but what *you* honor, deeds. Listen, then, to what happened to me, so that you may see that I would not yield even to one man against justice because of my fear of death, even if I were to perish by refusing to yield. I will tell you vulgar things, typical of the law courts, but true. I, men of Athens, never held any other

b   office in the city except for being once on the Council. And it happened that our tribe (Antiochis) held the prytany[92] when you wished to judge the ten generals (the ones who did not pick up the men from the naval battle) as a group—contrary to law, as it seemed to all of you in the time afterwards. I alone of the prytanes opposed your doing anything against the laws then, and I voted against it. And although the orators were ready to indict me and arrest me, and you were ordering and shouting, I

c   supposed that I should run the risk on the side of the law and justice rather than go along with you because of fear of prison or death, when you were counseling injustice.[93]

Now this was when the city was still under a democracy. But again, when the oligarchy came to be, the Thirty summoned myself and four others into the Tholos,[94] and they ordered us to arrest Leon the Salaminian and bring him from Salamis to die.[95] They ordered many others to do things of this sort, wishing that as many as possible would be implicated in the responsibility.

Then, however, I showed again, not in speech but in deed, that I   32d
do not care about death in any way at all—if it is not too crude to
say so—but that my only care is to commit no unjust or impious
deed. That rule, as strong as it was, did not shock me into doing
anything unjust. When we came out of the Tholos, the other
four went to Salamis and arrested Leon, but I departed and
went home. And perhaps I would have died because of this, if
that rule had not been quickly dissolved. And you will have
many witnesses of these things.   e

Do you suppose, then, that I could have survived so many
years if I had been publicly active and had acted in a way worthy
of a good man, coming to the aid of the just things and, as one
ought, regarding this as most important? Far from it, men of
Athens; nor could any other human being.

But through all my life, if I was ever active in public, it was   33a
apparent that I was the sort of man (and in private I was the
same) who never conceded anything to anyone contrary to
justice—neither to anyone else, nor to any of those who my
slanderers declare to be my students.[96] I never became anyone's
teacher; but if anyone, whether younger or older, ever desired
to hear me speaking and minding my own business, I never
begrudged it to anyone. And I do not converse only when I
receive money, and not when I do not receive it. On the con-   b
trary, I offer myself for questioning to rich and poor alike, and if
anyone wishes to answer, he may hear what I say. And whether
any of these becomes an upright man or not, I would not justly
be held responsible, since I never promised or taught any
instruction[97] to any of them. If someone asserts that he ever
learned anything from me or heard privately what everyone else
did not, know well that he does not speak the truth. But why,
then, do certain ones enjoy spending so much time with me?
You have heard it, men of Athens, I told you the whole truth. It   c
is because they enjoy hearing men examined who suppose they
are wise, but are not. For it is not unpleasant.

I have been ordered to practice this, as I affirm, by the god,
through divinations, and through dreams, and in every way
that any divine allotment ever ordered a human being to practice anything at all. These things, men of Athens, are both true
and easy to test.[98]

Now if I am corrupting some of the young, and have already   d

33d corrupted others, and if any of them, when they became older, recognized that I ever counseled them badly while they were young, then now, no doubt, they should have come forward to accuse me and take their vengeance. If they themselves were not willing to, then some of their families—fathers and brothers and their other relatives—should now have remembered it and taken their vengeance if their kinsmen had suffered harm from me.

In any event, I see many of them present here: first of all Crito
e here, of my age and deme, the father of Critobulus here; and next Lysanias the Sphettian, the father of Aeschines here; and then Antiphon the Cephisean is here, the father of Epigenes. And here are others whose brothers have spent time in this way: Theozotides' son Nicostratus, the brother of Theodotus—and Theodotus has died, so he could not beg him off—and Demodocus' son Paralus, whose brother was Theages. And here is
34a Adeimantus, son of Ariston, whose brother is Plato here, and Aeantodorus, whose brother is Apollodorus here.[99]

And I can tell you of many others, from among whom Meletus should certainly have offered someone as a witness during his own speech. If he forgot then, let him offer one now—I make way—and let him say if he has any such thing. But you will discover that it is wholly opposite to this, men, that everyone is ready to come to aid *me*, the corrupter, the one who does evil to their families,[100] as Meletus and Anytus assert. Now the cor-
b rupted ones themselves would perhaps have a reason to come to my aid. But the uncorrupted ones, their relatives, are now older men, so what other reason would they have to come to my aid except the correct and just one, that they know that Meletus speaks falsely, and that I am being truthful?

Well then, men. These, and perhaps other such things, are about all I would have to say in my defense. Perhaps someone
c among you may be vexed when he recalls himself, if, in contesting a trial even smaller than this trial, he begged and supplicated the judges with many tears, bringing forward his own children and many others of his family and friends, so as to be pitied as much as possible, while I will do none of these things, although in this I am risking, as I might seem, the extreme danger. Perhaps, then, someone thinking about this may be rather stub-

born toward me, and, angered by this, he may set down his vote   34c
in anger. If there is someone among you like this—for I do not   d
deem that there is, but if there is—to me it seems decent for me
to say to this man, "I too, best of men, no doubt have some
family; for just as Homer has it, not even I have grown up 'from
an oak or a rock,' but from human beings."[101] So I do have a
family, and sons too, men of Athens, three of them, one already
a young man, and two still children. Nevertheless I will bring
none of them forward here in order to beg you to acquit me.

Why, then, will I do none of these things? Not because I am
stubborn, men of Athens, nor because I dishonor you. Whether   e
I am daring with regard to death or not is another story;[102] but as
to reputation, mine and yours and the whole city's, to me it does
not seem to be noble for me to do any of these things. For I am
old and have this name—and whether it is true or false, it is   35a
reputed at any rate that Socrates is distinguished from the many
human beings in some way. If, then, those of you who are
reputed to be distinguished, whether in wisdom or courage or
any other virtue at all, are to act in this way, it would be shameful. I have often seen some such men when they are judged,
who, although they are reputed to be something, do amazing
deeds, since they suppose that they will suffer something terrible if they die—as though they would be deathless if you did not
kill them. They seem to me to attach shame to the city, so that
anyone, even a foreigner, would assume that those Athenians   b
who are distinguished in virtue—the ones whom they pick out
from among themselves for their offices[103] and other honors—
are not distinguished from women. For those of you, men of
Athens, who are reputed to be something in any way at all,
should not do these things; nor, whenever we do them, should
you allow it. Instead, you should show that you would much
rather vote to convict the one who brings in these piteous
dramas and makes the city ridiculous, than the one who keeps
quiet.

Apart from reputation, men, to me it also does not seem to be
just to beg the judge, nor to be acquitted by begging; one should   c
rather teach and persuade. For the judge is not seated to give the
just things away by favor, but to judge them. For he has not
sworn to favor whoever he pleases,[104] but to give judgment

35c   according to the laws. Therefore we should not accustom you to swear falsely, nor should you become accustomed to it. For neither of us would be pious.

    So do not deem that I, men of Athens, should practice such things before you which I hold to be neither noble nor just nor

d   pious, and certainly, by Zeus, above all when I am being prosecuted for impiety by Meletus here. Clearly, if I should persuade you and force you by begging, after you have sworn an oath, I would be teaching you to hold that there are no gods, and in making my defense speech I would simply be accusing myself of not believing in gods. But that is far from being so. For I believe, men of Athens, as none of my accusers does. I turn it over to you and to the god to judge me in whatever way it will be best both for me and for you.

    [*The jury votes on Socrates' innocence or guilt, and a majority finds him guilty as charged. Meletus then makes a speech proposing the death penalty, and Socrates must offer a counterproposal.*]

e

36a   I am not vexed, men of Athens, at what has happened—that you voted to convict me—for many reasons, among which is that what has happened was not unexpected[105] by me. But I am much more amazed at the number of the votes on each side. For I at least did not suppose it would be by a little, but by much. Now, as it appears, if only thirty of the votes had fallen differently, I would have been acquitted. So as it seems to me, I have even now been acquitted as far as Meletus is concerned; and not only have I been acquitted, but it is clear to everyone that if Anytus (and Lycon) had not come forward to accuse me, he would have had to pay a fine of a thousand drachmae, since

b   he would not have gotten a fifth of the votes.[106]

    At any rate, the man proposes death as my desert.[107] Well, then. What counterproposal shall I make to you, men of Athens? Or is it not clear that it should be whatever I am worthy of? What then? What am I worthy to suffer or to pay, just because I did not keep quiet during my life and did not care for the things that the many do—money-making and management of the household, and generalships, and public oratory, and the other offices and conspiracies and the factions that come to be in

42

the city—because I held that I was really too decent to survive if I   36c
went into these things? I did not go into matters where, if I did
go, I was going to be of no help either to you or to myself;
instead, I went to each of you privately to perform the greatest
benefit, as I affirm, and I tried to persuade each of you not to
care for any of his own things, until he cares for himself, how he
will be the best and most prudent possible, nor to care for the
things of the city, until he cares for the city itself, and so to care
for the other things in the same way. What, then, am I worthy to   d
suffer, being such a man? Something good, men of Athens, if
you give me what I deserve according to my worth in truth—
and besides, a good of a sort that would be fitting for me. What,
then, is fitting for a poor man, a benefactor, who needs to have
leisure to exhort you? There is nothing more fitting, men of
Athens, than for such a man to be given his meals in the
prytaneum, much more so than if someone among you has won
a victory at Olympia with a horse or a two- or four-horse
chariot.[108] For he makes you seem to be happy, while I make
you be happy; and he is not in need of sustenance, while I am in   e
need of it. So if I must propose what I am worthy of in accordance with justice, I propose this: to be given my meals in the   37a
prytaneum.

Perhaps, then, when I say this, I seem to you to speak in
nearly the same way as when I spoke about the lament and
supplication—quite stubbornly. That is not so, men of Athens,
but rather it is something like this: I am convinced that I do not
do injustice to any human being voluntarily, but I do not persuade you of this. For we have conversed[109] with each other a
short time. Since, as I suppose, if you had a law, like other
peoples,[110] not to judge anyone in a matter of death in one day,
but over many days, you would be persuaded. Now, however,   b
it is not easy in a short time to do away with great prejudices.

Being convinced that I do not do injustice to anyone, I am far
from doing myself an injustice, and from saying against myself
that I am worthy of something bad, and from proposing this sort
of thing as my desert. Fearing what? That I might suffer what
Meletus proposes for me, about which I declare that I do not
know whether it is good or bad? Or instead of this, should I
choose to propose something from among the things which I

43

37b
c

know well are bad? Should it be prison? And why should I live in jail, enslaved to the authority which is regularly set up there, the Eleven?[111] Or money, and imprisonment until I pay? But for me, this is the same as what I just now said, for I have no money to pay.

But then should I propose exile? For perhaps you would give this as my desert. I would certainly be possessed by excessive love of life,[112] men of Athens, if I were so unreasonable that I were not able to reckon that you, who are my fellow citizens, were not able to bear my ways of spending time and my speeches, but that instead, they have become quite grave and hateful to you, so that you are now seeking to get rid of them. Will others, then, bear them easily? Far from it, men of Athens. Fine, indeed, would life be for me, a human being of my age, to go into exile and to live exchanging one city for another, always being driven out. For I know well that wherever I go, the young will listen to me speaking, just as here. And if I drive them away, they themselves will drive me out by persuading their elders. But if I do not drive them away, their fathers and families will drive me out, for the sake of these same young men.

d

e

Perhaps, then, someone might say, "By being silent and keeping quiet, Socrates, will you not be able to live in exile for us?" It is of all things the hardest to persuade some of you about this. For if I say that this is to disobey the god, and that because of this it is impossible to keep quiet, you will not believe me, since you will suppose that I am being ironic.[113] But again, if I say that this does happen to be the greatest good for a human being, to make speeches every day about virtue and the other things about which you hear me conversing and examining both myself and others, and that the unexamined life is not worth living for a human being, you will believe me even less when I say these things. This is the way it is, as I affirm, men; but to persuade you is not easy.

38a

And at the same time, I am not accustomed to deem myself worthy of anything bad. If I had money, I would have proposed as much money as I could pay, for that would not harm me. But now I do not have any, unless you wish me to propose as much money as I am able to pay. Perhaps I would be able to pay you about a mina of silver.[114] So I propose that much.

b

44

But Plato here, men of Athens, and Crito and Critobulus and   38b
Apollodorus bid me to propose thirty minae,[115] and they themselves will stand surety. So I propose that much, and these men
will be trustworthy sureties of the silver for you.

*[Voting between the penalties proposed by the accuser and the ac-
cused, the jury condemns Socrates to death. He has time to make some
further remarks before he is taken away to prison to await execution.]*

For the sake of not much time, men of Athens, you will be   c
given the name and the responsibility, by those wishing to
abuse the city, for having killed Socrates, a wise man. For those
wishing to reproach you will assert that I am wise, even if I am
not. At any rate, if you had waited a short time, this would have
come about for you of its own accord. For you see that my age is
already far advanced in life and close to death. I say this not to
all of you, but to those who voted to condemn me to death.   d
I also say this to these same ones: Perhaps you suppose, men
of Athens, that I have been convicted because I was at a loss for
the sort of speeches that would have persuaded you, if I had
supposed that I should do and say anything at all to escape[116]
the penalty.[117] Far from it. But I have been convicted because I
was at a loss, not however for speeches, but for daring and
shamelessness and for not being willing to say the sorts of
things to you that you would have been most pleased to hear:
me wailing and lamenting, and doing and saying many other
things unworthy of me, as I affirm—such things as you have   e
been accustomed to hear from others. But neither did I then
suppose that I should do anything slavish[118] because of the
danger, nor do I now regret that I made my defense speech like
this: I much prefer to die having made my defense speech like
this, than to live like that.
For neither in a court case nor in war should I or anyone else
devise a way to escape death by being willing to do anything at   39a
all. In battles it often becomes clear that one might escape death
by letting go of his arms and turning around to supplicate his
pursuers.[119] And there are many other devices to escape death
in each of the dangers, if one dares to do and say anything at all.
But I suppose it is not hard, men, to escape death, but it is much

45

39b   harder to escape villainy. For it runs faster than death.[120] And
now I, since I am slow and old, am caught by the slower, while
my accusers, since they are clever and sharp, are caught by the
faster, by evil. And now I go away, condemned by you to pay
the penalty of death, but they have been convicted by the truth
of wretchedness and injustice. And I abide by my penalty, and
so do they. Perhaps these things had to be so, and I suppose
there is due measure in them.

c   After this, I desire to deliver oracles to you, O you who voted
to condemn me. For I am now where human beings most of all
deliver oracles—when they are about to die.[121] I declare, you
men who have condemned me to death, that vengeance will
come upon you right after my death, and much harsher, by
Zeus, than the sort you give me by killing me. You have done
this now supposing that you will be let off from giving an account of your life, but it will turn out much the opposite for you,

d   as I affirm. There will be more who will put you to the test,
whom I am now holding back; you did not perceive them. And
they will be harsher, since they are younger, and you will be
more vexed. For if you suppose that by killing human beings
you will prevent someone from reproaching you for not living
correctly, you do not think nobly. For to be let off is not at all
possible or noble; but it is both noblest and easiest, not to re-
strain others, but to equip oneself to be the best possible. And
so, having divined these things for you who voted against me, I
take my leave.

e   Yet with those who voted for me I would be pleased to converse about this matter which has happened, while the officials
are occupied and I do not yet go to the place where, when I do
go, I must die. But stay with me, men, for this much time;
nothing prevents our telling tales[122] to one another as long as it
is possible. For I am willing to show clearly to you, as to friends,

40a   what this thing means which has occurred to me now. Since,
judges—for by calling you judges I would address you
correctly[123]—something amazing has happened to me. My customary divination from the *daimonion* was always very frequent
in all the former time, opposing me even in very small matters, if
I were about to do something incorrectly. Now, you yourselves
see what has occurred to me, this thing which someone might

suppose and believe to be the extreme of evils. But the sign of
the god did not oppose me when I left my house this morning,
nor when I came up here to the law court, nor anywhere in the
speech when I was about to say anything. And yet in other
speeches it has often stopped me in the middle when I was
speaking. But now it has nowhere opposed me concerning this
action—not in any deed or speech. What, then, do I take to be
responsible for this? I will tell you. What has occurred to me is
likely to be good, and there is no way that we take it correctly
if we suppose that being dead is an evil. For me, a great proof
of this has happened. For there is no way that the accustomed
sign would not have opposed me, if I were not about to do something good.

Let us also think in this way how great a hope there is that it is
good: For being dead is either of two things. Either it is such as
to be nothing and the dead man has no perception of anything,
or else, in accordance with the things that are said,[124] it happens
to be a certain change and migration of the soul from the place
here to another place.

And if there is no perception, but it is like a sleep in which the
sleeper has no dream, death would be a marvelous gain. For I
would suppose that if someone had to select the night in which
he slept so soundly that he did not even dream, and had to
contrast the other nights and days of his own life with that night,
and then had to say on consideration how many days and nights
in his own life he had spent better and more pleasantly than that
night, I would suppose, not that some private man, but that the
Great King himself[125] would find that they are easy to count
compared with the other days and nights. If, then, death is such
a thing, I at least say it is a gain. For all time appears thus to be
nothing more than one night.

But again, if death is something like a journey from here to
another place, and if the things that are said are true, that all the
dead are there, then what greater good could there be than this,
judges? For if someone who arrives in Hades, leaving behind
those here who claim to be judges, shall find the true judges—
those who are said to give judgment there, Minos and
Rhadamanthys, and Aeacus, and Triptolemus,[126] and as many
of the other demigods who were just in their own life—would

41a this journey be anything paltry? Or again, to associate with Orpheus and Musaeus and Hesiod and Homer,[127] how much would any of you give? I am willing to die many times if these

b things are true. Since for myself, at least, spending time there would be marvelous: when I would happen upon Palamedes and Telemonian Ajax,[128] or anyone else of the ancients who has died because of an unjust judgment, I would compare my own experiences with theirs. As I suppose, it would not be unpleasant. But certainly the greatest thing is that I would pass my time examining and searching out among those there—just like those here—who among them is wise, and who supposes he is, but is not. How much would one give, judges, to examine the one

c who led the great army against Troy, or Odysseus, or Sisyphus,[129] or countless others whom one might mention, both men and women? To converse and to associate with them and to examine them there would be inconceivable[130] happiness. Surely those there do not kill on this account. For not only in other things are those there happier than those here: they are also deathless henceforth for the rest of time, at least if the things that are said are true.

But you too, judges, should be of good hope toward death, and you should think this one thing to be true: that there is

d nothing bad for a good man, whether living or dead, and that the gods are not without care for his troubles.[131] Nor have my present troubles arisen of their own accord, but it is clear to me that it was now better for me to be dead and to have left troubles behind. Because of this, the sign also nowhere turned me away, and I at least am not very vexed at those who voted to condemn me and at my accusers. And yet it was not with this thought that they voted to condemn me and accused me: they supposed they

e would harm me. For this they are worthy of blame.

This much, however, I beg of them: When my sons grow up, punish them, men, and pain them in the very same way I pained you, if they seem to you to care for money or anything else before virtue. And if they are reputed to be something when they are nothing, reproach them just as I did you: tell them that they do not care for the things they should, and that they suppose they are something when they are worth nothing. And if

you will do these things, we will have been treated justly by 42a
you, both I myself and my sons.

But now it is time to go away, I to die and you to live. Which
of us goes to a better thing is unclear to everyone except to the
god. [132]

Notes to the

Translation

1. "Clever" translates the Greek *deinon*, which I have elsewhere rendered as "dangerous" or "terrible." It can mean anything from "terrific" to "terrible" to "terrifying"; the common root of these English words reveals the root sense of *deinon*. Cf. Martin Heidegger, *An Introduction to Metaphysics* (Garden City, N.Y., 1961), pp. 123–138.

2. "Seem" or "be reputed" will always be used to translate *dokein*, from which is derived *doxa*, "opinion," "reputation," or "fame." In its root sense, *doxa* is (1) the visible appearance of someone or something, the regard or aspect in which he or it stands. (2) If this aspect is an outstanding one, *doxa* is understood as respect or glory. (3) If the respect is grasped only as partial, as a perspective, *doxa* is opinion, the way something looks to someone. (4) Finally, *doxa* may be mere appearance, empty show. (Heidegger, *Metaphysics*, pp. 87–89.) Socrates describes his own investigation of *doxa* and *dokein* at 21c–22e and returns to the theme at 34e.

3. "Speech" is *logos*, whose meaning ranges from "argument," "account," or "reason" to "statement" or "story." For the Greeks, speech (as opposed to mere chatter) implies a coherent, orderly account of something, presented in such a way that the thing comes to sight as it is. The original sense of the word seems to have been a "collection" or "gathering" into a binding unity which then manifests itself *as* that unity. (Heidegger, *Metaphysics*, pp. 104–114, 141–146.) A consistent translation of the term is impossible, but "speech" has been preferred wherever feasible. *Logos* describes both the activity (conversation) and the focus (the opinions spoken by oneself and others about how one should live) of Socrates' philosophizing (cf. 38a).

4. "Ordered and adorned" translates *kekosmēmenon*, from the verb *kosmein*. Its original sense of "arrange" or "order" came to be used by analogy for "adorn" or "embellish." In the present context both "ordered" and "adorned" seem to be the intended meanings. We derive "cosmetic" from *kosmein*, and the Greeks called the world *kosmos* from its orderly arrangement.

50

5. "At random" translates *eikē*, which might also be rendered "as I please," "just as I like." The word may mean, but does not have to mean, that Socrates speaks without any order at all.

6. The Greek for "fabricate" is *plattein* (in the form used in the text, *plattonti*), and it is not impossible that Plato intends a pun here on his own name.

7. The Greek *apologein* will always be translated "speak in (my) defense," because of the narrow meaning of our English word "apologize." *Apologia* will be "defense speech" instead of "apology."

8. The public life of the city, both political and commercial, centered on the "market" or *agora*. Neither Plato nor Xenophon ever portrays Socrates speaking "in the market at the money-tables." His usual haunt is the Lyceum, one of the places of exercise (*gymnasia*) in the suburbs of Athens where the youths often spent their time. (See Plato *Euthyphro* 2a, *Symposium* 223d.) Socrates says he once heard the sophist Hippias (below, n. 29) boasting of his wisdom "in the market at the money-tables" (*Hippias Minor* 368b). The sophists, with their desire for public acclaim and tuition-paying students, would probably have spent more time there than Socrates.

9. The large Athenian juries often made known their approval or disapproval of a speaker by applause, shouts of anger, or jeers.

10. "Simply" in Greek is *atechnōs*; in the context of Socrates' introductory remarks, the word is a pun on *atéchnos*, "artlessly." (Socrates' speech and manner lack the artful arrangement of his accusers'.) *Atechnōs* recurs at 18c7, 18d6, 26e8, 30e2, 35d4.

11. "Really" will always be used to translate *tō onti* and *ontōs*, literally "in being" and "beingly" (from the participle of "to be").

12. "Dialect" is *phōnē*, literally "voice."

13. "Virtue" or *aretē* is the specific excellence of a thing. That excellence may or may not imply what we call "morality": Socrates speaks of the "virtue" of colts and cattle at 20b. The meaning of Socratic virtue must be culled from the contexts in which he uses the word. For an excellent extended discussion of Socrates' understanding of virtue, see Jacob Klein, *A Commentary on Plato's Meno* (Chapel Hill, N.C., 1965).

14. Anytus was the most important of Socrates' three accusers or prosecutors, although he did not himself initiate the prosecution. (That was done by Meletus: see n. 21 below.) Anytus also appears in Plato's *Meno* (89e–95a), where he becomes angry with Socrates in a discussion about the education of the young. In that conversation Socrates appears to praise the sophists and to attack the politicians in their capacity as educators. Anytus was said to be a tanner by trade (Xenophon *Apology of Socrates to the Jury* 29). Cf. also Aristotle *Athenian Constitution* 27.5, 34.3.

15. "Wisdom," for the Greeks as for us, can denote the highest achievement of the mind, but in this context the epithet "wise" (*sophos*) suggests a frivolous cleverness not consistent with a man's proper seriousness. Even among us, the term "philosopher" or "intellectual" is

sometimes applied derisively to those whose impracticality appears to stem from too much "thinking." ("Wisdom" [*sophia*] may also be mere technical skill in a manual or fine art: cf. 22d–e.)

16. Socrates is accused of being a *phrontistēs*, a "thinker" or "worrier"; when used as a noun, the word implies excessive intellectuality. In Aristophanes' *Clouds*, Socrates' school is called a *phrontistērion* or "thinkery." *Phrontistēs* was a generally used, uncomplimentary epithet for Socrates (Xenophon *Symposium* 6.6). Cf. the frequent use of *phrontistēs* and cognates in Aristophanes' *Clouds*, listed in Eric A. Havelock, "The Socratic Self as It Is Parodied in Aristophanes' *Clouds*," *Yale Classical Studies* 22 (1972), 9–10, n. 24.

17. "To make the weaker speech (*logos*) the stronger," or "to render the worse argument the better," is to use clever speech to accomplish an unjust or improper purpose. See n. 23 below.

18. The word translated "believe in" (*nomizein*) may also mean "acknowledge" or "respect." It is related to *nomos*, "custom" or "law." Belief in gods may be understood, then, either as the inward conviction that they exist or as the outward demonstration of respect—by performing the proper sacrifices, for example. Socrates plays on this ambiguity of believe/acknowledge in his cross-examination of Meletus (26b–27e). Cf. the comment of John Sallis, *Being and Logos* (Pittsburgh, 1975), p. 33, n. 8, and the literature cited there.

19. The poet is Aristophanes, who portrayed Socrates as a comic figure in his *Clouds*, first produced in 424/3 (twenty-four years before the trial). See K. J. Dover's annotated edition of *Aristophanes: Clouds* (Oxford, 1968), p. lxxx, and n. 23 below.

20. *Diabolē* will always be translated by "slander" or "prejudice." The Greeks used a single word for both, since prejudice is nothing more than slander that is believed.

21. Meletus led the prosecution of Socrates (see 36a and *Euthyphro* 2a–b). He was young and unknown in Athens, but he is thought to have been a poet, since Socrates says Meletus indicted him "on behalf of the poets" (23e). Cf. John Burnet's annotated edition of *Plato's Euthyphro, Apology of Socrates, and Crito* (Oxford, 1924), pp. 9–11.

22. "To do injustice," in the context of an indictment, means "to commit a crime"; the specific counts of the indictment follow.

23. Socrates refers to a passage in the *Clouds* where he is first brought on stage, in a basket suspended in the air. When he is asked what he is doing in a basket, Socrates responds: "I tread on air and contemplate the sun." His interlocutor then comments: "Then you look down on [or: despise] the gods from a perch" (lines 218–234). Throughout the *Clouds* Socrates is shown to be concerned with the study of natural things, such as animals and the "things aloft," and of the gods (143–173, 365–407). He is also skillful in the use of speech, and he is said to be able to make the weaker speech defeat the stronger (112–115). He pays little attention to the moral and political themes that are so prominent in the Socratic dialogues of Plato and Xenophon. If allowances are

made for comic exaggeration, Aristophanes' Socrates seems quite similar to Plato's Socrates as a young man, as he describes himself in the *Phaedo* (96a–99d).

24. "Understanding" has always been used to translate *epistēmē*, a word whose original meaning is skill or knowledge of how to do something. (*Epistēmē* is derived from *epistasthai*, "understand.") In translations of Aristotle *epistēmē* is often rendered by "science," but Socrates' use of the term remains closer to its meaning in ordinary discourse. I have used "understanding" instead of "knowledge" in this translation, so that *epistēmē* and its cognates can be distinguished from *eidenai*, which is always translated by "know," and from *gignōskein*, translated by "know" or "recognize."

25. The word for "indictments" is the plural of *dikē*, literally "justice." Cf. n. 117 below.

26. "The many" (*hoi polloi*), an expression referring here to the majority of the jurymen, also suggests the "vulgar multitude" that we still associate with the words *hoi polloi*. Socrates points to the difficulty of his defense at the end of this paragraph, where he says he expects "the many" of the jurymen (chosen at random from the Athenian citizen body) to refute the slanders of "the many."

27. "Human being" is *anthrōpos*, a member of the human race, as opposed to *anēr*, a man or male human being. In ordinary discourse there is nothing outstanding about being an *anthrōpos*—one need possess only the minimal qualities of the species. Women, children, and slaves are also *anthrōpoi*. The life of an *anēr* is distinguished by its dedication to manly excellence, which shows itself above all in politics and war. ("Manliness"—*andreia*—is the Greek word for courage.)

No English word adequately corresponds to *anēr* since "man" must often be used to translate an adjective or pronoun used as a substantive (for example, "this" is sometimes translated "this man"). But *anthrōpos* will always be translated "human being." (Allan Bloom, ed., *The Republic of Plato* [New York, 1968], pp. 441–442, n. 14.)

28. "Noble" translates *kalon*, the crucial term meaning beautiful, noble, splendid, or fine. The word suggests the brilliance of something that shines forth, with the capacity for both deception and illumination. Its rich meaning ranges from the superficial attractiveness of bodily beauty to the inward nobility of the speech and deed of moral or intellectual excellence. *Kalon* will be translated "beautiful," "noble," or "fine." Heidegger discusses Plato's understanding of *kalon* in *Nietzsche*, 2d ed. (Pfullingen, 1961), I, 218–231.

29. These three men were known as "sophists" (the word is related to *sophos* or wise), and all were foreigners, as Socrates emphasizes. The sophists were held in low esteem by both the old-fashioned aristocratic gentlemen and the democratic politicians. Socrates' accuser Anytus says in the *Meno*, "It is apparent that they maim and corrupt those who associate with them" (91c).

Gorgias (from Leontini, a Greek city in Sicily), a famous teacher of rhetoric, is shown in conversation with Socrates in Plato's *Gorgias*. He taught that knowledge of rhetoric, the art of persuasion, is the chief part of a complete education, and that the possession of that art enables one to accomplish anything one likes by ruling other men (*Gorgias* 449–452). Prodicus (from Ceos, an island in the Aegean Sea), a grammarian and philologist, stressed the need for precision in the use of words (Plato *Protagoras* 339e–341c). Hippias (from Elis, a city of southern Greece), prided himself on the scope and diversity of his knowledge, which included the natural phenomena of the stars and the heavens (*Protagoras* 315c, *Hippias Major* 285c). The remarkable money-making abilities of these three sophists are discussed at the beginning of the *Hippias Major*.

30. Callias was an Athenian notorious for his dissolute and corrupt manner of life, wherein he rejected everything old-fashioned. Aristophanes derided him for it in his *Birds* (283–286) and *Frogs* (428–430). His father Hipponicus was thought to be the richest man in Greece, but Callias' free-spending habits dissipated the family fortune (Lysias *On the Property of Aristophanes* 48). Callias was a generous patron of the sophists, as we learn from the *Protagoras*, where two of the three sophists mentioned at 19e appear as guests at his house. He was said to have married a woman whose mother he later took as a mistress, having one son by the daughter and another later by the mother. At first he acknowledged only the first son, but he later confirmed that both sons were his. Socrates' repeated mention here of Callias' *two* sons may allude to this scandal, which became public knowledge during a trial that probably occurred a few months before the trial of Socrates. It is not known whether this information about Callias' family affairs is accurate. (Andocides *On the Mysteries* 124–132; Douglas MacDowell's edition thereof [Oxford, 1962], pp. 10–11, 204–205; cf. Leo Strauss, *Xenophon's Socratic Discourse* [Ithaca, N.Y., 1970], pp. 157–158.) Cf. Xenophon *Symposium* passim; *Hellenica* VI.3.3.

31. In Greek a "noble and good man" (*kalos kai agathos*, or, contracted, *kalos kagathos*) is the normal expression for a "perfect gentleman." I have translated the phrase literally whenever it occurs in order to preserve the original force of the words, but the reader should also remember this idiomatic meaning of the combination "noble and good."

32. Socrates puns on the words "master" (*epistatēs*) and "one who understands" (*epistēmōn*) in his question to Callias. He implies that the only suitable "master" or educator is one who "understands"—one who knows the art of education (20c).

33. Evenus (from Paros, an island in the Aegean Sea), besides teaching for pay, wrote lyric poetry and discussed rhetorical technique (*Phaedo* 60d–61c and *Phaedrus* 267a). A few fragments of his poetry are preserved in M. L. West, ed., *Iambi et Elegi Graeci ante Alexandrum Cantati* (Oxford, 1972), II, 63–67.

Five minae was a small fee to pay a sophist. Protagoras was said to have been the first to charge 100 minae, and Zeno was paid as much by some of his students (Diogenes Laertius IX.52, Plato *Alcibiades I* 119a). Cf. n. 114 below.

34. "Art" is *technē*, a skill or craft whose principles can be known and described in speech. "Art" is to be understood in contrast to "nature" (*physis*; see n. 51 below). Nature includes whatever grows up, persists, and passes away back into itself of its own accord, uncompelled to do anything other than to be what it is. When men seek to establish and make a place for themselves within things natural, their action is guided by an understanding. This understanding is called *technē* or art. *Technē* is as such *not* the word for making and producing things; in fact, since *technē* is the knowledge that guides every fundamental human action, the word is sometimes used in Greek to designate human understanding simply. But in particular, since the production of tools and implements and the making of poetry and other "works of art" manifest themselves to us obtrusively in our everyday lives, the understanding that guides such activity is called *technē* in an emphatic sense. (This account is taken from Heidegger, *Nietzsche*, I, 96–97.)

35. "To plume oneself" (*kallynesthai*) contains the stem *kal-*, "beautiful" or "noble" (n. 28 above).

36. This sentence—"What is your *pragma*?"—might be translated "What is your affair?" or "What is the trouble about you?" See nn. 70 and 131 below.

37. "Name" (*onoma*) here refers to reputation or fame. *Onoma* in its primary sense means "proper name" (e.g. Socrates, Zeus). The Greeks also used *onoma* for the "name" of any thing at all, like the English "word." *Onoma* is always translated by "name" except at 17c, where "word" is used.

38. Socrates seems to quote a verse from Euripides' lost tragedy *Melanippe the Wise*, "not mine is the story," but he replaces Euripides' word for story, *mythos*, with *logos*. Eryximachus quotes the word correctly in Plato's *Symposium*, 177a. The complete verse is:

Not mine is the story, but from my mother....

The passage continues in a naturalistic vein:

[She told me] how heaven and earth were one form;
and when they gained a place apart from each other,
they gave birth to all things and gave them up to the light:
trees, winged creatures, beasts that the brine nourishes,
and the race of mortals.

(August Nauck, ed., *Tragicorum Graecorum Fragmenta*, 2d ed. [Leipzig, 1889], p. 511, Fr. 484.)

39. Chaerephon is the principal companion of Socrates in the *Clouds*. He shows his impetuosity at the beginning of Plato's *Charmides*. He also appears in the *Gorgias*, where Socrates orders him to question the venerable Gorgias, who, like an oracle, has offered to answer any question.

40. On the "recent exile" of the democratic party of Athens, see the Introduction to the Translation.

41. "The Pythia" was the title of the priestess who delivered Apollo's oracles at Delphi.

42. The word for "lawful" here is *themis*, a somewhat exalted term with overtones of divine sanction. (Socrates uses the related word *themiton* at 30c.) For its use, cf. Plato *Gorgias* 497c4. Emile Benveniste explains the root sense of *themis* in *Indo-European Language and Society* (Coral Gables, Fla., 1973), pp. 379–384.

43. The reader should remember that the words "reputed," "seem," and "reputation," which occur frequently throughout this section (21b–23c), are translations of *dokein* (n. 2 above).

44. "Divination" is *manteion*, which may also be rendered "prophecy." From the same root comes *mantis* (diviner, seer, prophet). Words of this *mant-* root will be translated consistently.

45. "Politician" is *politikos*, one engaged in the public life of the *polis* (city). The negative associations of "politician" are not heard in *politikos*; the term approaches our word "statesman."

46. Swearing "by the dog" was an unusual, perhaps even improper, way to affirm something. The normal Greek oath was "by Zeus" (as at 17b, 26d, 35d, and 39c) or by one of the other Olympians. In the *Gorgias* (482b) Socrates swears "by the dog, god of the Egyptians."

47. "Prudence" (*phronēsis*) in ordinary speech denotes "being sensible"—speaking and behaving in a sensible manner. (The Greek word used here is literally "prudently," *phronimōs*.) Aristotle later gave prudence the more limited signification of "practical wisdom," knowledge of how to act well (as opposed to *sophia*, the theoretical wisdom of contemplation) (*Nicomachean Ethics* VI). *Phronēsis* is a cognate of *phrontistēs* ("thinker" or "worrier": n. 16 above); prudence may therefore be understood, and Socrates does understand it, as a kind of thoughtfulness. The word occurs below at 29e1 and 36c7.

48. The expression "certain labors" recalls the famous labors of Heracles, the traditional Greek hero; less obviously, Socrates' "wandering" may allude to the wise Odysseus' long voyages (narrated in Homer's *Odyssey*).

49. "What they [the poems] meant" is literally "what they said" (the verb is *legein*).

50. The word for "make" here is *poiein*, which means "compose [poetry]" when applied to poets, but has the more general meaning "do" or "make" when used for human action in general. The English and Greek words for poetry and poem derive from *poiein*.

51. According to Joseph Cropsey, " 'Nature' is taken to mean many things, but primarily it means the things, or the principles of the things, that do not owe their being to human agency. The natural is opposed in the first place to the artificial." Yet nature exhibits regular motions and changes which are like the products of artful intention, although in the case of nature no manifestly embodied intelligence initiates the

motion. (Joseph Cropsey, "Political Life and a Natural Order," in *Political Philosophy and the Issues of Politics* [Chicago, 1977], p. 223.) Cf. n. 34 above.

A poet who composes "by some nature" writes without the guidance of his own plan and thought. Socrates elsewhere (*Ion* 534c) speaks of such composition as directed by "divine allotment" (*theia moira*): like the works of nature, such poetry allows no clear explanation of the origins of its orderly form.

52. "While inspired" (*enthousiazontes*) is from the verb *enthousiazein*, "to have a god within."

53. "My own things" translates *ta oikeia*, literally "the things of one's own household or family" or "the things familiar and peculiar to oneself and one's closest relations." *Oikos* is the word for household or family, from which comes *oikonomikē* or "economics," the art of household management. Socrates' way of life turns away from *ta oikeia*—all that is private, personal, uniquely one's own—toward a wisdom that can be shared by anyone through conversation and thought. On the original sense of *oikos* as household, see Benveniste, pp. 251–254.

54. "Well-ordered" (*syntetagmenon*) is the reading of all the Greek manuscripts of the *Apology*. Burnet has emended this to "vigorously" (*syntetamenon*).

55. "From among these men" (*ek toutōn*, literally "out of these") might also be translated "as a result of these things."

56. Little is known of Lycon, the insignificant third accuser of Socrates. He is probably the Lycon of Xenophon's *Symposium*, a slow-witted but decent gentleman, whose son was the beloved of Callias (n. 30 above).

57. "Patriotic" (*philopolis*) is rendered more literally by "city-loving."

58. *Daimonia*, the neuter plural of the adjective *daimonion* ("daimonic"), may be translated "daimonic things" or "daimonic beings," or perhaps even "divinities." I have left the word untranslated wherever it is used as a substantive, as it is here, in order to leave open whether the "daimonics" in question are supernatural beings or something else. Otherwise it will be translated "daimonic."

For Socrates, "the daimonic" seems to be the realm between the divine (the gods) and the merely human. A daimon, as explained at 27d–e, is a being half divine and half human. See also Plato *Symposium* 201d–204c and n. 91 below.

59. The original of the indictment seems best preserved in Diogenes Laertius (II.40): "Socrates does injustice by not believing in the gods in whom the city believes, and by bringing in other *daimonia* that are new; he also does injustice by corrupting the young." Xenophon's version differs in only one word: instead of "bringing in" he has "carrying in" (*Memorabilia* I.1.1; *Apology of Socrates to the Jury* 10). In Socrates' present restatement of the indictment (admittedly not accurate, since he says it is "something like this" and "of this sort"), (1) he reverses the original

order of the impiety and corruption charges, and (2) he drops the word "bringing in," changing the meaning of the charge from "introducing" to "believing in" new *daimonia*.

60. "Care," in Greek, is *melete*: "Meletus" sounds almost like "care." Socrates puns on his name and tries to prove that "Mr. Care doesn't really care."

61. The oath "by Hera" is a feminine oath (E. R. Dodds, ed., *Plato: Gorgias* [Oxford, 1959], note on 449d5). Hera, the wife of Zeus, was "a deity of marriage and of the life, especially the sexual life, of women." She is "also frequently connected with birth and the nurture of children" (*Oxford Classical Dictionary*, s.v.).

62. There were quite a few persons in attendance at the trial besides the five hundred jurors, as it seems; some of Socrates' acquaintances were among them (33d–34a).

63. The Council or *boule* was an administrative body of five hundred members, which supervised the day-to-day domestic affairs of the city. Its members were selected by lot for a one-year term of office. (Aristotle *Athenian Constitution* 43–49.) See n. 92 below.

64. The Assembly or *ekklesia*, the highest authority in Athens, was open to all adult male citizens. All important questions of public policy were determined by it.

65. In this single instance "to understand" is *manthanein*, literally, "to learn."

66. See n. 123 below on "judges."

67. Anaxagoras, a native of Clazomenae (on the coast of Asia Minor, in Ionia), lived and taught in Athens when Socrates was a young man. He was a friend of Pericles, the leading Athenian statesman during the early years of the war with Sparta. Like the other so-called pre-Socratic philosophers, Anaxagoras tried to give an account of the nature of things, a *physiologia* (a *logos* of nature, of *physis*). He apparently taught that the nature of things can be understood without reference to the city's gods or traditions. He thereby implied that the city's gods exist only by convention or law, and not by nature or in truth. (For a general discussion of "pre-Socratic philosophy," see Plato *Laws* 886a–892c.) Anaxagoras was indicted on a charge of impiety, under the provision of a decree against "those who do not believe in the divine, or who teach *logoi* about the things aloft." He avoided prosecution by fleeing the city (Plutarch *Life of Pericles* 32). For a selection of the fragments of his surviving writings, see G. S. Kirk and J. E. Raven, *The Presocratic Philosophers* (Cambridge, 1957), pp. 362–394. Cf. *Phaedo* 97b–99c.

68. Young men in training to be military officers were allotted one drachma per day for their rations. For common soldiers the ration was 4 obols (6 obols equal one drachma). The food dole for poor disabled citizens unable to work was 2 obols per day, which would probably have provided a minimal subsistence. So one drachma for a book is a quite small amount of money. (Aristotle *Athenian Constitution* 42.3, 49.4.)

The "orchestra" was apparently an area of the market place where books were sold (Burnet's note on 26e1).

69. The Greek for "insolence" is *hybris*.

70. "Matters" translates *pragmata,* things we handle and touch, or with which we concern ourselves in everyday life. *Pragmata* in other contexts is translated "affairs" or "troubles" (just as we say in English, "What's the matter?"). Cf. nn. 36 and 131.

71. Socrates alludes to the notorious stories of gods having children by intercourse with human beings.

72. An "ass" in Greek is *onos,* and a "mule" is *hemionos,* "half-ass." The word *hemionos* is analogous to *hemitheos,* "demigod" (literally, "half-god") (28c).

73. Socrates concludes his argument with a complex flourish. The last sentence means: if someone believes in *daimonia* (daimonic things) and *theia* (divine things), then he must also believe in daimons, gods, and heroes. ("Heroes" were demigods or "half-gods," like Achilles, children of one mortal and one divine parent, as Socrates explains at 28b–c. On heroes and daimons, cf. Plato *Cratylus* 397d–398e, where Socrates presents the account of the *Apology* in a more playful manner.)

74. Socrates may use the term "just speech" here in deliberate response to Aristophanes' *Clouds,* where he was portrayed as indifferent or hostile to the "just speech," which was personified as a character in the play (lines 889–1106).

75. It is generally a sign of contempt to address someone as a mere "human being" in Greek. Cf. n. 27 above.

76. Achilles was the son of the goddess (sea nymph) Thetis and the mortal Peleus, as Homer describes in the *Iliad* (XVIII.84–85, 432–434, XXIV.534–540).

77. "To be eager" is *prothymeisthai,* containing the root *thym-,* from which comes *thymos* ("anger" or "heart"). Achilles is preeminently a man of *thymos;* Socrates is not. Cf. *Republic,* Books II–IV, for an extended explication of the nature of *thymos.*

78. "Penalty" in Greek is *dikē,* also the word for "justice." Cf. n. 117 below.

79. Socrates refers in this passage to Homer's *Iliad,* the epic poem about the Greek war against Troy, whose story would have been familiar to every Athenian. Achilles, whose youthful beauty and excellence as a warrior distinguish him from the other heroes, proudly and then angrily insists that he be honored as the best of the Greeks. He withdraws from the war when he is publicly insulted by Agamemnon, the leader of the Greek expedition against Troy (cf. 41b). When Patroclus, Achilles' closest friend, is killed by the Trojan hero Hector, Achilles' desire for revenge leads him back into the fight, although he knows that when he kills Hector, he must die soon thereafter. (This crucial choice, the turning-point of the *Iliad,* is what Socrates recounts here.) There follows a crescendo of violence which culminates in the slaying of Hector and in his funeral.

Socrates makes some changes in his "quotation" from the *Iliad*. In the original the passage reads:

"Swiftly doomed, child, you will be for me, since you say such things, for directly after Hector, your fate is ready at hand."
Greatly burdened, Achilles swift of feet addressed her:
"Directly may I die, since I was not
to aid my comrade when he was killed. Very far from his fatherland he has perished; he needed me to become his protector from destruction. But now—since I am not returning to my dear fatherland's earth, and did not in any way become a light [of safety] to Patroclus and to my other comrades, many of whom went down before glorious Hector,
I sit beside the ships, a vain burden on the land." [XVIII.95–104]

Patroclus' death is not called a "murder," nor does Achilles speak of "inflicting a penalty on the one doing injustice [injury]." Socrates makes Achilles dwell on Hector, the "criminal" to be "punished," not on Patroclus, the dear lost friend. Socrates' Achilles acts out of fear of doing something shameful (he introduces the word "ridiculous" or "laughable": *katagelaston*), not out of a passionate sorrow at losing the man he loved and honored "equally to my own head."
In Homer the passage continues:

". . . I being such as is no one of the bronze-coated Achaeans
in war, though there are others better in speaking." [105–106]

In this regard, Socrates and Achilles are opposites, Socrates being a master of speech and less outstanding in military virtue. Cf. Seth Benardete, "Some Misquotations of Homer in Plato," *Phronesis* 8 (1963), 173–178.

80. A "ruler" is an *archōn*, in this instance a military commander appointed by the city. Cf. the term *archē*, translated "rule" (i.e., "government"), used at 32d.

81. These three battles of the war between Athens and Sparta are described in Thucydides' history. (Potideia: I.56–65, II.58,70; Amphipolis: V.6–10; Delium: IV.90–101.) Socrates is said to have behaved bravely at Potideia and to have retreated bravely at the defeat of Delium (Plato *Symposium* 220d–221b, *Laches* 189b). Potideia was a costly and inconclusive victory; Amphipolis and Delium were decisive Athenian defeats. On each occasion the Athenian commander who stationed Socrates at his post died during the battle (George Anastaplo, "Human Being and Citizen: A Beginning to the Study of the *Apology of Socrates*," in *Human Being and Citizen* [Chicago, 1975], p. 24).

82. When Socrates says, "they fear it," he seems to mean "most men fear it."

83. In Greek poetry Hades is the insubstantial abode for the shades or shadows of men after death (Homer *Odyssey* XI). Literally, the word "Hades" means only "the unseen"; to speak of "Hades" does not necessarily imply a belief in the immortality of the soul. (Cf. the use of "Hades" in the *Phaedo*.)

84. In this sentence Socrates is saying: I would rather do things whose worth is unknown to me than things I know are evil. That is, he would rather risk death than do injustice and disobey his better.

85. In Greek the word "kill," used in a legal context, may mean "condemn to death."

86. "Lawful" is *themiton*, related to *themis* (n. 42 above).

87. An alternative reading of the Greek text, not found in the principal manuscripts, would change "dishonor" (*atimaseien*) to "punish with loss of citizens' rights and privileges" (*atimōseien*) (Burnet's note on 30d2).

88. "Well-bred" translates *gennaion*, identical in meaning to the English word "gentle" in its original sense (well-born, of good family, noble, honorable).

89. "It does not seem human" may be more literally translated, "it is not like the human."

90. "The things of my household" is a translation of *ta oikeia*; cf. n. 53 above.

91. Socrates mentions his "daimonic thing" (*daimonion*) again at 40a–c below. See also Plato *Theages* 128d–131a, *Republic* 496c, *Theaetetus* 151a, *Phaedrus* 242b–c, and *Euthydemus* 272e. Euthyphro, like Socrates in the present context, traces the impiety charge against Socrates to his professed guidance by the *daimonion* (*Euthyphro* 3b). Cf. Xenophon *Memorabilia* I.1.2–9; *Apology of Socrates to the Jury* 4, 12–13. See also nn. 58 and 73 above.

92. The citizen-body of Athens was divided into ten administrative units called "tribes" (*phylai*), which were originally supposed to be based upon ties of kinship. Each year fifty men were selected by lot from each of the tribes to serve on the Council for a one-year term. (See n. 63 above.) The year was divided into ten parts, and each group of fifty served as prytanes during one of these periods; each period was called a prytany. Among other responsibilities, the prytanes arranged for meetings of the Council and Assembly. When the Assembly met, certain of the prytanes were chosen by lot to be the chairmen of the Assembly. (Aristotle *Athenian Constitution* 43–44.)

93. Near the end of the war against Sparta (in 406, seven years before Socrates' trial) the Athenians won a considerable victory in a naval battle fought near Arginusae island in the Aegean Sea. On account of the confusion following the battle and a storm which arose soon afterwards, the disabled ships and Athenians still at the scene of the battle, both alive and dead, were unable to be rescued as the generals had originally intended. When the generals returned to Athens, they were accused by Theramenes, an unscrupulous and ambitious politician, of neglecting their duty. (In fact, one of the ten was not accused, and one had died after the battle.) (Socrates uses here the word *anaireisthai* for "pick up"; in this context, the word means particularly "to take up dead bodies for burial." He implies thereby that the most important omission by the generals was the failure to pick up the dead for burial, a crucial

rite in the Greek tradition of piety.) Theramenes cleverly manipulated the Assembly of the people, and the people were led to condemn the eight generals to death as a group, although it was evident that many or perhaps all were innocent of wrongdoing. Socrates happened to be one of the prytanes who were chairmen of the Assembly, and he maintained that such a procedure was against the law, since the men should have been tried separately. His protest was ineffectual, for his fellow prytanes easily yielded to the threats of the politicians and the Assembly. The multitude shouted out that it would be terrible if the people should not be permitted to do whatever they wished. But, as Socrates says, the people soon afterwards regretted their hasty condemnation of the generals. (A thorough account of the battle and trial is given in Xenophon *Hellenica* I.6–7. For other contemporary sources see Burnet, pp. 131–135.)

94. The Tholos was the round building where, under the democracy, the prytanes dined. The Thirty apparently made it their chief government building.

95. The arrest and execution of Leon of Salamis was said to be one of the most flagrantly unjust acts of the Thirty. According to a speaker in Xenophon's *Hellenica,* Leon never committed a single injustice. Socrates and the four others who were ordered to arrest Leon knew that he would be executed without a trial. (Xenophon *Hellenica* II.3.39; Andocides *On the Mysteries* 94.)

Andocides tells us that one of the men sent to arrest Leon was a certain Meletus, who was also one of the prosecutors at Andocides' own trial on a charge of impiety (*On the Mysteries* 94; cf. n. 30 above). It is possible that this was the same Meletus who is now accusing Socrates (MacDowell, pp. 208–210).

96. Socrates refers obliquely to the claim that Critias and Alcibiades were his students. (This claim could not be raised explicitly by the accusers because the amnesty of 403, proclaimed when the democracy was reestablished, prohibited prosecutions for crimes committed before that date. See Burnet, pp. 100–101, on the legal situation in 399.) Critias and Alcibiades had both spent time with Socrates when they were younger, and they later became the two most notorious figures of the democracy and the oligarchy. Indeed, Critias was one of the Thirty responsible for the arrest and execution of Leon of Salamis. Xenophon reports that Critias was said to be "the most avaricious and violent and murderous of all those in the oligarchy," while Alcibiades "became the most unrestrained and insolent and violent of all those in the democracy" (*Memorabilia* I.2.12).

97. "Instruction" is *mathēma*, a discipline, a specific object of learning. *Mathēma* comes from *manthanein*, "to learn." Our word mathematics derives from it.

98. "Easy to test" is *euelenkton*, which can also mean "easy to refute" (see *Theaetetus* 157b8).

99. Crito: He was a sober gentleman of ordinary intelligence, a friend to Socrates, not because of philosophy, but because of their common life in near proximity. They came from the same neighborhood or deme. (A deme was a sort of township; each tribe [n. 92 above] was divided into ten demes.) Crito offers to pay for Socrates' escape from prison in the *Crito*. He helps Socrates care for his body in the *Phaedo*, concerning himself with Socrates' wife and children, his final bath, and his burial. He also appears in the *Euthydemus*. Cf. Xenophon *Memorabilia* I.2.48, II.9.

Critobulus: Crito calls his son "puny" and despairs of educating him in the *Euthydemus*, 271b and 306d–307a. Critobulus seems to be a rather silly boy who spends his time going to comedies and has no serious friends (Xenophon *Oeconomicus* 3.7, *Memorabilia* II.6; cf. I.3.8–10, 3.13). Cf. *Phaedo* 59b (present at Socrates' death).

Lysanias: He is otherwise unknown. Sphettos was the name of an Athenian deme.

Aeschines: He wrote Socratic dialogues, of which a few fragments survive. He was once prosecuted for nonpayment of a debt (Athenaeus XIII.611d). Cf. *Phaedo* 59b (present at Socrates' death).

Antiphon: He is otherwise unknown. Cephisus was an Athenian deme.

Epigenes: Socrates exhorts him to remedy his poor bodily condition by exercise (Xenophon *Memorabilia* III.12). Cf. *Phaedo* 59b (present at Socrates' death).

Nicostratus, Theozotides, Theodotus, and Paralus are otherwise unknown.

Demodocus: An older man than Socrates, he held in his lifetime many of the highest offices in Athens (*Theages* 127e). In the *Theages* he requests that Socrates undertake to educate his son Theages. One of the spurious dialogues attributed to Plato is entitled *Demodocus*.

Theages: In the *Theages* Socrates is reluctant to accept him as a student. Socrates remarks in the *Republic*: "The bridle of our comrade Theages would be the sort of thing that would hold him back. For in everything else Theages was ready to fall away from philosophy, but the sickliness of his body, keeping him away from politics, holds him back" (496b–c). Nothing else is known of him.

Adeimantus: This elder brother of Plato converses with Socrates in the *Republic*. He is presented there as a serious, rather stodgy young man without outstanding gifts.

Plato: The author mentions himself only three times in his dialogues: the other two places are below, 38b, and *Phaedo* 59b, where he is said to have been prevented by sickness from attending Socrates on the day he died.

Aeantodorus: He is otherwise unknown.

Apollodorus: Xenophon says he was a "strong desirer [i.e., loving admirer] of Socrates, but otherwise simple" (*Apology of Socrates to the*

Jury 28). He narrates Plato's *Symposium* to a comrade, who says, "You are always alike, Apollodorus. For you always speak badly of yourself and others, and you seem to me to believe that simply everyone, beginning with yourself, is wretched except Socrates." Apollodorus also had the nickname of "the soft" (*Symposium* 173d). Cf. Xenophon *Memorabilia* III.11.16–17, where Socrates playfully calls him his *philē*, "girl friend," and *Phaedo* 117d, where Apollodorus cannot control his lament at the sight of Socrates dying. Socrates chastises him, as well as the others attending him, for their womanlike conduct.

100. "Families" (also "kinsmen" at 33d) translates *oikeioi*, literally "those of the household" or "their own." The same word occurs at 34c–d and 37e. Cf. nn. 53 and 90 above.

101. The phrase "from an oak or a rock" occurs twice in Homer. (1) In the *Odyssey*, when Penelope asks her husband Odysseus, who has returned home in disguise, to tell her of his ancestry, she says, "for you are not of an oak of ancient story, or a rock." Odysseus responds with a tale full of "many falsehoods" (XIX 163, 203). (2) In the *Iliad* the Trojan warrior Hector utters this phrase in his last speech to himself before he is killed by Achilles (XXII.126).

The word for "I have grown up" (*pephyka*) contains the root *phy-*, indicating growth in accordance with nature (*physis*). See n. 51 above.

102. "Story" is *logos*.

103. "Offices" is *archai*, literally "rules"; cf. n. 80 above and 32d.

104. "Whoever he pleases" may be rendered more literally as "those whom it seems [good or pleasing] to himself [to favor]." "To favor" (*charieisthai*, related to *charis*, "grace") may also be translated "to gratify."

105. "Not unexpected" (*ouk anelpiston*) can also mean "not unhoped for."

106. In order to discourage frivolous prosecutions, Athenian law prescribed a fine against the accuser if less than one-fifth of the jury voted for conviction. Out of Socrates' jury of 500, 280 voted for conviction and 220 for acquittal. (Two hundred eighty is one-half of 500, plus 30: Socrates says that a change of 30 votes would have acquitted him.) When he says that Meletus would not have gotten one-fifth of the votes without the other two accusers, Socrates may be assuming playfully that each accuser contributed precisely one-third of the total votes for conviction. (One-fifth of the votes is 100; one-third of 280 is ninety-three and one-third, six and two-thirds less than 100.)

107. The Greek word for "propose as (one's) desert" is *timasthai*, whose root meaning is simply "estimate or value at a certain publicly recognized price," or "honor or reward [someone with something]" (cf. *timē*, "honor" or "price"). By extension the word came to be used in court to mean "assess the punishment due." But Socrates insists upon using the word in its original, nonjudicial sense, whereby it may refer to the worth or value of a man, good or bad. When Socrates says, "What shall I propose [as my punishment]," he is also saying, "What

[good or bad thing] do I deserve?" or "How shall I honor myself?" This ambiguity cannot be translated, but the reader should keep it in mind throughout this section. (The word "counterproposal" has the same ambiguity.) *Timasthai* will be variously translated as "propose as [my] desert," "propose [i.e., as a penalty or reward]," "give [me] what I deserve."

108. Maintenance in the prytaneum at public expense was an honor reserved for victors at the Olympic games, outstanding generals, and representatives of families whose ancestors had performed great deeds for the city. The prytaneum was the old common hearth of the city, closely associated with the city's ancestral roots in the sacred and in "one's own." From the point of view of the jury Socrates is making "a monstrous claim" (Burnet's note on 36d7).

109. "Converse" is *dialegesthai*; by using this word, Socrates implies that the *Apology of Socrates* is a dialogue or conversation with the people of Athens.

110. "Peoples" is literally "human beings" (n. 27 above). Sparta, the arch-enemy of Athens, had a policy such as Socrates describes (Burnet's note on 37a8).

111. "The Eleven" were the administrators, chosen by lot, in charge of the prison and executions (cf. *Phaedo* 59e; Aristotle *Athenian Constitution* 52.1).

112. "Excessive love of life" translates *pollē philopsychia*, literally "much love of soul." (*Psychē* here is used in its oldest meaning, "life" or "breath of life.") Cf. *Laws* 944e.

113. "To be ironic" (*eirōneuesthai*) is to dissemble, to say less than one thinks, to present oneself as less than one is. The opposite of irony is boastfulness, claiming to be more than one is. For a discussion, see Aristotle *Nicomachean Ethics* 1127a21–b31.

114. It is impossible to convey the value of "a mina of silver" in terms of current American money, because we are so wealthy. In Xenophon's *Oeconomicus* (2.3) Socrates estimates his worth at five minae, at which the wealthy Critobulus laughs; his fortune is over a hundred times as great as Socrates'. According to Aristotle, citizens possessing less than three minae were eligible for a dole if they were unable to work because of bodily disability (*Athenian Constitution* 49.4). A mina consisted of 100 drachmae (see n. 68 above).

115. Thirty minae was "a handsome sum for a man of moderate fortune to give as dowry to his sisters" (Burnet's note on 38b7, citing Lysias *Defense of Mantitheus* 10). Since a standard ransom for prisoners of war was one mina (Aristotle *Nicomachean Ethics* 1134b22), we may infer that thirty minae was a considerable sum of money.

116. "Escape" throughout this passage translates *pheugein* and its derivatives, more literally "flee." In Greek "flee" can also mean "be prosecuted" (as at 19c, 35d). *Diapheugein* ("flee through") means "be acquitted" (29c and 35c).

117. The word for "penalty" is *dikē*, literally "justice" (also at 39b

below). *Dikē* may also mean "court case" (38e), "penalty" (28d), or "indictment" (19c). Benveniste (pp. 385–388) gives an illuminating account of the root sense of *dikē*.

118. "Slavish" (*aneleutheros*) is literally "unfree," that is, unworthy of a free man.

119. In Greek the word for "pursue" may also mean "prosecute" (cf. *Euthyphro* 3e–4a). Cf. n. 116 above.

120. "It runs faster than death" is an alliterative jingle in Greek: *thatton thanatou thei.*

121. Socrates may allude here to two famous death scenes in Homer's *Iliad*: Patroclus' last words when he is slain by Hector, and Hector's last words when he is slain by Achilles. In each case the man about to die forecasts oracularly the impending death of his slayer. (*Iliad* XVI.843–857, XXII.355–363.) Cf. Xenophon *Apology* 30.

122. "To tell tales" is *diamythologein*, which contains the word *mythos*, "tale" or "story," often associated with the tales told by the poets.

123. Throughout the trial Socrates has studiously avoided the usual practice of addressing the jurymen by the name of "judges" (see the Introduction to the Translation).

124. The expression "the things that are said" (*ta legomena*, repeated at 40e and 41c) refers particularly to the poetic traditions about the afterlife which had gradually become public dogma for the Greeks (cf. *Republic* 330d–e, 362–366b). In his account of Hades (40e–41c) Socrates draws upon that tradition while introducing novel aspects of his own (nn. 126–129 below), the most characteristic of which is the opportunity for him to continue his customary philosophic examinations.

125. The King of Persia, called the "Great King" by the Greeks, was popularly believed to be the happiest of men because of his enormous wealth and empire. (On the Persian King, cf. *Laws* 693d–696a; Xenophon *Cyropaedia* and *Oeconomicus* 4.)

126. Minos: In Homer's *Odyssey* Odysseus pays a visit to Hades; among those he says he saw there was Minos, "brilliant son of Zeus, holding a golden sceptre, and seated, giving laws to the dead, while they, seated and standing around the lord through the wide-gated dwelling of Hades, asked for judgments" (XI.568–571). Minos was an ancient king of Crete, the first to clear the seas of pirates (Thucydides I.4, I.8). There was a tradition that he exacted an annual Athenian tribute of seven youths and seven maidens, whom he would feed to a great beast. Theseus freed Athens from the tribute by going to Crete and killing this Minotaur (*Phaedo* 58a–c). Minos was said to have been the original lawgiver for the Cretans and to have been a just man while he lived (Plato *Minos* 318d–321b, *Laws* beginning).

Rhadamanthys: The brother of Minos, he too had a reputation for great justice. (See above references to *Minos* and *Laws*.) The poet Pindar speaks of the "straight counsel" of Rhadamanthys, who was placed in authority in the Isles of the Blessed, where men who have lived just lives go to live after their deaths (*Olympian* II.68–77).

Aeacus: Pindar (in *Isthmian* VIII.22–24) says that he was "most careful" of mortals and "gave judgments even to gods."

Triptolemus: Legendary king of Eleusis, near Athens, he learned from the goddess Demeter the mysteries of the seasonal growth and harvest of grain; he passed on to men these "Eleusinian mysteries" and the art of farming. Triptolemus is seen as a judge of the dead, together with Rhadamanthys and Aeacus, on Athenian vase-painting (Minos was apparently left out because he was thought harsh and unjust by the Athenians on account of the tribute). Socrates seems to have been the first to include both Minos and Triptolemus among the judges of the dead (Burnet's note on 41a4). In the *Gorgias* he speaks at length about the judgments of the dead (523e–527a). There he names Minos, Rhadamanthys, and Aeacus as the judges. Cf. also *Crito* 54b–c.

127. These are the four seminal poets of the Greeks, although little is known of Orpheus and Musaeus, and some think they are merely legendary. Hesiod's chief poems are *Works and Days* and *Theogony*. In Aristophanes' *Frogs* Aeschylus mentions the four poets in the same order as here:

> For Orpheus showed us our rites, and how to hold back from murders;
> Musaeus cures for diseases, and oracles; Hesiod
> how to work the earth, and seasons of harvest and tilling; and the divine Homer,
> did he get his fame from anything but this: that he taught uprightness,
> orders [of battle], virtues, and armings of men? [lines 1032–1036]

These four poets are quoted or named together by Adeimantus (in the *Republic*, 364c–365a) as teachers of injustice (Leo Strauss, "On Plato's *Apology of Socrates* and *Crito*," in *Essays in Honor of Jacob Klein* [Annapolis, Md., 1976], p. 163.)

128. "Marvelous" (*thaumaston*, "amazing," "wonderful") may suggest a tinge of doubt about the existence of such an afterlife (cf. 40d).

Palamedes was the subject of lost tragedies by Aeschylus, Sophocles, and Euripides. According to the story, "Odysseus hid gold in the tent of Palamedes and forged a letter which compromised him. He was then accused of treason by Odysseus and stoned" to death by the Greeks (Burnet's note on 41b2).

Odysseus outwitted and tricked Ajax, one of the foremost Greek warriors at Troy, in a contest over the arms of Achilles, which had been set for a prize after Achilles' death. Odysseus apparently won the contest by manipulating the voting. Ajax sought to avenge his defeat by killing Odysseus and Agamemnon, but instead, he slaughtered a flock of sheep in a fit of angry madness sent by the goddess Athena. When he came to his senses, Ajax was overcome with shame and humiliation, whereupon he committed suicide. (*Odyssey* XI.541–562; Sophocles *Ajax*.)

129. "The one who led the great campaign" was Agamemnon, whose quarrel with Achilles touches off the action of the *Iliad*.

Sisyphus, in Odysseus' description of Hades, labors to move a huge stone over a hill, but it always rolls down again just as he reaches the hilltop (*Odyssey* XI.593–600). In the *Iliad* Sisyphus is called "craftiest of men" (VI.153).

130. "Inconceivable" (*amēchanon*) is more literally rendered as "unable to be devised" or "unable to be contrived." The word is used as we use the word "incredible" to praise something highly.

131. "Troubles" is *pragmata*, which may also be translated "affairs" or "circumstances." Cf. nn. 36 and 70 above.

132. A variant manuscript reading would change "except" (*plēn ē*) to "unless perhaps" (*plēn ei*). If the latter reading is correct, Socrates would be professing doubt even of the god's knowledge of the good. (This reading is preferred by Maurice Croiset, ed., *Platon: Oeuvres Complètes*, I [Paris, 1920].)

PART TWO

Plato's Defense of Socrates

INTERPRETATION

CHAPTER 1

The Introduction
(Proem) (17a–18a6)

An "apology" is a speech of defense against an accusation of injustice. The word *apo-logia* itself denotes a "speaking-away," an explanatory discourse intended to repulse a charge against oneself. Most readers of Plato's *Apology of Socrates* feel a strong sense of injustice in the conviction of Socrates on a charge of impiety and corruption of the young.[1] Socrates' present-day

1. Some examples of the usual interpretation are: Thomas Meyer, *Platons Apologie* (Stuttgart, 1962); W. K. C. Guthrie, *Socrates* (Cambridge, 1971); Romano Guardini, *The Death of Socrates* (Cleveland and New York, 1962); John Burnet, in his annotated edition of *Plato's Euthyphro, Apology of Socrates, and Crito* (Oxford, 1924); A. E. Taylor, *Socrates* (Garden City, N.Y., 1953); Reginald Hackforth, *The Composition of Plato's "Apology"* (Cambridge, 1933); Paul Friedländer, *Plato*, II (New York, 1964), 157–172; Kurt Hildebrandt, *Platon*, 2d ed. (Berlin, 1959), pp. 50–68; Erwin Wolff, *Platos Apologie* (Berlin, 1929); Maurice Croiset, "Notice," in *Platon: Oeuvres Complètes*, I (Paris, 1920), 117–139. Hegel's account, which argues that Socrates' case is tragic because both sides were right, is a partial exception: Georg W. F. Hegel, *Vorlesungen über die Geschichte der Philosophie* (Frankfurt a. M., 1971), I, 441–516. There have been some notable recent exceptions to this trend: Eva Brann, "The Offense of Socrates," *Interpretation* 7 (May 1978), 1–21; James Redfield, "A Lecture on Plato's *Apology*," *Journal of General Education* 15 (July 1963), 93–108; Alexander Sesonske, "To Make the Weaker Argument Defeat the Stronger," *Journal of the History of Philosophy* 6 (July 1968), 217–231; John Sallis, *Being and Logos* (Pittsburgh, 1975), pp. 25–63; Willmoore Kendall, "The People versus Socrates Revisited," in *Willmoore Kendall Contra Mundum* (New Rochelle, N.Y., 1971), pp. 149–167; Harry Neumann, "Plato's Defense of Socrates," *Liberal Education* 56 (October 1970), 458–475; Diskin Clay, "Socrates' Mulishness and Heroism," *Phronesis* 17 (1972), 53–60; George Anastaplo, "Human Being and Citizen: A Beginning to the Study of Plato's *Apology of Socrates*," in *Human Being and Citizen* (Chicago, 1975), pp. 8–29; Leo Strauss, "On Plato's *Apology of Socrates* and *Crito*," in *Essays in Honor of Jacob Klein* (Annapolis, Md., 1976), pp. 155–170; Alan F. Blum, *Socrates* (London, 1978).

71

advocates commend his speech as a model of truth and nobility. Yet his defense failed before the jury to whom he addressed himself at his trial. We are provoked to wonder why he fared so badly with his immediate audience when the judgment of posterity favors him so overwhelmingly. His scholarly admirers have often attributed his conviction to such causes as political intrigue, petty vindictiveness, and mindless superstition; but Socrates himself provides a simpler explanation in the introduction (proem) of his defense speech.

He begins by comparing the unprepossessing manner of his own speech with the forceful manner of his accusers. "I nearly forgot myself because of them, so persuasively did they speak," he says. Socrates professes to be amazed at his accusers' assertion that he is a clever (that is, persuasive) speaker. He even calls this the most shameful of the many lies they have spoken, since, so he claims, it will immediately come to sight that his only "cleverness" is to speak the truth. What made the accusers' speech so persuasive? Socrates says that their speeches were "beautifully spoken, ... ordered and adorned [kekosmēmenon]"[2] with phrases and words." Socrates, on the other hand, promises to speak at random (eikē), using whatever words he chances upon; he refuses to "fabricate speeches like a youth." He implies that his own speaking style is that of an old man—unattractive, without beauty, adornment, or order—and therefore far less suited to impress his listeners than the youthful, vigorous, engaging manner of the accusers. Their graceful and popular diction is at home in the Athenian law courts, and Socrates appropriately compares himself to a foreigner in the court who is confined to his barely intelligible native dialect because he is unfamiliar with the language of the place.

If Socrates had restricted himself to an ironic contrast of his own simplicity with his accusers' deviousness, his remarks would not be particularly noteworthy. But by comparing himself to a foreigner, he ungraciously suggests that he alone among Athenians speaks the truth. He self-righteously distinguishes his own manner from the way of speech "here" in court—and,

2. The related word kosmos, "order," and the English derivative "cosmetic" suggest the two primary senses of the term, which is here translated "ordered and adorned."

by implication, in Athenian public life generally. This abjuration of the accepted canons of court oratory casts doubt not merely upon his accusers, but upon the entire way of life popularly approved by the "men of Athens" he addresses, who identify the peak of human excellence with the successful pursuit of public honors through persuasive speaking in law courts and before the Assembly of the people (cf. 36b6–9[3]).[4] In his presentation persuasive and truthful speeches seem to be wholly incompatible, with the result that a man is limited to the single choice between being an orator "of their [the accusers'] sort" (persuasively false) or of Socrates' sort (unpersuasively truthful). His is no conventional exhortation to live up to one's reputation by telling the truth about oneself so that one may be what one is thought to be. He denies, in effect, that the truth about a man can ever coincide with the way he appears to others, since a truth-teller will always seem paltry or disgusting beside a skillful practitioner of persuasive oratory. Later in the *Apology* Socrates describes his inquiry into human wisdom, wherein he discovered that men with lesser reputations invariably proved more sensible than those reputed to be superior (22a3–6). Or, as he states it still later, a good man simply cannot survive if he is active in political life (32e). For Socrates, as it seems, every successful politician is a villain, and a decent statesmanship based upon rational choice and deliberation is impossible.

When Socrates links youthfulness, adornment, beauty, and

3. Citations in the text to the *Apology of Socrates* and to other works of Plato refer to Plato, *Opera Omnia*, ed. John Burnet, 5 vols. (Oxford, 1900–1907). The page numbers follow the Stephanus pages and divisions used therein. Passages of the *Apology* quoted or paraphrased in the text will normally not be cited when they occur within the section under immediate consideration. Thirty-five dialogues and thirteen letters have come down to us from antiquity as Plato's authentic writings. During the past two centuries classical scholars have attacked many of these works as spurious. In recent years, however, all of them have again obtained scholarly defenders, although much disagreement remains. As a convenience I will cite them in my notes as written by Plato. Translations from the Greek and German, unless otherwise noted, are my own.

4. When Socrates' friend Crito calls the conduct of the trial "ridiculous," "shameful [ugly]," and "unmanly," he is expressing the common opinion about Socrates' manner of speech—and, by inference, his way of life (*Crito* 45d8–46a4). Cf. Callicles' criticisms of Socrates on both grounds in Plato's *Gorgias*, 482c–486d and passim. See also Arthur W. H. Adkins, *Merit and Responsibility* (Oxford, 1960), pp. 153–168.

order to falsely persuasive speech, he severs from truthfulness the artful appointments it needs in order to appear to be what it is. Not only ornamentation but even coherent arrangement deceive and mislead.[5] Socrates seems to reject the *kalon*, the beautiful or noble, as the basis of right speech and action. He opposes here a long Greek tradition, which used the term *kalon* as high praise for an outstanding man's appearance and deeds. The leading poets, the spokesmen and teachers of Greece, celebrated the excellences of gods and outstanding men, lending them a manifest presence in beautiful poetic images that the people could grasp and trust.[6] The poets' praise of glory and honor was tempered by their appreciation of the precarious tension that accompanies the union of visible grace and true worth.[7] Socrates denies that such a union can be; he repudiates the beauty of outward form; he speaks the whole truth and nothing but the truth.

Yet Socrates does not simply abandon nobility, for he also calls his accusers' speech shameful or ugly (*aischron*), suggesting that speech *should* be beautiful or noble. He thereby propounds a standard of beauty that distinguishes the superficial beauty of adornment and order from the genuine beauty of truth. Socrates criticizes popular opinion concerning beauty and nobility and counters it with a new understanding, one which he elaborates throughout his defense. When he says that it would be unbecoming to him as an old man to speak as his accusers did, he implies that he *could* speak in their manner but chooses not to. Scholars have noticed that even while Socrates disclaims knowledge of court procedure and diction, he uses commonplaces of

5. Cf. Crassus' critical remarks on Socrates' separation of eloquent speech from wisdom in Cicero's *De Oratore* (III.60–61).

6. The paradigm is Homer's portrayal of Achilles and the Olympian gods in the *Iliad* (cf. *Apology* 28c–d). Cf. Plato *Republic* 606e1–5, *Phaedrus* 245a1–5; Xenophanes, Fr. 10, in Hermann Diels, ed., *Die Fragmente der Vorsokratiker*, 16th ed. (Zurich, 1972), I, 131; H. I. Marrou, *A History of Education in Antiquity* (New York, 1956), pp. 9–13; Werner Jaeger, *Paideia*, I, 2d ed. (New York, 1945), 35–56.

7. Tragedy occurs when the coherence of beauty and truth is visibly sundered. Sophocles' Oedipus, the ruler of Thebes who solved the riddle of the Sphinx, in appearance the wisest and most glorious of men, discovers his concealed ugliness and brings it into the light of day. Pindar's odes to the lustrous fame of kings and tyrants might be compared.

74

that diction in nearly every sentence of the proem.[8] But he deliberately uses those commonplaces unpersuasively, in order to show that his truthfulness arises from choice and not incompetence (cf. 38d3–8). An orator aiming at success would employ such devices to conciliate his audience, but Socrates uses them to prepare the way for his unexpected assertion that "[the virtue] of an orator is to speak the truth." He is proposing a reversal of the generally accepted view, which held that the noblest achievement of forensic rhetoric was to secure an acquittal.[9]

In Plato's *Gorgias*, one of whose major themes concerns how one should speak in public, Socrates maintains that a good man should speak with a view to order and arrangement (*kekosmēmenon*) and not at random (*eikē*).[10] He apparently prescribes a manner of defense there that contradicts his procedure in the *Apology*. Yet Socrates' truthful speech does have an order—although not the sort that results from deploying schematic devices and clever embellishments. The coherence of his discourse derives from an invisible beauty and arrangement discernible behind its apparent disorder. However, the closest attention of the mind is required to look upon that latent beauty. Consequently, only those jurymen who are thoughtful will discover the charm of Socrates' truthful speech beneath its surface disarray. He ironically dissembles the degree to which his speech will display order, but this self-depreciation is justified by his knowledge that its arrangement will not shine forth unambiguously from the bland surface. Indeed, it is simply true, without any ironic allowance, that order is not "present" in the speech at all, since it only comes to be seen on second sight, that is, upon

8. James Riddell, in the Introduction to his edition of *The Apology of Plato* (1877; repr. New York, 1973), p. xxi; Burnet, pp. 66–73; Meyer, *Platons Apologie*, pp. 26, 45–46, 51–52, 59.

9. Burnet, p. 67, says that Socrates "improves on the current rhetorical commonplaces by giving them deeper meaning"; they "are all made to lead up to the genuinely Socratic paradox that the function of a good orator is to tell the truth." Meyer, p. 25, remarks: "There is something unusual about this formulation. When one proclaims to tell the 'whole truth' in an [ordinary] defense speech, one does so only in relation to a concrete assertion, not in general, not in such a solemn way as here."

10. *Gorgias* 503d6–504a1.

conscientious reflection. If beauty and order comprise persuasive speech, then we must say that Socrates' speech is persuasive only in theory. In practice most of his audience will remain oblivious to its intricate articulation and hence ignorant of its subtle grace.

Does this mean, then, that readers of the *Apology*, most of whom, both ancient and modern, come away from the work favorably inclined toward Socrates, are superior in intellect to the jurymen who found him guilty? The readers' vanity may be flattered by such a conceit, but it is probably more fruitful to consider the different effects of Socrates' words on the two audiences of the *Apology*: the dramatic audience, the jury present at the trial itself, and the literary audience consisting of readers of Plato's defense of Socrates. The same words that the jury cannot abide evoke the strongest sympathy in readers of the *Apology of Socrates*. The unpersuasiveness of Socrates' speech, as we will see, lies particularly in its arrogant, insulting attitude toward the jury of Athenian citizens. Socrates affirms his own justice against their injustice; his wakefulness against their drowsy sloth; his concern for virtue against their pursuit of wealth and honor; his divine mission against their all-too-human cares; and finally, his own wisdom against their ignorance.[11] When he says such things, the jurymen are likely to take offense—to be "vexed," as he says (34c1). But we, the readers, looking on from our detached position as outside observers, applaud the misunderstood sage, as he appears to us, in his lonely defiance of the mob. Since we are not part of the jury he treats so rudely, we easily imagine, as human beings are wont to do, that we are quite superior to the vulgar men chastised by Socrates.

For the men of the jury, an ugly old man stands before them, boastfully and offensively proclaiming his divine stature and his surpassing excellence. But for us, Socrates' ugliness has become invisible, transmogrified by the healing power of the artist's craft. Plato makes Socrates the admired hero of a drama whose fatal outcome we anticipate with fear and pity. In the succeeding dialogue *Crito*, Socrates turns down his friends'

11. *Apology* 32b1–c3, 30e1–31a7, 29d7–30b4, 23c1 and elsewhere, 29a4–b6.

offer to help him escape from prison, patiently explaining to Crito why he must obey the law and pay the penalty decreed by Athens. Finally, the *Phaedo* portrays Socrates on the day of his death, calmly discussing the nature of the soul with his friends, and just as calmly drinking down the poison that carries him off. For readers of Plato, Socrates has become an almost tragic figure, a man ennobled by his evident willingness to forfeit his life as witness to the cause of philosophy.

Plato reunites what Socrates disjoins, the appearance and the truth of things, by making the truthful Socrates attractive to his readers. In this respect Plato could be said to betray the very dictum that Socrates expounds in the proem. When we are led to see a Socrates become "young and beautiful"[12] through the drama, we forget the Socrates who stands before the court. Yet Plato faithfully permits his readers to discern the old and ugly Socrates who insists, in speech as well as in deed, upon the necessary separation of the true from the convincing. This simultaneous presence of the beautiful and the ugly Socrates, subtly portrayed by Plato's literary powers, gives to the *Apology* (as well as the other Socratic dialogues) its peculiar flavor and difficulty of interpretation.

Socrates, then, tells the truth. But telling the truth is hard, for in order to do so, one must know what the truth is. The *Apology of Socrates* will show that Socrates, more than anyone else in Athens, devotes his life to the task of seeking through conversation the truth about all things. Such an effort demands a rigorous and constant application of the mind and a renunciation of conventional pursuits. This is what Socrates calls his "philosophizing." Hence the theme of the proem—the difference between the manner of speech adopted by Socrates and that employed by his accusers—points to the fundamental Socratic theme of the relative merits of *the* two ways of life, philosophy and politics.[13] Later in his defense Socrates will offer a thorough account of his manner of life. But he will also have to show why a philosophic life should be preferred, or even tolerated, by the political community of Athens.

12. Plato *Second Letter* 314c4.
13. On the two ways of life, cf. *Gorgias* 500c.

The central difficulty of Socrates' defense can be seen by a preliminary reflection on the opposition between the way of life of Socrates and that of the city and its traditions. Any community, in order to be a community, presupposes something shared by its members. A political community in particular depends for its unity and ultimately for its survival upon opinions and traditions held in common. Socrates' demand for the truth questions and corrodes Athenian beliefs about nobility and beauty without providing an alternative accessible to the citizens. If the Athenians were to follow Socrates and forsake their political and poetic tradition, they would have to entrust themselves to a sea whose farther shore might remain forever unattainable to them. If, having cast themselves off from the firm land, they could find no time for extended reflection, were deficient in intellectual capacity, or lacked the firm desire to improve their ignorant state—if, in other words, they were like most men most of the time—they would be left adrift, for the publicly recognized standards of nobility and justice would no longer grant them any guidance. The city's justice is embodied in the public laws and customs, while its nobility is seen in the visible reputation, honor, and beauty of the outstanding public men, the heroes of the poetic tradition, and the gods as they appear in sculpture and stories. Without such public justice and nobility, the city's unity cannot rest upon anything except the mutual competition of self-interested factions or the outright rule of force. And the alternative is conquest by one's inevitable foreign enemies. The invisible truth by itself furnishes no foundation on which to build a public trust in shared institutions and paradigms of excellence.[14] Is Socrates, then, as an obscure but persistent tradition maintains, "opposed to nature and to the preservation of civilization and of the human race"?[15] Was the

14. Cf. Harvey C. Mansfield, Jr., "Liberal Democracy as a Mixed Regime," *The Alternative* 8 (June/July 1975), 9. Mansfield defines the task of the Aristotelian political scientist to be "to find a standard which makes invisible virtue visible so that men can see beauty of soul. Invisible virtue is the intellectual virtue that most men, including most rulers, cannot recognize or appreciate." Cf. Hegel, p. 507; "The state rests upon thought; its existence depends upon the sentiments of men."

15. Muhammed b. Zakariyya al-Razi, *The Book on the Way of the Philosopher*, trans. Edward J. Erler (mimeographed typescript), p. 1, translated from Paul Kraus, "Raziana I," *Orientalia* 4 (1935), 300–334.

comic poet Aristophanes right when he portrayed the outcome
of Socrates' teaching to be the destruction of the family order
and the city's laws?

Of course, the proem only alludes to such complications. But
the distance between Socrates and Athens—a distance which
his defense must try to overcome—can be grasped from the
outset. He appears to speak the truth baldly, without order or
ornament. He teaches that truth is beautiful, but not in the usual
and traditional sense. His defense would succeed, and the men
of Athens would listen to him, if truth appeared as beautiful to
them as it does to himself. But it manifestly does not, and probably cannot, for its beauty is too subtle and refined to reveal
itself to common men. What is the result? When Socrates says
he will tell the whole truth, yet refuses to give that truth an
outward order and attractiveness, he guarantees that the jurors
will not believe it. Consequently, his claims to beauty and nobility, instead of winning him sympathy, alienate his audience,
who must look upon him as an arrogant boaster. For the jury
can see no evident reasons for his pretensions to superiority.
Socrates' pride, whatever the hidden justice of its grounds,
must appear arrogant *hybris* to these Greeks nourished on noble
poetry and a memory of great politics. Just as Socrates' old and
ugly body wholly conceals his inner beauty,[16] so also the naked,
unadorned truth looks simply ugly to men not capable of pene-
trating thought. Only after Plato has turned the trial into a drama
does Socrates' defense attain an external splendor. Plato gives
Socrates' speech order and arrangement by showing it to be an
integral part of a noble action that culminates in Socrates' death.

Moreover, if the truth by itself is unpersuasive, and if Socrates
will not use the appropriate means to persuade the jurymen to
reach a just judgment, then is he himself not the cause of
injustice—namely, of his own unjust condemnation? And does
he not advocate a way of speech that leaves not only himself but
all other good men at the mercy of the unscrupulous, who are
willing to say and do anything? (38d5). He says in the proem
that "it is just, as it seems to me," for him to beg the judges to
"disregard the manner of my speech"; yet at the conclusion of
his defense he says that it seems just to him to teach and to

16. Plato *Symposium* 215a–217a; cf. Xenophon *Symposium* 4.19, 5.1–7.

persuade the judge (35b9–c2). How then can Socrates be just, if his speech is unpersuasive and justice necessarily entails persuasion? How can justice prevail in the city if just men are denied their only means of salvation? Justice seems to demand the contradictory combination of truth and persuasion. Socrates says that the jurymen should consider and apply their minds to whether what he says is just: "For this is the virtue of a judge." He "trusts" that what he says is just—but is it? It would seem that Socrates' defense is truthful but not entirely just, because he refuses to speak beautifully and therefore fails to persuade.

Only if truth and beauty, philosophic and political speech, could be united would a successful and truthful defense of Socrates become possible. This would mean that the "foreign dialect" of philosophy would have to learn how to speak the language of the political community, in order to show that philosophy and philosophers can be at home in the city. To do this, philosophy would have to discover a way of telling the truth that is politically responsible and respectable—one that could evoke from common men the conviction that the truth is noble, and that it can defend justice from injustice. Otherwise Socrates, by remaining incomprehensible to the city, will rightly be thought dangerous to the noble opinions and just deeds that the community admires and needs. And since he insists upon speaking out publicly before the young men of the city, he will be perceived as a corruptor of the young. As if to show that it cannot after all be done, Socrates will half-heartedly try to bring together subtle truth and beautiful persuasion in his speech. His inevitable failure leads directly to condemnation and the death sentence.[17]

17. Cf. the critique of Socrates implied in Plato *Statesman* 297d–302e.

CHAPTER 2

The Charge of the
First Accusers (18a7–24b2)

The Statement of the Case (Prothesis) (18a7–19a7)

In the proem Socrates delineates an inherent antagonism between truthful and persuasive oratory, and he affirms there his own choice for austere truth over artful persuasion. Now he begins to put into practice a sort of program of deliberately maladroit speech. In the prothesis, or statement of the case, he initiates this program with what must be judged an outright blunder by the standards of effective courtroom oratory: he expands the case against him by adding a further, unofficial accusation to the present charge.[1] He is said to be a "wise man, a thinker on the things aloft, who has investigated all things under the earth, and who makes the weaker speech the stronger." This charge of the "first accusers" has circulated for "many years" (at least twenty-five, judging by Socrates' reference to the "comic poet," Aristophanes),[2] and Socrates treats it as though almost everyone in Athens has come to believe it. True, his expansion of the indictment is not entirely inept, for he does bring up the charge in order to account for the extensive prejudice against him. Moreover, most readers of the *Apology* respond to this revelation with sympathy and pity, seeing in it

---

1. John Sallis, *Being and Logos* (Pittsburgh, 1975), pp. 31–32; Thomas Meyer, *Platons Apologie* (Stuttgart, 1962), p. 27.
2. Aristophanes' comedy portraying Socrates, the *Clouds*, was first performed in 424/3 B.C. (Translation n. 19).

the portrait of the much-maligned philosopher who, oppressed by anonymous slanders, cannot call to account the fomenters of this irresponsible libel. Readers may also admire Socrates' honesty. Yet this very honesty, recalling so vividly these long-standing and widely accepted rumors, can only lead his audience to suspect that there must be some truth behind them. Besides, by accusing his jurors of prejudice, Socrates is likely to dissipate whatever good will he might otherwise have engendered by his recitation of the lamentable causes of his present unpopularity. Socrates even points out that those who do the things of which he was accused have a reputation for atheism. Yet this remark calls attention to the fact that he himself refuses to affirm a belief in gods. If the proem shows in principle how difficult it will be for Socrates to defend himself by a manner of speech that scorns convincing rhetoric, the prothesis demonstrates in deed the dangers Socrates invites with his bold truth-telling.

Similarly, the tactic employed by Socrates of transferring the charges against himself back to the accusers and the jury scarcely promises a favorable outcome. He adopts the role of judge and counteraccuser, judging the court not by their accepted standards, but by criteria of his own that he imposes. He was said to be a clever speaker; now he accords both the earlier and later accusers the epithet of *deinon*, clever or dangerous. The present accusers charge that Socrates corrupts the young; he retorts that the first accusers persuaded the judges, when some of them were "children and youths," of false and malicious things about Socrates. In short, the first accusers corrupted the young by slandering Socrates.[3] Here he merely draws out the practical consequence of the posture he adopted in the proem, when he installed himself as critic of the received, traditional manner of speech and conduct. He refuses in his defense to limit himself to a refutation of the charge against him, choosing instead to address himself to the broadest possible significance of his trial: the opposition between his own unique way of life and the traditional *ēthos* of Athens. This is his deeper reason for discussing the first accusers. Their charge sums up the things

3. Cf. Sallis, pp. 33–34.

said by decent citizens about philosophers in general (23d4–5). Hence Socrates' procedure entails a thorough critique of the way of life of the city as such. In fact, this negative counteraccusation only presents the outward face of a positive, comprehensive alternative that Socrates makes fully explicit at the center of the *Apology* (28b–31c). Unfortunately for Socrates, the men he denounces and reproaches happen to be the very judges before whom he is on trial. Given his conception of the trial as a contest between the philosophic and political lives, his acquittal would require him to overcome the jurors' prejudices about him; that in turn would involve the colossal task of converting them to the Socratic way of life.

The first accusers call Socrates a "wise man" and a "thinker." In the context both terms suggest an intellectuality that exceeds the limits of propriety.[4] Just as Socrates implies in the proem that his intransigent truthfulness leads to his conflict with the prosecutors and the Athenians, so also the first accusers appear to trace his injustice back to his wisdom, which Socrates will declare to be the core of his way of life (20d6–23c1). For when Socrates repeats their charge in the next part of his speech, he replaces the statement that "there is a certain Socrates, a wise man, a thinker," with "Socrates does injustice and is meddlesome" (19b4). For the first accusers, his intellectual life is the source of his crimes.

Socrates concludes the opening remarks of his defense with a short statement expressing his reservations about making any plea at all. After he repeats that he expects great difficulty in making a defense, since the slander against him has had such long currency, he wonders whether or not it would be "better both for you and for me" if his speech succeeds in removing their prejudice. Is Socrates professing ignorance about whether the Athenians would live better in truth than in falsehood?[5] If so, he may be more aware of the necessarily limited character of political life than our discussion of the proem suggested. Yet Socrates may also mean that he would prefer not to defend

---

4. Translation nn. 15 and 16.
5. Leo Strauss, "On Plato's *Apology of Socrates* and *Crito*," in *Essays in Honor of Jacob Klein* (Annapolis, Md., 1976), p. 156.

himself at all, for he continues by saying, "Nevertheless, let this proceed in whatever way is dear to the god, but the law must be obeyed and a defense speech must be made." He implies that he would not even speak were it not for the compulsion of the law. As he indicates at the close of the trial (41d3–5), he may think it best in his own case not to be acquitted. Leaving us and his listeners with this odd appearance of insouciant lassitude, Socrates turns to the particulars of the charge.

Is Socrates a Student of Nature? (19a8–d7)

Before Socrates answers the charge of the first accusers, he begins again "from the beginning" by "reading" the fictitious "sworn statement" that he attributes to them: "Socrates does injustice and is meddlesome, by investigating the things under the earth and the heavenly things, and by making the weaker speech the stronger, and by teaching others these same things." He mentions in passing that Meletus, the author of the present accusation, trusted in the slander of the first accusers when he wrote his indictment. This offhand remark, suggesting that the present accusation is based upon the older one, implies a close affinity between the two charges. We will take note of other links connecting the earlier charge with the present indictment.

In the prothesis Socrates stressed the vague diffuseness of the first accusers' charge. Now he treats those early slanders as though they constituted a formal indictment. The prothesis first conveyed the impression that the numerous and nameless first accusers consisted mostly of the anonymous multitude. But now Socrates seems to trace the charge entirely to a poet who is called by name: "For you yourselves also saw these things in the comedy of Aristophanes." Socrates thus offers a specific basis for the distinction drawn in the prothesis between two kinds of first accusers: those (knowingly) using envy and slander to persuade others, and those (ignorantly) persuaded by the libels of these cunning slander-mongers. Among all these accusers Socrates professes to know only the name of a "comic poet"; all the rest are nameless (18c8–d4). Socrates thereby intimates that a single poet was a major source of the common opinion about him. Poets teach the people through the images they fabricate in their dramas. They are more powerful and seminal than the many and their popular mouthpieces, the democratic politicians. By turning our attention away from the political men (the politicians and the citizens), from the vulgar who believe in the first accusers' charge, and by refocusing it instead upon the poet Aristophanes, Socrates strengthens and sharpens the veracity of his account, for he now shows more precisely how the slander and prejudice against him came to be so widely believed. In keeping with this shift in perspective, Socrates mentions here another poet, Meletus, after mentioning the politician Anytus in the prothesis.[6] Socrates singled out Anytus there as though he were the true leader of the prosecution, since he is superficially the most powerful of the present accusers. But now Socrates takes Meletus more seriously, as the one who "wrote" the present charge (just as Aristophanes "wrote" the first charge in his comedy). It now appears that political power resides principally in the shadowlike images (cf. 18d6) staged by the poets for the admiring but ignorant multitude who are formed by what they see. The power of the opinion-makers takes precedence over the superficially impressive but derivative power of politicians. The poets' influence surpasses even the power of the public opinion that installs politicians in office and sustains them there. Political authority comes neither from the barrel of a gun nor from the consenting votes of the governed, but from the words indited by the poet's pen.

Socrates specifically refers to that part of Aristophanes' *Clouds* where "a certain Socrates was borne about there, asserting that he was treading on air, and spouting much other drivel about which I comprehend nothing, either much or little." This occurs in an early part of the play, when Aristophanes' Socrates first appears on stage suspended in a basket. Strepsiades, the impoverished father of an extravagant son, has arrived at Socrates' "thinkery" to become a student. He wants to learn the "unjust speech" so that he can escape paying his debts. He asks Socrates what he is doing, and the pedagogue loftily answers, "I tread on air and contemplate the sun." (The word "contemplate" [*periphronein*] can also mean "despise.") Strepsiades responds,

---

6. On Meletus and Anytus, see Translation nn. 14 and 21.

you look down on the gods. . . ." To look down on *nein*) is meant both literally and metaphorically: "to above" and "hold in contempt."[7] Socrates does not deny Strepsiades' interpretation of his contemplation. Like "other human beings," Strepsiades believes that the sun is a god (cf. 26d1–2).

By quoting from this section of the play, Socrates indicates why the search into the things aloft and under the earth was suspected by the Athenians. The scene following the line quoted shows a Socrates whose disbelief in the city's gods is a consequence of his study of nature. His considerations of "the heavenly things"—rain, sun, thunder, and clouds—have led him to give an account of all things through natural causes alone. (Such a natural account, a *logos* of *physis*, may be called a *physiologia*.)[8] Socrates openly denies that Zeus exists, and he argues that thunder is to be explained by the motion of the clouds, not by Zeus's thunderbolts. The orthodox traditions of the political community, given form and speech through the images of poets, teach that the first causes of all things are the gods. For the Socrates of the *Clouds*, "Chaos, Clouds, and Tongue" have taken the place of Zeus and the other Olympian deities. *Physiologia* replaces the city's *theologia*.[9] As Socrates said in the prothesis, it is thought that those who investigate the things aloft and under the earth also do not believe in gods (18c2–3). The plot of the *Clouds* explains why that inference is well founded.

It might seem strange to us that the study of nature should have been perceived as a danger to the city, even if that study should lead to disbelief in the accepted opinions about the divine. However, Aristophanes shows two harmful consequences of the denial of the city's gods. First, as the result of such impiety the divine oaths which pledge payment of debts and which

7. *Clouds* 218–234. For the translation, see K. J. Dover's annotated edition of *Aristophanes: Clouds* (Oxford, 1968), pp. 126–127.

8. Cf. Aristotle *De Sensu* 442b25 and Translation n. 65.

9. *Clouds* 365–407, 424. Cf. Socrates' use of the word "drivel" (*phluaria*) in line 365 with *Apology* 19c4. The poets Homer and Hesiod decisively formed the Greek opinions and traditions about the highest things: "They composed in poetry a theogony [account of the gods' origin] for the Greeks, and gave the gods their epithets, and alloted to them their honors and arts, and indicated their forms" (Herodotus II.53).

enforce honest testimony in the courts are rendered meaning-less, and the city's justice as expressed in its laws is thereby undermined. Second, the family depends upon the sanction of the gods, for divine law supports the father's authority and the mother's chastity. If the gods do not exist, father-beating and incest become permissible, and more generally, the grounds of filial and paternal love and respect are eroded. In the absence of trust in the divine order and the customs it sustains, the internal order of the city and family loses its self-evidence. Thoroughgo-ing doubt about the city's gods therefore reduces men's relations with one another in the community to considerations of mere nature, and those relations thereby become vulnerable to the depradations of violence, fraud, and self-interest.[10])

The indictment of the first accusers also charges Socrates with "making the weaker speech the stronger." In the *Clouds* Soc-rates is presented as a linguistic expert who willingly teaches clever speaking to Strepsiades and his son Pheidippides. In fact Socrates' indifference there to just and unjust speech—he pre-sents both kinds of speech impartially to the young man—is a consequence of his indifference to the city and its concerns. Yet he is extraordinarily adept in speech, making it one of his chief objects of investigation, and that skill enables his students to employ speech for whatever purpose they like. Strepsiades' creditors certainly believe that he uses unjust speech to escape his debts. And from the point of view of the father whose son has learned how to argue against the family order and the gods' existence, Socrates most obviously has taught Pheidippides how to make "the weaker speech the stronger."[11]

Dismissing the Aristophanic allegations against him, Socrates emphatically denies that he has any share in these matters whatever. His denial is supported by the massive evidence of both Plato's and Xenophon's Socratic writings. Not only does Socrates appear never to engage in *physiologia* in their works; he even seems to condemn such study as useless or improper. Moreover, although Socrates is shown to be a master of dialecti-

10. *Clouds* 1177–1477.
11. *Clouds* 112–117, 658–692, 882–1104. For the interpretation of the *Clouds* in this section see Leo Strauss, *Socrates and Aristophanes* (New York, 1966), pp. 11–53. Cf. Sallis, pp. 34–36.

cal argument, his linguistic dexterity always seems to be put into the service of justice and virtue.[12]

The apparent contradiction between the Platonic-Xenophontic and the Aristophanic accounts has given rise to a much-discussed controversy among classical philologists over the so-called Socratic problem. Much elaborate speculation and conjecture has been propounded to explain the differences, and the dominant opinion maintains that "Aristophanes attaches to Socrates the characteristics which belonged to the sophists in general but did not belong to Socrates." This view rests, as it must, upon an interpretation of the writings of Plato and Xenophon. Yet these very writings also raise doubts about Socrates' innocence of *physiologia* and of "making the weaker argument the stronger."[13]

12. Plato *Phaedrus* 229b4–230a6; Xenophon *Memorabilia* I.1.11, IV.7.

13. Dover, pp. xlix, xlv. It would be fruitless to treat Dover's argument in detail here. The key point, however, is stated on p. xlix: "Even if *Phaedo* 96a ff. were taken as evidence for Socrates' early interest in science, it would not touch the question of his teaching oratory for money." If the passage in the *Phaedo*, where Socrates explicitly affirms his early, and abiding, interest in "science," or the search for "the truth of the beings" (99e6), is not admitted as evidence, then Plato's status as an authority on the historical Socrates must be thrown into doubt. Why believe one Platonic utterance rather than another? If Plato is prepared to distort the truth about Socrates in a supposedly "later" work, there is no prima facie reason to assume that Plato portrays him faithfully in any of his "early" works. As to the question of teaching for pay, Dover refers to three passages in the *Clouds*: 98, 245 f., and 1146 ff. (p. xxxiv). At 98 Strepsiades, who does not even know the names of the "wise souls" in the "thinkery," states his *opinion* that "if you pay," they will teach the art of speaking so as to defeat both the just and the unjust. At 245 he spontaneously swears to Socrates to pay him as much as he likes; Socrates ignores the offer and discusses the question of oaths and gods. At 1146 Strepsiades, filled with joy at his son's educational progress in Socrates' hands, freely gives Socrates an honorarium, which was nowhere specifically requested. If Dover thinks Socrates' acceptance of a gift shows that he teaches for pay, he would have to admit that the Platonic Socrates too accepts gifts from his friend Crito, whose son was a follower of Socrates. (*Phaedo* 60a7–9, 118a7–9; *Apology* 33e1, 38b6–9; cf. Xenophon *Oeconomicus* 2.8). (Dover himself seems to admit as much on p. liv.) The apparent contradictions between the Aristophanic and the Platonic-Xenophontic Socrates can be accounted for by the rhetorical intention of Plato and Xenophon to furnish a defense against the Aristophanic critique, or else by the difference between the younger and older Socrates (Strauss, *Socrates and Aristophanes*, pp. 3–4, 8, 48–50, 314). A summary of the literature on the "Socratic problem" is given by Jaeger, *Paideia*, II (New York, 1943), 17–27. See also C. J. de Vogel, "The Present State of the Socratic Problem," *Phronesis* 1 (November 1955), 26–35; W. K. C. Guthrie, *Socrates* (Cambridge, 1971), pp. 5–55; the articles in Gregory Vlastos, ed., *The Philosophy of Socrates* (Garden City, N.Y., 1971), pp. 1–49; Eric A. Havelock, "The Socratic Self as It Is Parodied in Aristophanes' *Clouds*," *Yale Classical Studies* 22 (1972), 1–18.

In Plato's *Phaedo*, which portrays the conversation of Socrates on the day he died, Socrates discourses at length about "the things under the earth and the heavenly things." He admits there that he devoted his youth to the investigation of such matters. "When I was young," he says, "I had a wondrous desire for the wisdom that they call inquiry about nature." He wanted to learn "the causes of each thing: why each thing comes into being, why it perishes, and why it is." After a careful study of things "concerning the heaven and the earth" and other visible phenomena, he concluded that he could not thereby obtain the knowledge he desired, since the direct observation of things did not lead him to their causes. So he turned away from the investigation of beings "in deed," that is, in their visible manifestations, to their investigation "in speeches." "It seemed to me that I should take refuge in speeches and consider in *them* the truth about the beings."[14] Speeches (*logoi*) mean not merely arguments, but also what people say and believe about things, that is, their considered opinions. Men learn their opinions through the families and cities where they live, where the poetry and customs of the community form their views of things.[15] Hence Socrates' seeming renunciation of physics for political or ethical philosophy—his calling down of philosophy from the heavens and compelling it to inquire about morals and things good and bad[16]—continues his old search for "the truth about the beings," but in a new way.

According to this account, Socrates' career had two stages, one devoted to the inquiry about nature, and the other to the "refuge in speeches." In the first stage Socrates was a "pre-Socratic" philosopher, so to speak, a student of the things aloft and under the earth. This was evidently the stage to which Aristophanes addressed himself in the *Clouds*. In the second

14. *Phaedo* 96a6–100a7. Socrates is shown to be quite familiar with *physiologia* in Xenophon *Memorabilia* I.1.11–15, IV.7.5–8. In the *Oeconomicus* of Xenophon he is said to have had a reputation as "one who talks idly and measures the air" before he ever began his conversational investigations of human opinions about the noble and good (6.13–17, 11.3). Cf. Plato *Parmenides*; Xenophon *Symposium* 7.4; *Memorabilia* IV.6.1: "He [Socrates] never stopped considering with his companions what each of the beings is." See Sallis, pp. 38–43, for a more thorough discussion of this section of the *Phaedo*.

15. See n. 9 and ch. 1, n. 6, above.

16. Cicero *Tusculan Disputations* V.10.

stage Socrates conducted his inquiry through conversations in which he would examine men's opinions about things. The old and the new accusers apparently correspond to the "pre-Socratic" Socrates and the Socrates with whom we are familiar from Plato's dialogues.[17] Since Socrates cannot deny the charge of having once been an inquirer into nature, his defense, if it is to tell the whole truth, will have to give an account of his leaving behind this study. The story of the Delphic oracle and its consequences will provide that explanation.

When he turned his inquiry to speeches, Socrates was compelled to adopt a new respect for the decent speech of ordinary men. In the *Clouds* either he tries to perfect language artificially by purging it of its incongruous idiosyncrasies, or else he uses language as an indifferent tool to be manipulated for one's own private ends. In the play Socrates insists upon making up a word for "hen," since in Greek the word "chicken," being masculine in gender, does not distinguish between male and female chickens. And Pheidippides uses deft arguments learned from Socrates to justify beating his father and mother.[18] But after his departure from *physiologia*, Socrates, instead of trying to force speech to submit to his own purposes, was obliged to accept it as it was, so that he could learn what unreconstructed, unforced, "natural" speech could reveal about things. He shows in the *Phaedo* that in his attempt to understand the causes of things, he simply followed the implications of *logos* as it is used whenever someone speaks.[19] Yet this later inquiry, wherein he pressed the meaning of ordinary speech to the very limit, caused him to be easily confused with mere verbal quibblers. His relentless pursuit of the implications of men's opinions often led to blatantly paradoxical conclusions. In the *Gorgias*, for example, Callicles is outraged by Socrates' argument that since it does a man good to pay the penalty for injustice, one should make every effort to prevent one's enemies from being brought to trial for crimes committed, lest by being punished they might receive some benefit. From such examples one can appreciate why most

17. Strauss, *Socrates and Aristophanes*, p. 4.
18. *Clouds* 662–667, 1321–1446.
19. *Phaedo* 100a3–102a2.

men, and perhaps rightly so, thought Socrates to be an ingenious perverter of speech.[20]

We have seen that Socrates traces the first charge to the poet Aristophanes (among others), who is "more dangerous" (18b4) than the politician Anytus. Aristophanes' attack on Socrates in the *Clouds* seems to be that of a patriotic Athenian citizen. Yet Aristophanes claims not merely to be just, but also and emphatically to be wise. He calls the *Clouds* "the wisest of my comedies."[21] Socrates' principal defect, from Aristophanes' point of view, is his lack of wisdom, and particularly his lack of self-knowledge. When the Socrates of the *Clouds* imprudently dispenses his subversive thoughts about nature and the gods to a foolish man, he forgets that such talk has consequences on the political community in which he dwells. When the simple citizen Strepsiades finally comes to understand that the ultimate consequence of Socratic wisdom is the destruction of his family, he indignantly burns down Socrates' "thinkery." As he stands on the roof of that building, tearing it apart, he sarcastically calls out to Socrates, "I tread on air and contemplate the sun."[22] Socrates' quotation from this line is therefore doubly appropriate. It reminds us not only of his impious study of nature, but also of his imminent condemnation to death, a fate foreshadowed by the end of the *Clouds*.

The confrontation of Aristophanes and Socrates in the *Apology* is a manifestation of the "old quarrel between philosophy and poetry," which becomes an explicit theme of the tenth book of Plato's *Republic*.[23] Later in the *Apology*, Socrates will treat the poet Meletus, and not the politician Anytus, as his most important opponent in the trial. But Aristophanes in turn is "more dangerous" (and more clever) than Meletus and is therefore a

20. *Gorgias* 480e5–481b1. Plato's *Euthydemus* displays sophistic argumentation based upon equivocations in words and other verbal tricks. Socrates is accused of arguing in a like manner at *Republic* 338d3–4, 340d1, 341a5–b2; *Gorgias* 483a2–3, 489b2–c1, 497a6–b7.

21. *Clouds* 522.

22. *Clouds* 1476–1509.

23. *Republic* 601a4–b4, 607b5–6, c1, 608a6–7. Cf. also the contest between the philosopher Socrates and the poets Aristophanes and Agathon in Plato *Symposium* 175e, 212e5–8, 213e1–6; Gerhard Krüger, *Einsicht und Leidenschaft*, 4th ed. (Frankfurt a. M., 1973), pp. 80–85.

worthier poetic adversary. Socrates' willingness to bring up Aristophanes' criticism of philosophy is another example of the dangerously intrepid truthfulness of his defense.

After Socrates denies any expertise in the things of which he is accused in Aristophanes' play, he hurries to disabuse the jury of a possible but mistaken impression that he dishonors this sort of understanding—if anyone is in fact wise in such matters. "May I never be prosecuted with such indictments by Meletus!" Socrates playfully suggests that Meletus might prosecute him for dishonoring *physiologia*—precisely what arouses Meletus' anger (cf. 26d1–6). The word for "indictment" here is *dikē*, which is also the Greek word for justice. Socrates speaks as though it were a crime—or should be a crime—to dishonor knowledge, even the questionable knowledge of the Aristophanic Socrates. He is trying to bring the ordinary meaning of justice more into harmony with a respect for wisdom. He implies that Meletus and the Athenians are unjust because they do not honor knowledge.

How then does Socrates refute the first part of the charge of the first accusers? He simply asserts that he comprehends nothing of the matters portrayed in the *Clouds*, saying that "I, men of Athens, have no share in these matters." Does he mean that he has no expert understanding of them? Or does he deny absolutely that he thinks about or studies such things? This emphatic but ambiguous statement is not clarified by his "proof": he asks whether anyone among the judges has ever heard him conversing about such things. He does not deny that he converses about them, but he is confident that none of the jurymen ever heard him do so. The unstated premise of Socrates' "proof" of his innocence is that he has no secrets. Yet is it likely that Socrates always says the same things both "in the market at the money-tables," where many hear him speak, and "elsewhere," perhaps in more secluded surroundings? (17c8–9). Is it credible, as he later declares, that he never says anything in private that he does not also say publicly? (33b6–8). Episodes of silent meditation are recounted elsewhere in Plato. Yet Socrates implies that he has nothing whatever private or personal about him: he is simply open to everyone to be seen as he truly is. (In a similar context in his defense of Socrates, Xenophon says that Socrates "was always in the open.")[24] The identification of an outer unadorned appearance with a solidly reliable inner substance, applied in the proem to his manner of speech, is here extended to his whole life. His earlier refusal to give the truth a deceptively attractive form is but one sign of his persistent equation of what he is with what he says. Yet in spite of Socrates' perfect openness, virtually everyone in Athens misunderstands him. In our discussion of the proem we have already seen this equivocal sense in which Socrates' truthfulness both reveals and hides what he is, allowing him to proclaim that he has no secrets even while he eludes the comprehension of most men.

Socrates' affirmation of ignorance concerning the things under the earth and the heavenly things is not surprising, at any rate, if not necessarily for the reasons he avers. He generally maintains in other dialogues that he knows nothing certain about the gods and the afterlife (cf. 29b2–7). According to the account in the *Phaedo*, it was precisely because of his failure to achieve wisdom through the study of nature that he turned to the inquiry in speeches.[25]

When Socrates denies that he "comprehends" or has "understanding" of such things, he seems to address himself more to the charge of engaging in *physiologia* than to that of making the weaker speech the stronger. This impression is strengthened by his use of the expression "conversing about such things," for one does not converse *about* one's use of clever speech, one simply uses it. Socrates never answers this central part of the first accusers' charge. Yet it is perhaps here that he is most clearly vulnerable, for his entire cross-examination of Meletus, not to speak of frequent instances of similar sophistic victories in other Platonic dialogues, would seem to confirm this part of the charge against Socrates.[26]

Socrates calls on the judges to teach and to tell each other that his defense is truthful. The difficulty is that they are the very ones who have been filled with the slander against him. Soc-

24. Plato *Symposium* 174d–175b, 220c–d; Xenophon *Memorabilia* I.1.10.
25. *Phaedrus* 229c–230a; *Phaedo* 96a–100a, 107a–b, 114d1–2.
26. Alexander Sesonske, "To Make the Weaker Argument Defeat the Stronger," *Journal of the History of Philosophy* 6 (July 1968), 222.

rates asserts that if the jurymen obey him and teach each other that he is innocent, they will realize that the other things that "the many" say about him are also untrue. But they themselves *are* the many: they are the very ones who accept and spread the slanders. Moreover, the impression created by Socrates' vehement praise of the knowledge of nature (if such knowledge exists) is not likely to be taken favorably. That praise cannot help intensifying the suspicions they already have about this "wise man."

When he presents the charge of the first accusers in the prothesis, Socrates says nothing about being accused of "teaching others these same things." As it is here restated, the charge is similar in form to that of the present accusers, which accuses Socrates of impiety and corruption of the young. Just as the investigation of the things under the earth and the heavenly things is impious because it questions the gods' existence, so also teaching others these same things is corrupting because it takes away their respect for gods, law, and tradition. (In his dialogue with Meletus, Socrates confirms that his corruption of the young is thought to be a product of his teaching on the gods [26b2-7].) These two parts of the two charges might be said to refer to Socrates' most characteristic private and public activities, his thought and his conversation. This would be correct. But we have already seen that Socrates admits no difference between his private thoughts and public deeds. They are complementary aspects of an existence distinguished by a greater degree of unity than other lives exhibit. Hence the third and central part of the first charge, "making the weaker speech the stronger," contains in itself both the private and public sides of Socrates' life as perceived by the first accusers. As an action directly or indirectly denying the gods of the city, "making the weaker speech the stronger" is *ipso facto* impious, but when listened to by others its subversion of the gods is corrupting. The privacy of thought comes to light in speech, and Socrates' speech, which is always conversation, is necessarily heard by others.

Xenophon has his Socrates divide human activity into three parts: things spoken, things done, and things silently deliberated.[27] These three parts correspond to the three items listed in the charge of the first accusers. "Making the weaker speech the stronger" is what Socrates speaks; "teaching others" is what he does; "investigating the things under the earth and the heavenly things" is what he silently deliberates. The ambiguous medium of Socrates' speech, which tells the truth while hiding it, binds together the openness of publicity and the secrecy of privacy into a seamless union. For his speech reveals his "silent deliberations" because it speaks the whole truth, while it simultaneously conceals that truth by its lack of external order and arrangement. The three parts of the charge therefore point to the three essential moments in the self-avowed perfect integrity of Socrates' life.

The structure of Socrates' defense speech proper, the first long speech of the *Apology* as a whole, consists of the introductory section (the proem and prothesis), followed by fifteen consecutive sections dealing alternately with the impiety and corruption charges: in each section Socrates deals first with the theme of impiety, then with corruption, and so on. This sequence is disturbed only once in the *Apology*, on an occasion to be noted later.[28] This studied arrangement running through the whole speech silently confirms how closely connected are the charges of the first and later accusers. Far from being an arbitrary, vague slander unrelated to the true Socrates, the earlier charge, like the later one, addresses itself to the very substance of Socrates' thought and conduct.

Does Socrates Try to Educate Human Beings? (19d8–20c3)

Socrates now turns to the last of the three counts of the first accusers' charge, the one which accuses him of "teaching others these same things." His response has two parts. The first is a single sentence in which he flatly denies that he tries to educate human beings and charges money for it. The rest of the section consists of a digression wherein he discusses those who *do* edu-

27. *Memorabilia* I.1.19; cf. Democritus Fr. 2, in Hermann Diels, ed., *Die Fragmente der Vorsokratiker*, 16th ed. (Zurich, 1972), II, 132.
28. See pp. 130 and 136 below.

cate, or try to educate, human beings for pay, those known as "sophists": "Although this also seems to me to be noble, if one is able to educate human beings, like Gorgias of Leontini, and Prodicus of Ceos, and Hippias of Elis."[29])

If Socrates "also" considers education noble, he must consider the understanding of *physiologia* noble as well. He has just proposed that justice requires that knowledge be honored (19c5–7); now he suggests that knowledge, whether of *physiologia* or education, is noble or beautiful (*kalon*). In the proem Socrates alluded to his conflict with justice and nobility as these qualities are understood by the city through its traditions. Now he intimates an alternative to the prevailing convention by proposing that wisdom or knowledge be considered both just and noble. In general Socrates' defense depends upon his attempt to correct the tradition by making the citizens more respectful of the pursuit of wisdom. He must teach the men of Athens to change their opinions about beauty and justice if philosophy as a way of life is to become respectable. We see here the beginning of that project. But once he embarks on such an educational mission, Socrates places himself into an antagonistic relation to the tradition accepted by the jurymen. He must therefore win them over completely to his side in order to avoid conviction and execution. Is he therefore guilty of "trying to educate human beings" in the very section of his speech where he denies it? This would indeed be the case, if his attempt were a serious one. But his offhand manner and deliberately unpersuasive speech indicate that he intends rather to show what he would have to do in order to achieve acquittal, than actually to try to be acquitted.

Just as Socrates alluded in the previous section to Aristophanes' claim to be wiser than Socrates, now he explicitly discusses the sophists' claim to know how to educate human beings. Beneath the surface of his conflict with the Athenian tradition is a profounder contest with the chief claimants to wisdom, the poets and sophists. Socrates mentions three sophists, of whom the central one is Prodicus, an expert on the use and

29. See Translation n. 29.

meanings of words.[30] It is appropriate that his should be the central place immediately after Socrates' precise use of the word "noble." Moreover, Socrates employs here the word *anthrōpos* (human being) for the first time in the *Apology*, to signify a broadened perspective, a human as opposed to a merely Athenian view.[31] The sophists mentioned are all foreigners. Socrates stresses their foreignness (as well as their cleverness) by describing how they are able to persuade the youth of each of the cities to pay them for their company, when it is possible for these young men to associate with their own citizens for free. Education is a matter whose importance transcends the attachment to one's own city; one seeks the best education possible, not merely the local one. (This is not to deny, of course, that most men believe the traditional education to be superior.)

Socrates seems to bring up the sophists in order to dispel the misconception that he is one of them. By using "wise man" synonymously with "sophist" (20a3, a4), he indicates that he is mistaken for a sophist by the first accusers. Some of the sophists did profess to teach *physiologia* (e.g. Hippias) and rhetoric, the art by which one can do anything one wishes in speech (e.g. Gorgias).[32] Socrates will prove his innocence of the charge of "teaching others these same things" by distinguishing himself from the sophists. He denies that he shares the two characteristic traits of sophistry: he neither charges money for teaching nor professes to be able to educate human beings. His notorious poverty provides plausible evidence against any suspicion of money-making, and in fact, even the present accusers do not accuse him of teaching for pay (31b7–c3). Socrates' innocence of the charge of teaching others depends upon his claim not to "understand" or "know" the art of education (20c1–3). Hence his refutation of the charge says nothing about whether he discusses *physiologia* and practices clever speaking in the presence of others. It is as though a lifelong student of mathematics, having conversed with young men for many years about num-

---

30. Plato *Euthydemus* 277e3–4, *Laches* 197d3–5.
31. See Translation n. 27.
32. See Translation n. 29.

bers, lines, triangles, and their relations, denies that he "educates" students in mathematics because he does not possess final knowledge about the mathematical inquiries he pursues. His denial would be particularly implausible if he were in the habit of demonstrating the inability of anyone else to speak adequately about mathematics. Socrates is admittedly as guilty as the sophists of drawing the young men away from their fathers and fellow citizens, the traditional educational authorities. The youth prefer to associate with Socrates, not only because they enjoy watching him refute pretentious men who profess to know something, but also because they suppose that he is "wise in the things about which [he] refutes someone else" (23c2–7, a4–5).[33] Socrates shows the young by example and by argument that most men, being ignorant, are incapable of educating anyone rightly (21b–23e, 25a9–c1). The accusers and the citizens are more concerned about these matters than about whether Socrates possesses the true "art of education" or only "human wisdom" (20d8). Indeed, this effect of his on the youth is precisely what his accusers call "corruption" (23d1–2, 29c3–5; cf. 37e1–2). In these respects, decisive for the accusers and the men of Athens, Socrates is indistinguishable from the sophists. Therefore he could refute the corruption charge to the Athenians' satisfaction only if he could persuade them of his superiority to themselves in his understanding of the virtue "of human being and citizen" and of how to achieve that virtue. Instead, he proclaims his ignorance of both.

Socrates continues his account of the sophists by telling a story. He narrates a conversation he had shortly before the trial with an Athenian named Callias. Socrates introduces him as the "man who has paid more money to sophists than all the others." (Two of the sophists mentioned by Socrates here, Prodicus and Hippias, appear as guests at Callias' house in Plato's *Protagoras*.) Callias, whose father was thought to be the richest man in Greece, is in regard to wealth wholly opposite to Socrates, who lives in ten-thousandfold poverty (23c1). In some

---

33. Cf. Plato *Meno* 91a–92e; Xenophon *Apology of Socrates to the Jury* 20, *Memorabilia* I.2.9, 49–55. Cf. Eric A. Havelock, "Why Was Socrates Tried?" in *Studies in Honour of Gilbert Norwood*, ed. Mary E. White, *Phoenix* suppl. vol. 1 (1952), 103–105.

contemporary comedies Callias is ridiculed for his dissolute manner of life.[34] In the *Apology* Socrates (or Plato) alludes to a particular scandal in which Callias was said to be involved. At another trial that took place about the same time as Socrates' (probably a few months earlier), Callias prosecuted an Athenian named Andocides on a charge of impiety. In his defense speech, which has been preserved, Andocides tells a shocking story about Callias. He asserts that Callias married a woman whose mother he later took as a mistress. For a time Callias kept both mother and daughter in his house together. He had one son by the daughter and another son later by the mother. At first he acknowledged only the daughter's son as his own, and he swore an oath that this was the only son he ever had. But later he swore that her mother's son was also his own.[35]

We do not know if this story was common knowledge in Athens at that time. We do not even know if it was true. Hence we cannot know whether or not the members of Socrates' jury were aware of these scandals surrounding Callias. However, certain features of Socrates' conversation with Callias hint that the matter was no secret to Socrates, at least. In any event, the author of the *Apology of Socrates* was well acquainted with the story.

Socrates emphasizes that Callias has two, and only two, sons. He first uses the word "two" explicitly, and then repeatedly uses the dual number in Greek to refer to the two sons. He seems to allude to Callias' broken oath and his former denial of one of his sons. According to Andocides, the youngest son was already grown up prior to the trial.[36] Thus Socrates' comparison of the two sons to "colts or calves" is singularly inappropriate. Socrates appears to offend Callias intentionally by drawing attention to the primary evidence of Callias' irregular family af-

---

34. Aristophanes *Birds* 283–286, *Frogs* 428–430.

35. Translation n. 30; for the exact date of Socrates' trial, see Eduard Zeller, *Die Philosophie der Griechen in ihrer geschichtlichen Entwicklung,* part 2, vol. 1 (5th ed., 1922; repr. Darmstadt, 1963), p. 45n; for the date of Andocides' trial, see Douglas MacDowell, ed., *Andokides: On the Mysteries* (Oxford, 1962), pp. 204–205; R. C. Jebb, *The Attic Orators from Antiphon to Isaeos,* 2d ed. (London: Macmillan, 1893), I, 81–82, argues less persuasively that Andocides' trial took place *after* Socrates'.

36. *On the Mysteries* 127.

fairs, the two sons. The conversation consists mostly of a long and windy question by Socrates. Callias gives the tersest possible answer to the three-part question about a fitting educator for his sons: "Evenus, Socrates, from Paros: five minae." If this conversation really did take place, it is not hard to imagine an irked Callias abruptly departing from the impertinent and tactless questions of Socrates after giving this curt response.

Why does Socrates choose to report a conversation on education which he had with Callias, of all people? An Athenian more notorious for improper behavior and questionable associations can hardly be recalled. If the outcome of Callias' suit against Andocides is any indication, he cannot have been very popular or powerful, for Andocides won an acquittal. Callias, especially in the year of Socrates' trial, seems to embody the height of personal depravity and corruption. With such a man Socrates seeks to inform himself on the subject of educating the young, on how to make them "noble and good in their appropriate virtue."[37] Socrates, on trial for corrupting the young, discusses with a corrupt interlocutor an art whose product is supposed to be the opposite of corruption (24e4–5, 25a9–10). Most obviously Socrates intends to contrast the manifest failure of the sophists' education on Callias with the fact that he has spent more money on them than others. Callias is a vivid refutation in deed of the sophistic promise to teach the virtue of human being and citizen.

A further reason for bringing Callias into a discussion on education may be indicated by the following considerations. Socrates compares the art of education to the art of training colts and calves. (An "art" or techne is a teachable skill in making or doing some particular thing that is not simply natural.)[38] Expertise in the arts of animal training is wholly independent of what we would call the moral character of the artisan. An expert horse-trainer would also know best how to injure horses, just as an expert guardian of money could also be an expert thief.[39] When one looks to competence alone, abstracting from the propriety of the intention or disposition of the individual arti-

37. See Translation n. 31.
38. See Translation n. 34.
39. Plato *Republic* 333e3–334a10.

san, the moral attitude becomes irrelevant. So Callias, whose moral character is most doubtful, could be sensibly approached by Socrates as a man who might well direct him to a knower of the art of education.

However, the analogy between the arts of animal training and human education is not easy to defend because of the complexity of human virtue. Socrates asks Callias, "Who understands such virtue, that of human being and citizen?" An educated man must perfect himself as an individual, but he must also learn his proper place in the order of the community. But if the community happens not to be a well-ordered one, then he may find that citizen virtue opposes human virtue. A good citizen loyal to the political order in Hitler's Germany would not necessarily have been a good man. Callias is himself a model—almost a caricature—of a man whose pursuit of human virtue (through the sophistic education) coexists uneasily with his manifest neglect of the citizen virtue approved by the political community. What is the sophists' response to this potential disharmony between virtue simply and virtue as taught by the city? Like so many professors down through the ages, they act as though their cosmopolitan manner could be transmitted to young men without great difficulty—as though "academic freedom" could be guaranteed by effective speech alone. They pay too little attention to the conditions or limits imposed by the political regimes. They tend to forget this restraint because they suppose that their dextrous speech and quick intelligence can overcome it.[40] Gorgias boasts that a man who has mastered the art of rhetoric is able, by his speech alone, to rule other men and even to make them his slaves if he likes.[41] The sophists' identification of wisdom and virtue with persuasive speech causes them to comport themselves with boastful vanity wherever they appear in the Platonic dialogues.[42]

The sophistic education aims at making a man capable of ruling in his city. But for what is that rule to be used? Here the

40. Socrates has to interrupt Hippias' boasts about his successes everywhere in the Greek world to remind him that he is not permitted to deliver his usual course of lectures at Sparta (*Hippias Major* 283b–286b).
41. *Gorgias* 452d–e, 456a–c.
42. This may be seen in Plato's *Gorgias, Hippias Major,* and *Protagoras.*

sophists have no answer but the conventional one: wealth, honor, and the gratification of one's every desire. In spite of its apparent repudiation and transcendence of convention, sophistry embraces the most vulgar opinions about human happiness. The "virtue" that it teaches enables a man to attain political power, but it cannot direct him to its proper use once it is obtained. Hence sophistry can offer no adequate *logos* or account of what its education understands virtue or nobility to be. Since the sophists teach for pay, they are compelled to make their wares palatable to the market—to the demand of vulgar opinion. Being dependent upon popularity, they cannot refuse to pander to the young men's most powerful ambitions. Socrates' discussions in other dialogues with Gorgias, Protagoras, and Hippias all display the sophists' thoughtless acceptance of tradition and common opinion in such matters and their consequent inability to present a coherent discussion of human excellence. In the end, as Socrates states it in the *Republic*, the sophists "educate in nothing else but in those opinions of the many which they opine whenever they are gathered together, and they [the sophists] call this wisdom."[43]

That Socrates asks Callias where the expert educator of the young is from indicates that he does not necessarily expect him to be an Athenian. Like Callias, Socrates is not satisfied with the citizens' answer to the question of the best teacher of virtue. The citizens believe that any Athenian is fully competent to teach virtue, as Meletus maintains later (25a9–11).[44] But unlike Callias, Socrates is not convinced that the sophists possess the art of education. Such knowledge may not be available to human beings at all, since "human wisdom" will turn out in the sequel to be knowledge of ignorance.

Socrates wants to know who is an appropriate master (*epistatēs*) who understands (*epistēmōn*) the virtue of a human being and citizen. His pun on the words for "master" and "knower" points to a serious teaching: the educator should be in a position to rule his students—in principle, absolutely. The following

43. See the dialogues listed in the previous note; cf. *Republic* 336b–354c. The quotation is from *Republic* 493a6–9.

44. In the *Meno* (92e) Anytus declares that any Athenian gentleman is a more capable educator than the sophists.

considerations may help to explain why an educator must have the power to implement his training with force if necessary. The sophists, as foreigners traveling from city to city merchandizing their educational wares, are at the mercy of the established political authorities, who may forbid sophistry whenever they like; hence the sophists are never really "masters" of their pupils. Cleverness of speech has little effect if the cities or their leaders refuse to listen. Just as horses and cattle cannot be trained by speeches alone (to say the least), so also the sophists neglect "the fact that sheer bodily force is a necessary ingredient of the rule of men over men."[45] By its very nature, the education of the young involves the political question of who rules. The laws and customs of the community decisively affect the formation of character and the conception of virtue that guides the young. The art of education in its most comprehensive sense includes the authority to make or remake those laws. If the original legislator of the polity did not enact his institutions with adequate knowledge of the nature and end of human life, then the virtue of a human being will be at odds with the virtue of a citizen. There will be only imperfect and limited occasions for an effective art of education unless the potential educator can be the lawgiver of the political community. Sophistry, then, is a sham image of the true art of making men good, which is the art of education or legislation.[46] This art provides a common ground on which the two kinds of virtue, human and political, can meet. In this best case the legislator would make laws that teach "the virtue appropriate to a *human being*" to the *citizens* of his city. On the level of legislation, the tension between the human and the political would achieve a resolution—if, in fact, there *is* an art of legislation. Concerning this question Socrates professes his ignorance.

---

45. *Republic* 327b–c; Leo Strauss, "Plato," in *History of Political Philosophy,* ed. Leo Strauss and Joseph Cropsey, 2d ed. (Chicago, 1972), p. 44; cf. Strauss, "Niccolo Machiavelli," in ibid., pp. 291–292.

46. In the *Gorgias* Socrates maintains that sophistry, which professes itself able to make men better (i.e., educate them), is a deceptive pretense that apes the genuine art of legislation (464b2–466a3, 519c–520b). The Athenian stranger in Plato's *Laws* says that the purpose of legislation is to care for "how a man becomes good, possessing the virtue of soul proper to a human being" (770c7–d2). Cf. Aristotle *Nicomachean Ethics* 1179a33–1181b15.

The Origin of Socratic Philosophy (20c4–23c1)

The Oracle (20c4–21c2)

Socrates has completed his defense against the first accusers. He has discussed the parts of the charge in order (scanting, it is true, the charge of making the weaker speech the stronger). But the speech goes on, which seems to indicate that Socrates is not unaware of the weakness of his defense so far. He freely brings up an objection which "one of you" might raise. The hypothetical contradictor wants to know what is Socrates' *pragma* (activity, business, "thing"). "For surely if you were practicing nothing more uncommon than others, such a report and account would not have come to be, unless you were doing something different from the many." In other words Socrates' unconditional denial of the charge is unconvincing, given the prejudice against him.[47] He agrees to show the jury "what it is that has brought me this name and slander." His explanation, as we will see, takes the form of an ironic intellectual autobiography.

Socrates expects some of the jurors to think he is playing or joking. "Know well, however," he says, "that I will tell you the whole truth." He does not deny that he will joke. In fact, playfulness and truthfulness, so far from being opposites, go together in Socrates' speech. Moreover, Socrates also indulges in both irony and boasting. Playing or joking in speech is akin to irony and boasting, since all seem to involve disproportions. Strictly speaking, irony is self-depreciation, an understatement of one's worth, while boasting is an overstatement of one's worth.[48] Exaggeration as such might seem to be a form of lying, but one can also exaggerate in order to highlight important differences—to reveal the truth. Socrates' speech in the *Apology* is both ironic and boastful, and he jokes while telling the truth. As Plato's *Sixth Letter* has it, seriousness and play are "sisters."[49] Socrates combines irony and boasting in his account

---

47. Cf. Strauss, "On Plato's *Apology*," p. 156.
48. Aristotle *Nicomachean Ethics* 1127a13–b32.
49. 323d1–2; cf. Xenophon *Memorabilia* I.3.8.

of the origin of his way of life. He boastfully claims to possess "human wisdom"—to be wiser than anyone he has ever met—but he ironically maintains that such wisdom is worth little or nothing. He boastfully recounts the Delphic oracle's pronouncement that no one is wiser than Socrates—but his interpretation of that oracle leads him to an ironic humility in the face of divine wisdom.

The theme of this section as a whole (20c4–23c1) is Socrates' wisdom or his "service to the god" (23c1). So far in the *Apology* Socrates has shown himself "negatively," from the three perspectives of the politicians and the many (18a7–e4), the poets (19a8–d7), and the sophists (19d8–20c3). He has distinguished himself from the political tradition of Athens, from those who discourse on nature, and from those who profess the art of education. Now he presents himself from the perspective of "the god" or of his own wisdom, distinguishing himself from the god's divine wisdom. Accordingly, his way of speech becomes more boastful than before. He says he expects his listeners to think he is boasting. Socrates no longer holds himself back: supported by "the god," he lets his true superiority shine forth.

Immediately after he admits that he will seem to be boasting, he quotes or rather misquotes a line from Euripides. The original of the line was "not mine is the tale" (*mythos*); Socrates' version is "not mine is the story" or "speech" (*logos*).[50] The "myth" or tale of the original line has been changed by Socrates to a "speech" or reasoned account. The substitution may imply that the story he is about to tell is a *mythos* pretending to be a *logos*, that he is presenting as true something which is a mere tale. This tale is probably what Socrates expects to be taken for a boast. In any event this story of the oracle could not be very well known in Athens if he expects people to believe that he is joking or boasting here.

Socrates says that his companion Chaerephon once went to Delphi and asked the oracle whether there is anyone wiser than Socrates. The Pythian priestess replied that no one is wiser. Although he says at first that he will provide the god in Delphi

50. See Translation n. 38.

as witness, we cannot help noticing a rather long intervening chain of informants. The god at Delphi first had to tell or inspire his Pythian priestess; she then told Chaerephon, who is unfortunately now dead; Chaerephon in turn told his brother, who is present at the trial, and Socrates. In the end, Socrates says that Chaerephon's brother will be the witness, although he never calls upon him to testify, as he was permitted to do.

What sort of man was Chaerephon, the "witness" of this fantastic story? Socrates says that he was "vehement... in whatever he would set out to do." At the beginning of Plato's *Charmides*, Socrates calls him a "madman." References to Chaerephon in Aristophanes are far from flattering. In the *Clouds* Strepsiades calls him "miserably unhappy and half dead." In the *Birds* he receives the epithet "the bat." These descriptions conjure up a rather odd character. As the chief companion of Socrates in the *Clouds* he seems to have been even more ascetic than Socrates himself.[51] Socrates mentions that Chaerephon was a member of the democratic party in Athens, and should therefore be a trustworthy witness to the jurors, but when Socrates emphasizes his unseemly boldness in approaching the oracle, he seems to detract from Chaerephon's value as a sympathetic witness. It is apparently at this point that the members of the jury shout out their disbelief in or disapproval of the story (21a5).

Socrates says that he could not understand the oracle, for he was aware that he himself was not wise at all. Although he hesitated to suppose that the god could be lying or mistaken, he proceeded to try to prove just that. He undertook a search—"very reluctantly," to be sure—for a man wiser than himself, so that he could "refute the divination and show the oracle, 'This man is wiser than I, but you declared that I was.'" The fact that Socrates eventually becomes the pious champion of the god's veracity draws attention away from his original impious intention and expectation: to show up the Delphic Apollo as a liar or a fool. Socrates gives the judges two choices. If they disbelieve the story of the oracle, they must conclude that Socrates is not only

---

51. *Charmides* 153b2; *Clouds* 504, 144, 104; *Birds* 1296, 1564; cf. John Burnet, ed., *Plato's Euthyphro, Apology of Socrates, and Crito* (Oxford, 1924), note on 20e8.

a braggart, but that he makes up stories about the highest beings the city looks up to, the gods—and in his own interest. If, on the other hand, they believe his tale, they cannot help observing Socrates' initial doubt of the god's truthfulness. Indeed, on the basis of Socrates' belief that it is not "lawful" for a god to speak falsely, his attempted refutation amounted to a tacit denial either of Apollo's divinity or of the priestess' inspiration by the god. It should be noted that these alternatives are compatible with the beliefs of the Aristophanic Socrates: in the *Clouds* he simply denied that the Olympian gods exist. His attempt to refute the oracle looks like a debunking of the Delphic Apollo. In any event Socrates sets himself up as judge of the god's utterance, and hence as the god's superior. The story which is supposed to show Socrates' piety barely conceals his *hybris*.[52]

The Examination of the Politicians, the Poets, the Artisans—and Socrates (21c3 –22e5)

Socrates began an examination of those who seemed to be wise in order to refute the oracle. At the beginning of his search he was aware that he himself knew nothing, but he was unaware of the knowledge of those around him. At first he expected to find someone wiser than himself. Prior to the oracle he cannot have yet conversed in a serious way with anyone in Athens reputed to know something. He apparently paid little attention to the world and city in which he lived until after Chaerephon's trip to Delphi. Before that, like the Socrates of the *Clouds*, his gaze was presumably directed upward, and he thought of the rest of mankind as mere "ephemerals." Chaerephon's question to the oracle shows that Socrates had a reputation for wisdom before he turned exclusively to conversation as his peculiar activity: he only began his questioning examinations after the oracle was delivered. This pre-Delphic wisdom had nothing to do with the "human wisdom" which Socrates only discovered after his examination of the men of Athens. He was probably engaged at the time before the oracle in the sorts of studies depicted or caricatured in the *Clouds*. At least Socrates

52. Sallis, pp. 47–49; cf. however Burnet's note on 21b8. Cf. Xenophon *Apology* 14.

agrees with Aristophanes that Chaerephon was his companion prior to his discoursing on virtue.

Socrates' turn away from "nature," or the things in the world as they appear in and by themselves, was a turn to opinion. After he heard the oracle and pondered it for a long time, he went to one of those who were reputed to be wise. (The word for "reputed" here is from *dokein*, to seem or to be opined. From this word comes *doxa*, opinion or reputation or glory.)[53] At first Socrates followed the opinion of the public, of "everyone," in seeking someone wiser than himself. Those whom the public holds to be wise are the political men, the men whom the many honor by choosing them for the city's offices (35b1–3).

Socrates went to one of the political men and considered him thoroughly. This examination, unlike Socrates' pre-Delphic investigations, is nothing more than a conversation. In the *Apology* Socrates sketches his examinations altogether too briefly to give a typical account of his conversations with politicians. Socrates presumably had many such conversations, but Plato has given us only one example of them, in the *Meno,* where Socrates argues with his future accuser Anytus.[54] In the *Apology* Socrates contents himself with a summary of the result of such a conversation: "It seemed to me that this man seemed to be wise, both to many other human beings and most of all to himself, but that he was not." The "wisdom" that Socrates sought was knowledge of something "noble [fine, beautiful] and good" (21d4). This expression is also the Greek term for a gentleman, a man who is "noble and good." It reminds one of the Callias conversation, where Socrates asked Callias who could make his two sons "noble and good in their appropriate virtue" (20b1–2). Socrates indicates that the subject of his conversation with the statesmen (just as with Anytus in the *Meno*) was virtue, the object of the art of education.

Meanwhile Socrates could not help noticing that in his examination of this politician he "became hateful both to him and to many of those present." He continued to conduct his examinations of the politicians, in front of "many others." Socrates

53. See Translation n. 2.
54. *Meno* 89e–95a.

recounts the story as though he were so caught up by the fervor of his attempt to prove the god wrong that he was oblivious to normal considerations of tact and politeness. Why could he not talk to these statesmen alone in private, for example? But Socrates, behaving rather like a religious fanatic (although here his intention is so to speak antitheological), pressed on with his investigations, making enemies out of almost everyone in Athens, as might be inferred from his exaggerated description of his public mode of interrogation.

He concluded from his examination of the politicians that the greater their public reputation for knowledge may have been, the less knowledge they possessed in fact; while those who were reputed to be of a paltrier capacity were in fact more fit in regard to prudence. Socrates' first attempt after turning away from his unsuccessful study of nature, which itself rejected all received opinions from the outset, was to go to the opposite extreme and seek out those who were wise according to the most universal opinion, that of the public. When his first examination of a politician failed, he went to "one of those reputed to be wiser than that man": he went even further in the direction indicated by public opinion. But he discovered that the extreme of public opinion was no more helpful in his search for wisdom than the extreme of the study of heavenly and subterranean phenomena divorced from all opinion.

Accordingly, Socrates went from the politicians, who seemed to *many* to be wise (21c6), to the poets, or rather to those of the poets who seemed to *Socrates* likely to be wise (22b1–4). With the poets he had somewhat better results than with the politicians. For although the poets "know nothing of what they speak," they do speak "many beautiful [noble] things." (The politicians apparently neither know nor say anything beautiful or noble.) The poets "supposed, on account of their poetry, that they were the wisest of human beings also in the other things in which they were not." We infer from the word "also" that they are wise in their poetry, at least. Their wisdom, however, is a transmitted wisdom. Like those who deliver oracles, they are "inspired" from outside, or moved from within by some inarticulate "nature," serving as vehicles for a higher (or lower) uncomprehended wisdom to reach their readers and listeners.

Since they are unable to present a *logos* of what it is they are saying in their poems, Socrates concludes that they literally do not know what they are doing. In this important respect they are the same as the politicians: they too think they are wise, but are not. Socrates does not hesitate to affirm in 'the strongest language the truth about the politicians' lack of knowledge (22a1–2). Yet when he comes to expose the poets, he is "ashamed to tell you the truth, men; nevertheless it must be said." For Socrates, the poets are more worthy of respect than the politicians. Their poems are carefully "worked on" and contain much that is beautiful and wise. The politicians, on the other hand, are vain reflections of the opinion and reputation that elevate them to the city's offices.

Why did Socrates turn to the poets after his search for a wise man among the politicans failed? He says that he went first to the politicians because of their high standing in public opinion. Poets are also looked up to by the multitude; the people are the poets' main audience. Tragedies and dithyrambs (the two kinds of poetry mentioned here) were performed in popular festivals and contests in Athens. The poets were reputed to be wise by the public as well as by Socrates himself. By investigating the poets Socrates remained within the boundaries set by public opinion, but he began to correct that opinion by reflecting on the results of his conversations with the politicians (22a3–6).

Poetry portrays the splendid attractions of the multitudinous variety of human ends. The heroic warrior, the commander in chief of the expedition, the faithful wife, and the wily traveler and storyteller seem to take on substance by virtue of the poet's vivid images. Through the order of the poem, and of the world of gods and heroes it presents, the poet gives to his audience a sense of the completeness of things. In poetry's *mythoi* the world appears as a *kosmos*, not a *chaos*.[55] Yet the poet typically indicates no clear and definitive criteria for preferring one mode of life or quality of soul over another. He allows his words to convey an impression of human excellence without explicating a rational basis for that impression. When Socrates questioned the

55. Socrates' poetic reconstitution of the afterlife, in the third speech of the *Apology*, is an example. Cf. Allan Bloom, "An Interpretation of Plato's *Ion*," *Interpretation* 1 (Summer 1970), 58.

poets, he found them almost stupidly inarticulate about their own poetry. He concluded that they composed their works "by a certain nature and while inspired," and not with the self-possessed awareness of precise craftsmen. For Socrates a truly artful poet would write with a sober knowledge of man and world; he would not produce his seductive images without the mediation of calculating thought.[56]

Finally he went to the true artisans, the lowly handworkers—the carpenters, house-builders, shoemakers, and so on. For he knew that he would discover "that they understood many beautiful things." Socrates took the poets' inability to give an account of their poems to be a sign of their ignorance. The artisans correct that defect, for they do understand what they do or make in their arts. Apparently, unlike the poets, they are able to explain their activities in coherent speech.

The transition from poets to artisans was perhaps initiated by the reflection that poetry, while aspiring to be an art, is defective because it is not based upon understanding. Guided by the outcome of his conversations with politicians and poets, Socrates now leaves the realm of opinion and enters the realm of art proper. Far from being reputed wise, the craftsmen are generally held in low esteem by the public. And yet, while the poets "speak many beautiful things," the artisans "understand many beautiful things," and they are thereby superior to the poets to a greater degree than the poets to the politicians. The artisans' knowledge distinguishes them from the poets' and politicians' ignorance.

But even the artisans' wisdom is blemished: "the good craftsmen also seemed to me to make the same mistake as the poets: because he performed his art beautifully, each one deemed himself wisest also in the other things, the greatest things." The artisans succumb to the "charm of competence."[57] They mistake their expertise in a coherent but partial pursuit for an adequate general understanding of human life as a whole. Whether it be the planning and construction of houses, the understanding of mathematics, or the command of an army,

56. Cf. Plato *Ion* 533d–536b.
57. The expression is taken from Leo Strauss, *What Is Political Philosophy?* (New York, 1959), pp. 39–40.

they falsely identify their precise knowledge of a particular productive art or craft with the comprehensive vision of "the virtue of human being and citizen."[58] This understanding would know the proper place within a man's life for all the partial arts and actions open to men to pursue. It would be an art of arts, an architectonic or governing art that would allot to each particular craft or pursuit its place and purpose in life's overall economy.[59]

Socrates' mission, as he originally conceived it, was to find someone wiser than himself in order to refute the oracle. If he was honest in his search, he must in principle have examined every kind of human being in Athens—or, for that matter, everywhere. Yet Socrates tells us of only three groups—politicians, poets, and artisans. If Socrates' account is to make sense, these three groups must represent the most important human possibilities. How are we to understand this?

In this short outline Socrates gives us the bare bones of his Odyssean wandering and Heraclean labors (cf. 22a6–7). It is incumbent on the listener to infer the complete body of which these bones mark the frame. In our analysis of the *Apology of Socrates* so far, we have seen the following order: the proem (introduction), the prothesis (Socrates from the political perspective of the politicians and citizens), the reply to the first accusers' "impiety" charge (Socrates from the point of view of a poet), and the reply to their "corruption" charge (Socrates from the sophistic perspective). The three sections which come between the proem and Socrates' own account of himself show how he looks to the politicians and the many, to the poets, and to the sophists.

This list reminds one of the three groups that Socrates examined in his attempt to refute the oracle: the politicians, poets, and artisans. The most noticeable difference is that the sophists have been replaced by the artisans in the later list. Is there a relationship between sophists and artisans? The word "art" (*technē*) occurs only twice in the *Apology*, once in the section on sophists, and once in the section presently under consideration

58. Bloom, "Plato's *Ion*," p. 47.
59. Cf. the action of *Republic*, Books II–IV, where Socrates undertakes this task for the city founded there in speech.

(20c1, 22d6). In our discussion of the section on sophists it became clear that education was the art to which the sophists unsuccessfully aspired, the true theme of that section being the art of education. The intricate correspondence of the earlier three sections of the defense to the three groups examined for their wisdom illustrates the deeper significance of those simple words: politician, poet, artisan. Socrates implicitly holds that these three groups comprise the three significant claimants to wisdom in human life. The story of their examination and his discussion of them in the three sections following the proem are meant to be compared and contrasted. They reflect upon each other in such a way as to enable the reader to achieve an articulate account of human life, and so to begin to understand Socrates' "human wisdom."

In our comparison of the prothesis with the Aristophanes section we discussed the relationship between politics in the vulgar sense and poetry as that between apparent and genuine political power.[60] The poets form the opinions and reputations of men more fundamentally than the everyday struggle of politicians and the competition of "popular ideas." But now we learn that the poets are not true artisans because they can provide no articulate *logos* of the images they compose. The "wisdom" of their beautiful words derives from a source external to their rational understanding. In a word, the poets are as much sham educators as the sophists, although for different reasons: the poets pass on a wisdom that is not their own, while the sophists retail vulgar opinions to their pupils as though they were wisdom. The poets are artless in their composition but comprehensive in their vision of human life. The sophists do proceed in the clear-sighted, calculating manner of the arts and with the poets' broad conception of human excellence. But their lack of adequate knowledge of the end—the virtue of human being and citizen—vitiates their artful unity of purpose.

We may infer from Socrates' remarks on sophists, poets, and artisans that the true art of education will include, in the first place, knowledge of the means to be adopted in order to accomplish the prescribed end. The educator must know the meaning

---

60. See pp. 84–85 above.

and probable effects of his words and deeds. To guide the young to their proper end, he cannot rely upon the self-forgetting intuitive procedure of the poets. He must keep the goal shining before his mind's eye, with a sure grasp of the material—the young souls to be educated, as well as his own resources—with which he must work. His arrangement of educational institutions will depend partly upon the temperament of the human beings, the climate and wealth of his community, and the past habits that the people have followed. He will order the pursuits to be practiced with a close view to the conception of human virtue he chooses to promote. Are the citizens to become a warrior race dedicated to the defense of their fatherland (as in ancient Sparta) or a free people permitted to pursue happiness in whatever way seems best to them (as in the United States)? Are glory and salvation to be won by extending the boundaries of the *imperium Romanum* or through a pious life of monastic contemplation (the high purpose of medieval Christianity)? Whatever the end may be, a craftsmanlike plan must guide the educator's activities.

Second, and most fundamental, the educator must know what it means for men to be "noble and good in their appropriate virtue": he must know "the virtue of human being and citizen." This knowledge must be grounded in sober reflections upon the nature of men, and not in instinctive insight or inspired imaginative frenzy. His understanding, like that of the poets, must embrace life as a whole, but unlike the productions of the poets, the educator's arrangements must emulate the precision of the lower productive arts. The educator must refuse to be deluded by either of the two opposite charms: the "charm of competence," encouraged by the expertise in small things found in the arts and crafts, and the "charm of humble awe," elicited especially by the mysterious resonances in the beautiful words of well-spoken poetry.[61] The educational art will comprise the grandeur of poetic vision, the sober competence of the arts, and the knowledge of virtue professed by the sophists.

61. See n. 57 above; cf. Allan Bloom, "Interpretive Essay," in *The Republic of Plato* (New York, 1968), pp. 405–406.

114

Such an art might easily be mistaken for poetry or sophistry, but it would surpass both.

The art of education would reconcile the tension, of which Socrates spoke in the proem, between persuasion which effectively moves the passions and unattractive, bald truth. If poetry were produced or informed by the dry intellect of the self-aware educational artisan, it could be used to establish habits of action conducive to a life of genuine excellence. But is this indispensable comprehensive knowledge of the purpose of life accessible to human beings? Or is Socrates correct in his conclusion that knowledge of ignorance is the peak of human wisdom? If so, the great educators of the past—above all those seminal "inventive" poets Homer and Hesiod, and the legislators Lycurgus of Sparta and Solon of Athens—have acted without adequate knowledge of man's proper virtue. These educators of Greece, "begetters of prudence and the rest of virtue," would differ from the sophists not in their knowledge of virtue, but in the scale of their ambition: not to make money, but to win lasting fame by shaping the souls of the young who are to be nurtured by their poetry and institutions.[62]

These educators, then, are clearly different from the poets whom Socrates examined in Athens, for although Homer too is a poet, he is a "good poet" (cf. 22d5–6) who wrote with clearsighted awareness of what he was doing and not by inspiration or "nature."[63] Since the art of education is "some wisdom greater than human" (20e1)—this may be the wisdom possessed by "the god" (23a5–6)—then Homer and the other educators seem like gods among men. (It was said that when Lycurgus, legislator of Sparta, went to Delphi, the priestess said, "I am pondering whether to call you a god or a human being.")[64] Homer and Hesiod taught the Greeks about gods and heroes,

---

62. The expressions quoted and educators named in this paragraph are from Plato *Symposium* 209a–e.

63. The term "good poet" is sometimes used in Plato's works to distinguish artful from "inspired" poetry, to the detriment of the latter: *Symposium* 209d2, *Republic* 598e3–5. Cf. Jacob Klein, "Plato's *Ion*," *Claremont Journal of Public Affairs* 2 (Spring 1973), 36.

64. Xenophon *Apology* 15.

those majestic figures to whose words and deeds they looked for guidance and meaning in their lives. The poets' tales instructed men about justice and injustice, good and evil. By molding the images that dominated the Greeks' horizon, these educators shaped their souls for centuries. Homer's image of the beautiful and noble Achilles provided a lasting standard for Greek youths and mothers in living their lives and raising their children.[65]

The "inventive" poets had many followers and imitators. These lesser spokesmen for the great poets and legislators are the poets whom Socrates examined in Athens. They are inspired "like the diviners and those who deliver oracles" because they are moved directly or indirectly by the great educators to compose their own beautiful but lesser works. Hence Socrates can say that "they know nothing of what they speak." As the unconscious transmitters of the wisdom of the past they become the immediate teachers of the present. Just as the politicians and citizens are instructed by these lesser poets, so the poets in turn are given their direction by educators of the first order. The three kinds of men examined by Socrates—politicians, poets, and artisans—happen to be the three segments of a chain that executes the educational process which in turn forms character and opinions generally. The ultimate source of the opinions that rule the political order can be traced back to those rare men who establish the images and customs that determine the *ēthos* in which men dwell.[66] Not the vulgar craftsman Anytus but the godlike teacher Homer is the true political authority in Athens.

Such is the tortuous path by which education becomes politically effective. It is unlikely that Socrates, in one short speech, could imitate the course of the reflective educator who sets forth the truth about virtue, and the inspired poet who transmits the images of that virtue to the people, and the contemporary politician who backs the teaching with threats of punishment for the recalcitrant. Yet that is the mammoth task he would have to accomplish in order to gain acquittal on the condition he estab-

65. Cf. ch. 1, n. 6, and ch. 2, n. 9 above.
66. On *ēthos* as both "dwelling" and "political regime" see Thomas G. West, "Phenomenological Psychology and Aristotelian Politics," revision of a paper delivered at the 1976 Annual Meeting of the American Political Science Association, mimeographed, pp. 22–24.

lishes at the beginning of his defense: the repudiation of the Athenian educational tradition in favor of the doctrine that the pursuit of wisdom is the noblest and most just life for man. Besides, does Socrates even wish to do this? Does not his separation of truth from persuasion compel him to decline any participation in the educational process? Moreover, genuine education, for Socrates, leads to truth, not belief, so that the linking together of educators, poets, and political men in a chain of received wisdom, passed on by persuasion and inspiration, excludes all but the educators themselves from genuine understanding.[67] For Socrates, therefore, education in the precise sense can never be a public matter, for knowledge is only attained through individual thought, never through shared dogma. Yet Socrates does propound a half-serious counterorthodoxy as a substitute for the poets' teachings. He raises the question, without answering it, of the philosopher's proper role in political education.

In our discussion of the three groups which Socrates investigated we have so far forgotten Socrates himself. Through his examinations he intended to find someone wiser than himself in order to refute the oracle. Accordingly, each time Socrates examined one of the three groups, he afterwards examined himself, in order to compare his wisdom with the wisdom of the others. When he went away from the first politician with whom he talked, he reckoned with regard to himself that although neither he nor the politician knew anything noble and good, he himself was wiser than the politician, because he did not deceive himself about his lack of knowledge. When he had completed his examination of the poets, he went away supposing that "I excelled them in the very same thing in which I did the politicians." Finally, after he had questioned the manual artisans, "I questioned myself on behalf of the oracle." He answered himself and the oracle that he was better off just as he was, neither "wise in their wisdom nor ignorant in their ignorance."

Socrates examined the politicians, poets, artisans—and himself. He constitutes a fourth "group" in addition to the other

---

67. Cf. Jacob Klein, *A Commentary on Plato's Meno* (Chapel Hill, N.C., 1965), ch. 4, esp. p. 106.

three, a group of which he is the only member. Only when he includes himself among those investigated does his treatment of the various human types become complete. He begins his "labors" believing that he is insignificant in regard to wisdom, but by the time he finishes, he sees himself as the wisest. His pre-Delphic study of nature led to the result that "I unlearned even the things I previously supposed that I knew."[68] From this state of complete ignorance, so to speak, he undertook the examination in speeches of the various kinds of human beings. At the end of his long wandering he has progressed far from the ignorance of his former state. Now that he has achieved "human wisdom"—the knowledge of his ignorance—he is in a position where he can speak for the god's oracle and even judge his wisdom (22e1, 23a5–6, b2–4).

We have noticed that the three sections preceding Socrates' account of the origin of his political philosophy concerned themselves respectively with political men, poets, and sophists (or educators). Socrates' "intellectual autobiography" itself forms the fourth section paralleling the fourth "group," Socrates himself. It is appropriate that this fourth section should contain within itself the account of all four of the human types. For Socrates, as philosophic inquirer, himself embodies the variety of men's characters. As Nietzsche said, "The most characteristic thing about Socrates was his participation in all temperaments."[69] In the prothesis Socrates presents himself from the point of view of the politicians and the many; in the two sections devoted to the charge of the first accusers, the point of view is that of the poets and the sophists. In the section concerning the origin of the prejudice against him he shows himself from the point of view of the Delphic god. Hence the four section-perspectives are political men, poets, sophists, god. The four groups Socrates examines are politicians, poets, artisans, Socrates. That Socrates should align himself with the Delphic god is in perfect keeping with the boastfulness of the autobiography section as well as of the *Apology* as a whole. We have discerned a "divine chain" of inspiration running from the highest artisan,

68. *Phaedo* 96c6.
69. *The Wanderer and His Shadow*, no. 86. Cf. *Republic* 576e6–577a5, 582a8–d2.

the educator, through the inspired poets, to the public and the politicians. The addition of a fourth "group," Socrates, raises this question: can or should the philosopher become an educator, the first link of the chain?

Socrates is the philosopher who asks questions to which he does not know the answers (23a3–5). His wisdom consists of an awareness of ignorance. It seems unlikely that such wisdom could provide the ground for any kind of definitive education. Such a philosophic education would be based upon a sort of emptiness at its very ground. An educational tradition requires a positive teaching, but Socrates' knowledge of ignorance seems to be a purely formal sort of wisdom, knowing nothing but its own inadequacy. If this is "human wisdom," the highest to which men can aspire, what education could it furnish to citizens born into such a philosophic community? How could Socrates' doubtful and doubting philosophy provide the foundation for an education which, as the start of a tradition of new modes and orders, would teach the citizens of a political regime the way of life they should follow? Is not the very conception of a philosophic founding an impossibility from the start? On the other hand, in the *Apology*, where Socrates seems least in command of firm answers to questions about the "greatest things," he also affirms most emphatically the superiority of the philosophic way of life. In spite of his ignorance, he knows that he is the wisest of human beings. On that foundation— simultaneously solid and empty—he builds the edifice which is unveiled later in the *Apology*. He is so sure that his way of life is the best that he even seems to be prepared to fight and die for it (28d–29c). Knowledge of ignorance leads directly to the care for "prudence, and truth, and how your soul will be the best possible" (29e1–2). Hence awareness of ignorance implies as its corollary the conscientious search for knowledge to remedy that ignorance. Philosophy as a way of life respectable to the community is the "new mode" which a Socratic public education could inspire. Yet such a life is one of endless motion, for Socrates promises no rest for men's striving to know the good for human life. Most men are likely to demand a sheet-anchor of more palpable solidity than the prospect of permanent progress without hope of reaching an end.

An image from another Socratic dialogue may help to elucidate further Socrates' understanding of education and the political order. In the *Republic* Socrates presents to his eager interlocutor Glaucon the celebrated parable of the cave, in order to
sketch an image of "our nature with respect to education and
lack of education." On the floor of the cave sit prisoners, human
beings whose heads are fastened with chains to keep them looking straight ahead. Behind them is a little wall, and behind the
wall men are walking back and forth carrying artifacts. A fire
behind the carriers projects the shadows of the artifacts onto the
wall of the cave which the prisoners face. The shadows of the
carriers themselves are not seen, because they remain below the
wall while they hold the artificial objects which they carry above
it. Some of the artifact-carriers speak, and some remain silent.
The prisoners believe the shadows are "the beings," and they
believe that the voices that accompany the shadows, uttered by
the carriers, belong to the beings themselves. Socrates then describes the education of one of the prisoners, how he is forced to
turn around and look up at the fire, how he is blinded by its
bright light, and then how he is dragged out of the cave into the
blinding light of day. This man, whose eyes eventually become
accustomed to the sunlight, is an image of the philosopher. He
contemplates the true beings in the light of the sun, and
gradually becomes aware of the falseness of the shadows in the
cave.

The inhabitants of the cave include the prisoners and the carriers of artifacts. In addition there is the philosopher, who,
when he returns to the cave from the sunlight, is temporarily
blinded by the darkness of the cave; consequently, he appears to
the prisoners to behave absurdly and criminally. If he should try
to free someone else and lead him up to the light, the prisoners
would say that his eyes were corrupted and they would try to
kill him if they could.[70]

Socrates' image is purposely incomplete. The lacuna occurs
around the fire. For, in order for the artifact-carriers to carry
artifacts, someone must produce them. Hence a fourth group of

70. *Republic* 514a–517a. On the cave, see Bloom, "Interpretive Essay," pp.
403–407; cf. Herman L. Sinaiko, *Love, Knowledge, and Discourse in Plato* (Chicago,
1965), pp. 167–184.

cave dwellers must be supposed, a group of artisans. It may be that the carriers make their own artifacts, but two distinct functions would still have to be performed: carrying artifacts and making artifacts. Hence there are four groups or kinds of cave dwellers: prisoners, artifact-carriers, artisans, and philosopher. These four groups are analogues to the four groups that Socrates examined in his long search for someone wiser than himself: politicians, poets, artisans, and philosopher. Socrates discovered that the politicians were utterly ignorant, that they were mere creatures of a more fundamental public opinion. These, the public and their politicians, are the prisoners of the cave image. They see nothing except the "shadows of artifacts" projected before them by the poets. Those who appear to hold power in the cave, the politicians, are nothing more than those prisoners who are the cleverest at discerning and remembering the passing shadows and are thus able to predict which ones are likely to appear in the future.[71] The politicians of the *Apology* are those who are held by the many to be wise, but who have no genuine knowledge. Just so the politicians of the cave: they too are prisoners of the public opinion there, an opinion no more substantial than shadows.

The ordinary poets of the *Apology*, corresponding to the cave's artifact-carriers, have no knowledge of what they do, although they speak many fine things. They are inspired but ignorant broadcasters of a higher divine wisdom to the many. The cave likeness expresses the same thought by having the poets' counterparts in the cave carry the artifacts whose shadows form the opinions of the prisoners about the beings. They carry the artifacts, but they may not themselves know how to make them. If the carrier did make his own artifacts, he would be like one of those good poets who produce their poetry by art.

In both the *Apology* and the cave likeness, Socrates compares the teachers and inspirers of the poets to the humble artisans. An analogy from these apparently most ordinary of men, the handworkers, illustrates the highest and most divine political task, establishing the educational institutions which form the souls of the citizens of their community. These institutions too

71. *Republic* 516c8–d4.

are artifacts: they are products of the human intellect which are made for a specific purpose. The shoemaker always chooses his tools and materials with a view to his end product, the shoe. The materials will differ if he makes a work shoe, a combat boot, or a dress shoe. The only limitation he faces is the availability of suitable materials. There are some kinds of shoes he will be unable to make, if his available leather is too stiff or thick or if he lacks the necessary nails, glue, tools, and other materials.

The end product that the educator has in view is the formation of a certain kind of human character. The educator's "artifacts"—images and pictures of the preferred kinds of human beings, their rewards, the punishments of the unjust, and so on—when transmitted convincingly by the poets to the multitude, and enforced by suitable legal prohibitions and encouragements, determine the way of life of the community. Like the artisan who is his analogue, the legislator-educator too is limited by the "material" of the community he inherits: the current laws and customs that he seeks to replace, whether the men are reasonably intelligent and spirited, and the resources of the land itself. But within these limits he can form the modes and orders of his community as he thinks best.

The cave likeness leaves the reader wondering about the role the philosopher might play in the making of artifacts. Socrates describes the philosopher's relation to the cave only from the point of view of the prisoners: when he tries to liberate one of the prisoners, the others try to kill him. On the first occasion when the philosopher is forced to try to learn about the carriers of artifacts, he is blinded by the bright light of the fire. Whether he understands and participates in the true hierarchy of power in the cave after his return from the sunlight, Socrates does not say. This doubt is repeated in the parallel in the *Apology*. It is difficult to decide whether or not the philosopher is the first link in the "divine chain" leading from legislation to public opinion. His role could be purely theoretical: he might be the man who holds a synoptic view of the whole political process without himself becoming a participant. Like the philosopher of the cave likeness, he might prefer to dwell far away from the politics of the cave, among the beings as they truly are, believing that he is living in the "Isles of the Blessed."[72] He might then live in a kind of noble isolation from the rest of humanity, like the Socrates of the *Clouds*. Yet the philosopher of the cave does not remain outside in the light of the sun. For some reason he returns to the prisoners he has left and tries to liberate someone else from his chains. There he becomes involved in a life and death fight with the other prisoners. The conclusion of his education is his learning about his own relationship to the prisoners. At first he cannot see clearly because his eyes have not yet gotten used to the darkness, and he therefore becomes an object of ridicule or hatred for the prisoners. Socrates does not describe what the fully educated philosopher does when his eyes become accustomed to the dim light of the cave. But the corresponding discussion at the beginning of Book VI shows that the legislators are expected to be philosophic, for they are said to look up, like painters, to "what is most true" while making laws about the noble, the just, and the good. What is not mentioned in the cave image itself is made clear here: the philosophers can also be educators.[73]

The cave image suggests that education, or the "making of artifacts," is not always directed by philosophic wisdom. The educator may be unaware of the truly best political order. If he has never left the cave, the artifacts he makes may have no relation to the truth of the beings. The regime he founds may be based on nothing more substantial than his own ambition for glory. But it is possible for the philosopher to become a maker of artifacts, although his own lack of desire might prevent it. If he loves his own enough to attempt to educate a future philosopher before his eyes have readjusted to the cave's darkness, would he not comprehend that the conditions for such education must be established for the community as a whole if he is not to be killed for his efforts? Prerequisite for the education of philosophers is the community's willingness to tolerate such education. The philosophic educator could make philosophy respectable by embodying it in appropriately popular images. In the *Republic*,

---

72. *Republic* 519c5.
73. *Republic* 484c8–d3; cf. 519c–520d.

which persistently (and intentionally) plays down the strength of love in human life, Socrates says the philosopher must be compelled to take care of the political affairs and public education of his city. But when the full power of love is admitted, as in the *Symposium* of Plato, that compulsion becomes superfluous.[74]

In the *Apology* Socrates acts like an educator-legislator. He redefines the noble, the just, and the good, and criticizes Athenian political practice and opinions from the point of view of his new understanding. By playing the role of judge of his accusers, he behaves as though his refounding has already taken place. This behavior is proved to be boastful by the vote that condemns him to death. The most that Socrates can do to enforce his attempted founding is to threaten vengeance by loosing the young men he was holding back (39d1). He asserts that it will not be long before those who accused him and voted to condemn him will be reproached for killing a wise man (38c1–3). According to unsubstantiated reports from antiquity, Socrates' prediction was fulfilled. Soon after his execution the Athenians regretted their condemnation of Socrates.[75] But was this turnabout in Athenian opinion due to Socrates himself, or to those who defended Socrates so successfully after his death, Plato and Xenophon? Who was the educator—Socrates, who mockingly and haltingly pointed the way, or Plato, who executed Socrates' "philosophic education"? This question lurks in the background throughout the *Apology of Socrates*.

The New Piety (22e6–23c1)

Let us look again at Socrates' treatment of the Delphic oracle in order to clarify his relationship with the divine. The principle that Socrates attributes to the Delphic god—that it is not lawful for him to say anything false (21b6)—is also stated in one of Pindar's poems. But it also reminds one of Socrates' "theology" in Book II of the *Republic*, where he argues that the gods cannot lie.[76] According to Homer, the Olympian gods sometimes do lie,

---

74. *Republic* 540a–b; Leo Strauss, *The City and Man* (Chicago, 1964), p. 128; *Symposium* 208c–210c.
75. For a compilation of these ancient reports see Zeller, p. 200, n. 4.
76. Pindar *Pythian* IX.42; *Republic* 381e8–383c.

although Apollo, the most truthful of the traditional pantheon, attains most nearly the character of Socrates' gods. When he perceived that he was becoming hateful because of his examinations, Socrates kept on because "it seemed to be necessary to regard the matter of the god as most important" (21e4–5). What does he mean by "the matter of the god"? He was still trying to refute the Delphic oracle, but he seems to say that since his attempt concerned "the god," it was justified. But soon afterwards, just after he swears by the dog (avoiding the usual oath "by Zeus"),[77] he refers to his "investigation in accordance with the god" (22a4). Socrates now speaks as though his attempt to refute the oracle was an attempt to sustain its truthfulness. The purpose of his labors had clearly changed by the time he completed his examination of the politicians. He now acted "so that the divination would become irrefutable for me" (22a7–8).

What is happening here? How could the attempted refutation of the oracle be in accordance with the god? Perhaps "the god" is not the Delphic god (Socrates never speaks of Apollo by name). It would be strange, at any rate, if the oracle approved of Socrates' efforts to overturn it. His oath "by the dog" and the discrepancy about the oracle suggest that the god in question is neither Apollo nor any of the other Olympians. But the obscurity of "the god" is not clarified, for the reference to the "divination" (oracle) points back to the Delphic god.

Socrates states unambiguously that at the beginning of his labors he was trying to refute the oracle. After he began his examinations, his attitude toward the oracle became unclear. However, by the end of the examinations, Socrates becomes the oracle's champion and spokesman. He questions himself "on behalf of" the oracle and answers "myself and the oracle" (22e). He declares that the god is wise. Socrates himself, "inspired" by the god's wisdom, recites his own explanation of the oracle as though it were itself the oracle and he its "priestess" (23b2–4).

Socrates did not stop his examinations when he discovered the true meaning of the oracle. "Even now" he continues his

---

77. See Translation n. 46. For an intriguing interpretation of this oath see Eva Brann, "The Music of the *Republic*," *Agon* 1 (April 1967), 4–5.

seeking and inquiring "in accordance with the god." And whenever he finds someone who seems to be wise but is not, "I come to the god's aid and show that he is not wise." And finally, he lives in "ten-thousandfold poverty" on account of his "service to the god." (Socrates boasts even when speaking of his poverty.)

We note that "service to the gods" is the third definition of piety discussed in Plato's *Euthyphro*.[78] The story of the origin of Socrates' philosophizing culminates in his becoming pious—if he is correct in construing his examinations as service to the god. (He expressed in the prothesis his concern for what is "dear to the god," another understanding of piety offered by Euthyphro.) It is true that these definitions are refuted by Socrates in that dialogue.[79] But he shows no evidence of having been pious in this or any other way before his examinations of the men of Athens.

The Origin of the Present Charge (23c2–24b2)

The words "in addition to these things" indicate the beginning of a new section. They are followed immediately by the words "the young who follow me." The previous section ended with the phrase "service to the god." The theme of that section was Socrates' piety or impiety, and the theme of the present section is his supposed corruption of the young.

Socrates explains here the origin of the corruption charge. During his examinations of the men of Athens, the sons of the rich, who have the most leisure, follow him around "of their own accord" as he questions those who pretend to know something. These idle, rich young men enjoy hearing human beings examined. It was not long before they began to imitate Socrates and to try out their newly learned skill on others who think they know something.[80] Socrates says he supposes that there is a great plenty of such men. Those who are cross-examined by his

78. *Euthyphro* 14d6 (cf. *Apology* 30a6–7).
79. *Euthyphro* 6e–11b, 12e–15c.
80. A charming example of such a conversation is reported in Xenophon (*Memorabilia* I.2.40–46), where the young Alcibiades examines the statesman Pericles on the question, "What is law?"

imitators become angry at Socrates and say that he corrupts the young. But when they are asked how Socrates corrupts the young, "they have nothing to say, but are ignorant. So in order not to seem to be at a loss, they say the things that are ready at hand against all who philosophize: 'the things aloft and under the earth' and 'not believing in gods' and 'making the weaker speech the stronger.'" The central charge of the three is that of atheism or impiety. By this account, the impiety charge arises out of the corruption charge almost as an afterthought. For it is because these men are "ambitious" (23d9) that they are vexed by their youthful examiners. The children deflate the puffed-up pretensions of their elders. The term "ambitious" seems to refer particularly to the political men. Their concern is not with Socrates' impiety or his study of nature. Instead, they add the impiety charge in order to attempt to justify their anger against the one who teaches the young how to show up the ignorance of those whom the city considers outstanding in virtue and therefore worthy of honor (cf. 35b1–3).

This section is an imperfect parallel of the prothesis. There as well as here, the subject is the origin of the great slander against Socrates. Both sections emphasize the intensity and length of time during which the prejudice against him came into being. The charge of the first accusers is repeated in this later section. But these parallels between the sections conceal important differences. The most decisive departure occurs in the account of the origin of the charge itself. In the prothesis Socrates was held to be a philosopher, a "wise man" seeking the things aloft and under the earth, and making the weaker speech the stronger. The people who heard these things believed that seekers of such matters also do not believe in gods. The charge of atheism was a conclusion people drew *after* they heard about his study of *physiologia* and clever speaking. Furthermore, the corruption charge, "teaching these same things to others," was mentioned by Socrates for the first time only when he repeated the charge in the section following the prothesis (19c1). In the prothesis his *impiety* constitutes the essence of the charge. His teaching or corruption of the young is the afterthought there.

We have two distinct and conflicting accounts of the origin of the prejudice against Socrates. The prothesis traces the corruption charge, apparently of only secondary importance, to the impiety charge, the charge that Socrates is a student of nature. The true author of that charge seems to have been the poet Aristophanes. The present section, on the other hand, presents the main charge as corrupting the young. This portrayal traces the origin of the charge to the injured dignity of the Athenian politicians and fathers who were cross-examined by Socrates' youthful imitators. The charge of impiety was added only afterwards, as a convenient slander ready at hand against philosophers. These divergent accounts surround the "autobiography," Socrates' story of the oracle and his turn to the conversational examination of human beings which it occasioned. The first account describes the charge against the "pre-Delphic" Socrates. We have seen that Socrates' defense against that charge was largely unsuccessful. It is probable that, prior to the oracle, Socrates truly did the things of which he was accused by the first accusers. The core of that charge was the impiety which seems to be a necessary consequence of the study of nature. The prejudice of the many was engendered by Aristophanes' comic critique of Socrates in the *Clouds*. Socrates bases this second account of the origin of the slander squarely upon his post-Delphic examinations of the Athenians. They were indifferent to the question of Socrates' atheism. They cared about themselves and their reputations, not about Socrates: they were angered because the children of Athens were making fools of them.

These two versions of the origin of the prejudice against Socrates deliberately confuse his pre- and post-Delphic ways of philosophizing. The reader could easily receive the impression that the charge of the first accusers is distinguished from the later charge only by time. For in the present section Socrates names Anytus and the others as nothing more than recent representatives of the three groups examined by him in his post-Delphic wandering. Almost without our noticing, the charge of the first accusers melts into the present charge. His concern with *physiologia* is "forgotten"—the true ground of the present charge is his corruption of the young. In the prothesis Socrates spoke of two distinct charges of the first and later accusers. But now, after having laid the ground for an illuminating contrast of his pre-

and post-Delphic activities, he scotches our expectations of a clarification by intentionally treating the two charges promiscuously. The reader, carried along by the reassuring flow of Socrates' superficially casual manner of speaking, tends to forget the earlier arguments about the origin of the prejudice. He is eager to applaud Socrates' honesty in openly confronting that prejudice, but he often fails to notice the gaps in the apparently tight logical chain of events.[81] He particularly forgets to ask what Socrates was doing before Chaerephon went to the oracle.

So, just as Socrates maintained at the beginning, there *are* two sets of accusers and two charges. The difference between the two is great. The earlier accusation emphasizes Socrates' impiety, which it deduces from his study of nature, while the later accusation emphasizes his corruption of the young and tacks on the impiety charge as a convenient appendage. (Socrates indicates his disdain for this addition by citing it in grammatically incomplete form.)[82] But there is also a great difference in the way the two charges arose. The first charge was based upon a comically exaggerated but essentially correct treatment of Socrates in the *Clouds*. But the later charge is based upon nothing more solid than the vexation of those Athenians who have been refuted in argument by Socrates and his young followers. The first charge is intelligibly and carefully articulated, while the later charge arises more from vanity than serious thought. It is the first, not the later charge which is founded upon a substantial consideration of Socrates himself. The first charge focuses on Socrates' true pursuits, while the later one begins from his effects. The first has the support of a highly intelligent comic poet; the later one is spread about by empty mediocrities. We are compelled to conclude that the earlier accusers had more truth and justice on their side than the later ones. The core of Socrates' injustice is his disbelief in the city's gods. His true corruption of the young consists not in his showing them how to reveal their elders' ignorance, but in teaching them to doubt that those

81. See, for example, Meyer, pp. 26–27; Erwin Wolff, *Platos Apologie* (Berlin, 1929), p. 14; Werner Jaekel and Siegfried Erasmus, *Lehrerkommentar zu Platons Apologie* (Stuttgart, n.d.), p. 41, n. 14.
82. Burnet's notes on 23d4 and d5.

gods exist. The indictment of the later accusers is correct, but it is correct for reasons that only the earlier charge can explain. The charge of disbelief in the city's gods lay "ready at hand" because of the successful work of Aristophanes and the others in bringing out the truth about Socrates.

An objection might be raised that Socrates changed his ways after the Delphic oracle. He seems to have given up his study of nature and to have turned exclusively to the examination of "ethical" questions. Socrates does imply that this is the case, since he clearly separates his pre- from his post-Delphic activity. But it is also the same Socrates who, having distinguished the periods before and after the oracle, proceeds to confuse them. He thereby indicates that there is no essential difference between the two periods with respect to his attachment to the public orthodoxy. Since he "knows nothing," he certainly does not know whether the city's gods exist. By his own admissions he is at least a confessed agnostic. As he declares later, he does not even know whether the stories told about the afterlife—traditional stories about some of the city's gods—are true (29a–b). Moreover, the very structure of the *Apology of Socrates* reflects the greater importance of the earlier charge. The first accusers considered Socrates' impiety to be a more serious injustice than his corruption of the young. Thus in their charge the crime of "impiety" was stated first. Socrates adheres to that order in the two pairs of sections (19a8–24b2) in which he responds to that charge. But when he quotes the charge of the present accusers in the next sections he reverses the order of its parts and places the corruption charge first. (We know that in the original indictment corruption was mentioned last.)[83] In this way he indicates the greater significance of the corruption charge to the present accusers. But in the second part of his defense (28b–35d) he reverts back to the order established by the first accusers in his alternating responses to the impiety and corruption parts of the charge. Thus the structure of the speech corresponds to Socrates' subtly stated opinion that the first charge is more truthful than the later one.[84]

83. See Translation n. 59.
84. In his summary of Socrates' indictment and trial in the *Seventh Letter* Plato mentions only the charge of impiety (325c1).

The Charge of the First Accusers

This section, like the prothesis, shows Socrates' conflict with the politicians and the many. The prothesis showed a passive Socrates who was utterly unable to do anything about the slanders of the first accusers. Now Socrates counterattacks. He and his followers cross-examine the politicians and bring their pretenses into the light of day. The pre-Delphic Socrates apparently was unable or unwilling to defend himself. In one respect, this is the most obvious lesson of the *Clouds*. Through his examinations of the Athenians he learns a new way of philosophizing, thereby also acquiring the virtue of courage or manliness. He learns how to defend himself against his enemies. The politicians were the first group questioned in Socrates' "autobiography"; they are the first group to be "attacked" by a newly rejuvenated post-Delphic Socrates.

Socrates now goes on to provide details about the origin of the present charge. Those ambitious men who were refuted by the young followers of Socrates have beaten their slanders into "your" ears. "From among these men, Meletus attacked me, and Anytus and Lycon, Meletus being vexed on behalf of the poets, Anytus on behalf of the craftsmen and the politicians, and Lycon on behalf of the orators." The difference between the first and later accusers has now entirely disappeared. The three present accusers are members of the three groups of human beings whom Socrates examines and his companions refute.

Meletus is listed first because he is the author of the written indictment.[85] He is an author by profession, a poet, and Socrates slyly intimates in the sequel that the charge is one of his shoddy poetic products. He maintains that Meletus is "joking" and making a comedy in the indictment (27a1–7, 31d1–2). It is Socrates, of course, who is joking. Meletus is a dedicated man who, of the three accusers, seems to be most truly concerned about Socrates' impiety. The answers he gives to Socrates' questions in the dialogue which follows are characterized by a small-minded but deadly seriousness (cf. 26b2–e5). Meletus "trusts" in the charge circulated by the first accusers (19b1): he does not think for himself.

Anytus' name stands in the center of Socrates' list. Socrates'

---

85. *Euthyphro* 2a1–b4, *Apology* 19b1–2.

conversation with Anytus in the *Meno* leads to the conclusion that the Athenian statesmen do not know how to educate their sons.[86] Anytus becomes angry, causing Socrates to observe that "he thinks he is one of these men," that is, one of the politicians with miseducated children. According to Xenophon's *Apology*, Anytus' son was brought up to be a tanner, like his father. Socrates says there that he had a brief association with the son, and he predicts a bad outcome for him. After Socrates was dead, says Xenophon, the son in fact did become a drunkard and brought Anytus a bad posthumous reputation.[87] We cannot know, of course, how far to trust this story. But if Anytus was having trouble with his son's upbringing, and if his son had spent time with Socrates, these things might help to explain why Anytus, rather than one of the other politicians, became an accuser of Socrates. Perhaps Anytus was cross-examined and refuted by his own son. Surely Anytus associated Socrates with the sophistic, impious circle which was, to him, the most visible token of the decline in the Athenian attachment to its venerable traditions.

About Lycon we know little that is certain. There is a Lycon in Xenophon's *Symposium* who may well be the accuser of Socrates. He is depicted there as a serious and slow-witted Athenian gentleman who has a handsome son. It so happens that Callias (whom we met earlier in the *Apology*) was in love with Lycon's son at the time of the banquet described in Xenophon's dialogue. Callias had just begun to lavish his attentions on the boy. From what we know of Callias' character, it is not difficult to imagine the worst in the further progress of his love affair with Lycon's son. He may well have introduced the good-looking but witless young man to his fashionable set of acquaintances, among whom were the leading sophists. In short, it is possible that Callias "corrupted" the boy in both senses. Lycon may well have held a vague grudge against Socrates for it, since Socrates and Callias were friendly acquaintances. Indeed, Xenophon's *Symposium* ends with a long speech of Socrates praising Callias' love for Lycon's son.[88]

86. See Translation n. 14.
87. Xenophon *Apology* 29–31.
88. Xenophon *Symposium* 1.2, 1.9, 3.12–13, 8.1–41. For "corruption" in the sense of homosexual seduction, see 4.52–54.

Our suggestions about Anytus and Lycon cannot be proved. But they do fit together well with Socrates' account here of the true cause of the origin of the present charge: the vexation of the older Athenians at the corruption of the young through "philosophy" (a term used loosely in ordinary discourse).[89]

The three accusers seem to represent the three groups examined by Socrates. But that is not quite correct. Meletus and Anytus between them represent the poets, politicians, and craftsmen. But in addition Lycon is mentioned as an orator. Socrates did not speak of examining the orators when he described his "wandering." The orators might seem to be practically the same as the politicians. Later in his speech Socrates says that "the orators" in the Assembly became angry with his refusal to accommodate a popular but illegal desire (32b8). From this point of view Lycon and Anytus both represent the politicians. But there may be another explanation for the incongruity. Socrates examined not three but four groups, the fourth group being Socrates himself. Does rhetoric have something to do with Socratic philosophy? If so, Lycon's rhetoric would be the sham image of Socratic speech. In the proem Socrates declares that he is a true orator, one who speaks the truth (17b6, 18a5–6). True rhetoric is truth-telling, the distinctive activity of the philosopher. Socrates implies that he is the only orator, properly so called, in Athens, which is why he will look like a foreigner to the jurymen (17d4).

Socratic rhetoric, as we will see, attempts to comprise political, poetic, and artful speech. Thus Socrates points the way to an answer to the question raised by his proem: how can truthful and persuasive speech be combined? Lycon the orator stands for the fourth term in the roster of claimants to wisdom; the philosopher, using his comprehensive craft of artful image-making, might accomplish in act what vulgar rhetoric attempts in vain. In the latter part of the *Apology* Socrates will undertake this very task; however, he must first provide a direct defense against the present accusers' charge.

89. Cf. Plato *Euthydemus* 304e7.

CHAPTER 3

The Charge of the
Present Accusers (24b3–28b2)

The foregoing considerations lead up to the explicit question of the *Apology*, Socrates' innocence or guilt. Socrates' defense speech, which makes up the bulk of the work, consists of three principal sections: the reply to the first accusers, the reply to the present charge, and the defense and glorification of the Socratic way of life. The first and third sections are lengthy monologues; the central section is a dialogue between Socrates and Meletus, the nominal leader of his accusers. Here, one might justly expect, will be found the core of his defense. Socrates himself states that his conversation with Meletus is the only part of his speech which undertakes a response to the charge of his "later accusers"—the charge for which he is now on trial. Socrates apparently treats the formal indictment frivolously by spending so little time on it and by arguing sophistically against it. However, we should not permit his superficial banter and disdain to distract attention from the substance of his defense.

Socrates turns to "Meletus, the 'good and patriotic,' as he asserts." Meletus indeed loves his city. In the *Euthyphro* Socrates says that Meletus accuses him "to the city as though to mother." He goes on there to praise Meletus' care for the youth, "the young plants" of the city.[1] Although Meletus is a poet—no

---

1. *Euthyphro* 2c7–d4.

doubt one of the artless, ordinary poets, possessed by someone else's wisdom—he is still higher than the politicians Anytus and Lycon. The two adjectives that Meletus applied to himself, "good" and "patriotic," are in a certain tension with each other. For in order to be good, Meletus would have to possess knowledge: the "good craftsmen" do what they do by art, not inspiration or nature (22d6). But if he acted by knowledge and art, he would not be driven by his inspired, enthusiastic patriotism. He would follow and teach his own understanding of good and bad instead of uncritically and passionately accepting the teachings of the tradition. The tension between "good" and "patriotic" is the same as that implied in Socrates' earlier distinction between the virtue of a human being and that of a citizen (20b4–5). The human being looks to the good for his standard, while the citizen looks to the city's laws—just as the ordinary poet in Socrates' scheme looks to the educator. We will see that the conflict inherent in Meletus' own self-characterization silently dominates his conversation with Socrates.

That the nominal leader of Socrates' accusers should be a poet again recalls that "old quarrel between philosophy and poetry." Socrates spoke of Aristophanes as the most important of his first accusers, and he treats Meletus as the most important of his present accusers. Aristophanes was inaccessible to Socrates in the prothesis (18d4), but Meletus is present and required by law (25d2–3) to answer Socrates' questions. Socrates' counterattack against the three groups he examined—out of which came the present accusers—continues. He has just completed his exposure of the politicians' pretensions (23c–e). He will now "defeat" a poet, having been "defeated" earlier by Aristophanes (in the *Clouds*). Indeed, Socrates will accept the premise of the *Clouds*—which presents his dialectic in exaggerated caricature—and use it successfully as a weapon against the poet Meletus, the present accusers' equivalent to Aristophanes. The arguments used by Socrates in this section are among the most ridiculous used by him anywhere in Plato. It is as though Socrates were saying, "See, Aristophanes, I can defeat your stand-in even with the kinds of speeches you gave to me in your *Clouds*. Nor is my comedy any less laughable than yours. I can beat you on your own ground."

Does Socrates Corrupt the Young? (24c4–26b2)

The charge of the present accusers is "something like" this, says Socrates: "It asserts that Socrates does injustice by corrupting the young, and by not believing in the gods in whom the city believes, but in other *daimonia* [daimonic things] that are new."[2] He proceeds to examine the points of the accusation in order— that is, in the order in which he states them. Beginning with the corruption charge, he does not affirm that he will prove himself innocent of that charge; instead, he answers with a counter-charge against Meletus. He says that Meletus does injustice because he "jests in a serious matter, . . . pretending to be serious and concerned about things for which he never cared at all." Just as Meletus' charge against Socrates has two parts, one on "impiety" and one on "corruption," so Socrates' counter-charge has two parts. He accuses Meletus of "joking in a serious matter" and "not caring."

Socrates' two-part conversation with Meletus would seem to aim at refuting Meletus' two-part charge against Socrates. But instead of following this sensible plan, Socrates devotes the two sections to the proof of the two parts of his own countercharge against Meletus. He responds to the two parts of the formal charge against him in reverse order from the original, discussing corruption before impiety. Similarly, he proves the second part of his countercharge ("Meletus doesn't care") first (24c4–26b2), and the first part ("Meletus jokes in a serious matter") second (26b2–28a1). Socrates continues to pose as judge of his accusers, just as he had earlier set himself up as judge of the Delphic god's wisdom. He even has the audacity to accuse Meletus of "crimes" that he himself commits. For "joking in earnest" is one of the most characteristic features of Socrates' speech throughout the conversation (cf. 20d4–5). In the culminating argument of the Meletus dialogue, he compares the gods and their off-spring to horses and asses and mules. The city regards its gods as beings of the highest dignity, yet Socrates treats them with seeming levity.[3]

2. See Translation n. 59 for the original version of the charge.
3. A marginal note on one of the medieval manuscripts of the *Apology* says: "You act nobly, Socrates, comparing the Athenians' gods to asses and horses." *Scholia Platonica*, ed. William Chase Greene (Haverford, Pa., 1938), p. 422.

Socrates begins his refutation of the corruption charge—or rather his proof that Meletus "doesn't care"—by asking him who makes the young better? His question assumes that the one who knows who corrupts the young also knows who makes them good. Whatever the final truth of Socrates' presupposition may be, as a practical matter it is surely easier to discern those who "corrupt" or ruin horses, dogs, and young men, than to know who makes them better. In order for Meletus to answer Socrates' question properly, he must know what is good for human beings. Socrates thinks that his own kind of philosophizing is "the greatest good for a human being" (38a2). Meletus, on the other hand, answers that the laws make the young better. Precisely here emerges the difference between Socrates' and Meletus' perspectives: Socrates looks toward individual human virtue through private philosophic inquiry, while Meletus looks to the established conventions of the political community for his guidance. To put it in Socratic terms: as an "inspired" poet, Meletus' fate is to "carry artifacts made by others," that is, to teach and to defend the laws and customs set down by the ancient legislator-educator. For the city, the laws provide a comforting and workable answer to the philosophic quest for knowledge of the good. The laws teach the citizens the good and evil, just and unjust things. According to Xenophon's parallel account in the *Memorabilia*, the accuser charged that Socrates taught his companions to despise the established laws. For Meletus and Anytus, "corrupting the young" means teaching them to question the laws of the democracy.[4]

Socrates now induces Meletus to assert that all the Athenians except Socrates make the young "noble and good" or perfect gentlemen. Behind this preposterous proposition lies the fundamental tenet of democracy: the many deserve to rule because they are the best citizens. (If the many admit that some other group in the city is superior to themselves in regard to excellence or virtue, their claim to rule would be weakened.) Socrates attacks Meletus' declaration with an "aristocratic" argument: the few, not the many, are the improvers of the young. He argues by analogy to horses and horse-trainers that only those skilled

4. *Memorabilia* I.2.9.

with horses improve horses, not the majority of men ignorant of the art of horse-training. Socrates encourages us to infer that he is a practitioner of the analogous art of education, although the inference is not a necessary one.

The discussion of those "skilled with horses" reminds one of Socrates' conversation with Callias reported earlier in the *Apology*. There Socrates also invoked the analogy of horse-managing with human education to raise the question of who understands the virtue of human being and citizen. Callias' answer was "Evenus of Paros," a sophist. He did not for a moment think of answering "the laws" as Meletus does. Callias was speaking as a private father, while Meletus speaks as a public-spirited citizen. Socrates' conversations with Callias and Meletus seem to presuppose that the virtue of human being and citizen are identical. But the widely divergent answers given by Callias and Meletus to the same question correct the tendency of Socrates' speech. Their answers point to a cleft between human and political excellence. Sophists and laws do not give the same answers to such questions as how to live, what is good for men, and what is justice.

This difference or conflict between the public and the private is generally ignored by both the sophists and the laws. The sophists are too sanguine about the possibilities of educating men without regard to the restraints imposed by the established political orders within which all human beings dwell. The laws, on the other hand, tend to speak as though men's lives were lived entirely through, by, and for the political community. When Socrates "personifies" the laws in Plato's *Crito*, he has them assert that "we generated you, raised you, and educated you."[5] The laws forget that part of men's lives which can never be public or political, while the sophists forget how far politics limits the private man's ability to shape men's lives.

Reflection upon Socrates' comparison of human beings to horses reveals important differences between human beings and horses which prevent any simple answer to the question of human education. Horses do not owe their obedience to cities; a good horse is one who obeys his master and who develops the

5. *Crito* 51c8–9.

excellence peculiar to horses (speed and strength, for example). Since they do not participate in the "public" life characteristic of human beings, their virtue is not problematic. Human beings, on the other hand, necessarily lead private, family, and civic lives. Their duties and inclinations are not always in harmony, because of the variety of their obligations and loves. What is good for the individual may not be good for the city. Nor does the city's good always help the individual. The city must order its young men to die in war whenever it is attacked. It preserves itself as a community only at the expense of some of its own members.

Socrates continues to "forget" the tension between the public and the private in the following argument (25c5–26a7), where he tries to prove that no one does evil voluntarily. Meletus is led to agree to the statement that the bad do something bad to those nearest them, and the good do something good. The most important difficulty in Socrates' argument is his transition from living among good "citizens" to "associates" (25c6, d1). Socrates' present predicament has come about because of the difference between citizens and associates, since he tends to draw his associates away from their civic duties and opinions. In Meletus' understanding good men are identical to good citizens. By exploiting his confusion, Socrates maneuvers Meletus into a contradition. The political good is not the same as the individual good; the "good" that someone does to those nearest him might be "bad" in another way. Socrates' concern with the human good in abstraction from the good of the city may have a harmful political effect. In all practical political situations—except the one described in the *Republic* where the philosophers hold political power—good men (for Socrates, the philosophers) are something other than good citizens, who as citizens must accept the laws rather than truth as their supreme teacher on all important questions.[6] Meletus' lack of awareness of the distinction between a good man and a good citizen enables Socrates to avoid meeting the corruption charge head-on. The charge of corrupting the young was written with a view to Socrates' public or

---

6. Cf. Aristotle *Politics* 1276b16–1277b32 on the difference between a good man and a good citizen.

political effect. It means that Socrates make the young worse as citizens. However, Socrates' dialectical skill enables him to shift the discussion to the question of whether he makes them worse as human beings.

The argument that no one harms another voluntarily implies that all harm to others is done in a state of ignorance. No one would knowingly choose to do anything bad to anyone, because he might be done some harm in return. Since all harm to others is done in a state of ignorance, with knowledge would come the cessation of injustice. If it is just to refrain from harming others, and if only the wise man performs all his actions with perfect awareness of what he is doing, then only the wise man is just. Here is a variant of the famous Socratic maxim, "knowledge is virtue." The conquest of injustice requires that the wise man replace the traditional authorities—the fathers and the laws—in order that men may be instructed in the true nature of "harm." Those who know best what is good and bad for human beings are best qualified to teach such things to the other citizens. Now the impracticability of this argument becomes manifest when one considers its implications for criminal law. If crime is involuntary, committed only through ignorance, all law that punishes the criminal is mistaken. If criminals are merely ignorant, the proper remedy for crime is education, not punishment. This conclusion which Socrates draws for his own case applies equally well to any other kind of injustice.[7] Socrates announces his subversive doctrine to the very men who must judge his innocence or guilt.

We have reached the center of Socrates' dialogue with Meletus. Socrates sums up the discussion so far with this remark: "What I said is already clear, that Meletus never cared about these things either much or little." There are six references to Meletus' "carelessness" in this first part of the Meletus dialogue and none in the remainder.[8] Socrates has completed his proof of the *second* part of his own countercharge against Meletus, that Meletus "doesn't care." In doing so Socrates puns

7. Cf. Aristotle's critique of the Socratic view that "virtue is knowledge" in *Magna Moralia* 1187a5–23.

8. At 24c8, d4, d9, two at 25c3, 26b2.

on Meletus' name, which sounds like the Greek word for care: "the one who cares" doesn't care. This Socratic joke contains, as usual, a serious thought which remains unspoken. Meletus, being *a-melēs*, a "non-Meletus," both is and is not "Meletus." Socrates thus indicates the character of the ordinary poet's and a fortiori the citizen's way of life. The poet forgets that he relies upon the received wisdom of the tradition in composing his poetry. The hidden natural or inspired source of his art blinds him to his own lack of independence. He remains ignorant of the serious opposition between city and man because he never needs to confront it in himself or in his art. Yet as a human being he necessarily cares for his own good, while as an "inspired" poet he cares about someone else's good, the good of the community as taught by the educator-legislator. Because of his split existence, he can never live a fully unified life. This unrecognized duality in his soul reveals itself in Meletus' self-contradictions. Socrates points to this internal opposition when he says, "You are unbelievable, Meletus, even ... to yourself" (26e6–7).

In an important sense, Meletus *does* care. He cares about the things for which most men care: the city, his profession, family, reputation, and property. Men's bodies draw them to the conflicting worldly concerns that often dominate our lives. We might say that Meletus speaks out of the kind of care that Goethe ascribes to the embodied human condition:

> Care nestles quickly in the depths of the heart,
> There it works secret pains;
> Restlessly it deludes and disturbs desire and rest;
> It constantly cloaks itself with new masks—
> It may appear as house and home, as wife and child,
> As fire, water, dagger, and poison. . . .[9]

As the last line of the quotation suggests, the strongest care that possesses us is that for life and the avoidance of death. The shortness of human life and the inevitable death that concludes it make us care for life, mere life, and everything that seems to protect and preserve that life.

Socrates' attack on "Meletus" is nothing less than an attack

9. *Faust,* Part I, 644–649.

upon care understood as attachment to one's own; it is a revolutionary attempt to shift the focus of human life from the pressing concerns of the everyday world ("the body") to an exclusive attention to the excellence of the individual human being ("the soul"). His attack on "care" in this sense carries with it as a corollary an attack on the fear of death itself (e.g. 29a4–6). This attack is the reverse side of his project to replace the powerful love of one's own city, family, and body with the fragile and questionable private love of wisdom.

The care for one's own is itself not free of contradictions. The conflict between one's own city and one's own body becomes clearest in the case of war, when one must sometimes risk one's life for the city. Socratic care is unitary because it transcends the split loyalties of "one's own." On the level of the soul, one's own city and one's own body become equally unimportant. Socrates' serene way of life, which accepts the demands of "one's own" as unpleasant but inevitable necessities, takes its bearings from the excellence of the soul, which is wisdom. Yet we have also seen that Socrates' vigorous insistence upon the inner soul as the locus of truth may cause a self-forgetting neglect of the outward beauty visible in bodily things. Socratic care and Meletean care may therefore be taken as the two extremes to be avoided by a careful artisan of education—and it is this most careful of all arts which can be glimpsed through Plato's portrayal of the excessively political poet and the insufficiently public-minded philosopher.

Socrates accuses Meletus—"Care"—of not caring about the education of the young. Meletus "cares" in the ordinary sense, but not in what Socrates considers the more important sense. True care requires training and diligence. Meletus and his fellow citizens live a lazy life, hardly distinguishable from sleep (cf. 31a7), and do not genuinely care for their pursuits or themselves. Care requires an exertion of the soul and assiduous effort. The ordinary poet and the citizens, thoughtlessly assimilating the traditions they inherit, do not concern themselves with the question of the best way of life for a human being.

Meletus charges Socrates with the corruption of the young. Socrates countercharges Meletus with careless irresponsibility about the education of the young. Meletus sees the laws of Athens as the youth's best educator, which Socrates' corrupting dialectic undermines: Socrates corrupts the young, but the laws improve them (24d3–11). However, from Socrates' point of view, it is precisely Meletus' "careless" acceptance of the laws which is objectionable. If he were truly dedicated, he would spend his life like Socrates, examining himself and others, "caring about how the soul will be the best possible," as Socrates says later (29d9). Socrates' very care for virtue corrupts the young from the point of view of Meletus. But Meletus is judged guilty of corrupting the young at the bar where Socrates' new justice presides. His "crime" is that he accepts the laws of Athens rather than the human good as his standard of conduct and teaches this to others. Socrates' countercharge of "not caring" is equivalent to a charge of "corrupting the young."

In the first part of his conversation with Meletus, Socrates appears to be trying to refute the charge that he corrupts the young. In fact he adduces only one argument to repulse that charge, the argument that no one voluntarily does evil to his associates. The weakness of this line of reasoning has been shown. Socrates' true concern has been his proof of Meletus' "carelessness," and not the disproof of the corruption charge.

Does Socrates Believe in Gods? (26b2–28a1)

Socrates now turns to the impiety charge. When he first stated the charge of the present accusers, he reversed the order of the original and quoted the corruption part first. He did this with a view to the present accusers, the most famous of whom is the politician Anytus. Anytus and the other public men were angry because the young were making them—the respectable politicians and fathers—look foolish. Meletus, on the other hand, seems to take a livelier interest in the "impiety" part of his conversation with Socrates. His answers are more emphatic, and he volunteers information about the details of Socrates' impiety. He swears twice by Zeus to strengthen his answers (26d4, e5). He has apparently even "researched" the impiety of the *physiologoi*: they say that "the sun is stone and the moon is earth" (26d4–5). Anytus is more concerned with Socrates as corrupter of the young, while Meletus is more concerned with Socrates' impiety.[10]

Meletus and Socrates agree that impiety is the most serious part of the charge. They agree that the corruption charge can be reduced to the impiety charge: Socrates corrupts by teaching the young not to believe in the city's gods, but in other *daimonia* that are new. Since the charge of impiety is more fundamental, we might expect that Socrates' attempt to refute that charge will be more serious than his treatment of the corruption charge. Instead, the argument seems to become even more flippant than before. The core of Socrates' procedure is this: after he goads Meletus into accusing him of total atheism, he points out that this statement contradicts the part of the charge that says that he believes in new *daimonia*.

The ease with which Socrates is able to induce Meletus to change his accusation from "not believing in the gods of the city" to "not believing in any gods" can probably be accounted for by Meletus' disbelief in Socrates' *daimonion*, his "daimonic thing," upon which the charge appears to be grounded.[11] When Socrates says that his daimonic sign prevents him from doing certain things, Meletus, like the other Athenians, thinks that Socrates is "being ironic" (38a1)—that is, lying. An invented god is no god at all. When Socrates summarizes the indictment against himself in the *Euthyphro*, he says he is accused by Meletus of being a *poiētēs theōn*, a poet or maker of gods.[12] A further incentive for Meletus' radicalization of the charge may be his irritation at what he probably considers Socrates' "making the weaker speech the stronger" in the preceding discussion. Many of the judges probably share Meletus' sentiment.

Socrates briefly recollects the corruption charge when he remarks that the youth can "laugh at Socrates" if he teaches the doctrines of Anaxagoras as his own.[13] He neither denies that he in fact teaches these doctrines, nor that he teaches other doc-

10. Socrates' sole quotation from Anytus' accusation speech concerns the corruption charge (29c).
11. *Apology* 31d1–2, *Euthyphro* 3b; cf. Xenophon *Memorabilia* I.1.2.
12. At 3b2.
13. Translation n. 67.

trines that encourage doubt about the existence of the city's gods or of gods in general. He admits that he himself is familiar with the books of Anaxagoras, and he is well informed about their price.

Socrates now proceeds to show that Meletus contradicts himself, having brought the indictment in a spirit of "insolence and unrestraint and youthful rashness." He is not even going to bother to try to refute the impiety charge. Instead, he is going to use Meletus' self-contradiction to prove that Meletus is "joking" (27a2, 7). Instead of dealing seriously with the corruption charge, Socrates has proved that Meletus "doesn't care." Now, instead of discussing the impiety charge, he will prove that Meletus "jokes in a serious matter." He cares more about proving his case against Meletus than refuting the indictment against himself.

Socrates asks Meletus, "Do I believe there is no god?" Meletus replies, "You certainly do not, by Zeus, not in any way at all." In the original indictment as stated by Socrates, he was accused not of complete atheism, but of disbelief in the gods of Athens. Socrates tries to show that the charge of atheism contradicts the charge of believing in new *daimonia*. But the whole argument is utterly superfluous. Meletus need only have said, "Socrates, you are accused of disbelief in the *city's* gods, not of atheism." Even if the argument proves that Meletus contradicts himself, it in no way proves Socrates' innocence of the charge of "not believing in the city's gods, but bringing in new *daimonia*." It does not even address that charge.[14] Socrates treats the impiety charge, a serious accusation of criminal activity, as though it were an object of ridicule in a comedy.

However, let us examine Socrates' proof that Meletus contradicts himself. In order to reveal a contradiction, Socrates must demonstrate that Meletus says, "Socrates does not believe in gods, but believes in gods." He must therefore argue that "bringing in new *daimonia*" implies "believing in gods." Socrates' argument depends upon two crucial steps, one of which is

14. Cf. Leo Strauss, "On Plato's *Apology of Socrates* and *Crito*," in *Essays in Honor of Jacob Klein* (Annapolis, Md., 1976), p. 158: "This refutation is so beautiful because it leaves entirely open whether Socrates believes in the gods of the city."

a subterfuge and the other a fallacy. Instead of accurately repeating the original charge of "bringing in new *daimonia*," he silently changes it to "believing in new *daimonia*." This is the first step (24c1).

But does belief in *daimonia* (daimonic things) imply belief in daimons? Socrates argues that if one believes in horse-matters (*hippika pragmata*) (he probably means things like saddles and bridles), then one must necessarily believe in horses. By analogy, therefore, he must believe in daimons. But does this follow? Someone could surely believe in "divine matters" (temples and priests) without believing in gods. Even the horse example is unsatisfactory, for if the species should ever die out, there would be no horses, but saddles and bridles might still remain. Similarly, the gods may not be immortal.[15] Further, Socrates' understanding of the "daimonic" may be different from the Athenian understanding. His *daimonion*, as opposed to what "we believe" (27d1) about daimons, may not have divine parentage.

Socrates draws the final premise of his argument from "what is said" about daimons. He presents the argument in the form of a condition (if... , then...) which he himself does not affirm. "If daimons are certain bastard children of gods, whether from nymphs or from certain others of whom it is also said they are born, then what human being would believe that there are children of gods, but not gods?" Does Socrates take seriously these stories passed on by obscure tradition? Shortly afterwards in his speech he declares his ignorance of whether death is a good thing: he does not know whether the stories told by tradition are true (29b5–6; cf. 41c6–7). From here on, however, the argument is flawless, given the premises. Unfortunately, all the premises are false or doubtful. If Socrates believes in children of gods, he must believe in gods. Otherwise, it would be as though he believed in children of horses or asses—namely, mules—but did not believe in horses and asses.

Let us summarize the argument of Socrates' answer to the impiety charge. The first step was a silent but bold change in the charge against him (from "bringing in" to "believing in" new

15. Leo Strauss, *Socrates and Aristophanes* (New York, 1966), pp. 169, 179.

daimonia). The second step was a weak argument by analogy (belief in *daimonia* implies belief in daimons). The third step relied upon a tradition which Socrates himself probably regards as doubtful (daimons are children of gods). The final step, although logically sound, raised the question of Socrates' reverence towards the divine through its incidental comparison of gods to beasts (belief in children of gods implies belief in gods). The members of the jury, whatever their attitude may have been at the beginning of the trial, are probably now more convinced than before that Socrates is impious.

Of course Socrates' concern was not to refute the impiety charge, but to prove that Meletus "jokes in a serious matter." But Meletus' attitude has hardly been that of a comic poet. Whatever hidden jokes Socrates may have brought to light were entirely unintentional on Meletus' part. Being generous to Socrates, we may say that he proves that Meletus "jokes in a serious matter" by inadvertently making jokes while trying to be serious.[16]

Socrates ironically treats Meletus as a comic poet (cf. 31d1–2) because part of his intention here is to defend himself against Aristophanes. Meletus, who trusts in the slander brought about partly by the author of the *Clouds* (19b1), stands for Aristophanes in this part of the *Apology*. Socrates' flippant dialogue with Meletus is a superficially comic but truly serious counterattack on Aristophanes. The issues of the conflict between poetry and philosophy are raised, and poetry is found wanting. By bringing Meletus' self-contradictions to light, Socrates implies that there is a serious problem in the poet's way of life.

In contrast to Meletus' unintentional joking is Socrates' obviously fully conscious joking. He appropriately adopts the devices of comedy in his critique of the master comedian. Meletus cannot help being ridiculous because he woodenly persists in trying to be serious. Unlike Meletus, Socrates jokes in a serious matter by intentionally making jokes about serious things. He treats the gods—the most serious things of the city—in a comic

16. Seeing the manifest inadequacy of Socrates' defense, Reginald Hackforth, in *The Composition of Plato's "Apology"* (Cambridge, 1933), pp. 80–88, argues implausibly that Plato deliberately failed to report those parts of Socrates' speech which directly refuted the impiety and corruption charges.

manner in a trial where his own life is at stake. There is a clear connection between Socrates' serious joking and his impiety, just as there was a connection between his care for wisdom and his corruption of the young. From the city's perspective, piety requires awe and reverence. Men are expected to look *up* to the splendor and power of the gods. But Socrates' playful banter appears to deprive the gods of their proper dignity. He seems to assume a position of superiority to the divine objects of his jesting.[17]

Socrates and Meletus agree that the impiety charge is more important than the corruption charge. They agree that the substance of the corruption charge lies in the impiety charge: Socrates corrupts the young by teaching them not to believe in the city's gods. We have seen the weakness of the defense against the corruption charge. But his defense against the impiety charge is merely laughable. Moreover, his countercharge against Meletus has not fared much better. He showed that Meletus "doesn't care" in the sense of one meaning of the word care; yet in another sense, Meletus' whole being is filled with care. His proof of the other part of the countercharge, that Meletus "jokes in a serious matter," is even less persuasive. The only joking here seems to be originated by Socrates. In sum, if Socrates' defense against the corruption charge and proof that Meletus "doesn't care" are weak, his defense against the impiety charge and proof that Meletus "jokes in a serious matter" are even weaker. Since the impiety charge is the core of the charge of both the first and present accusers, Socrates' defense speech to this point has failed utterly.

Conclusion and Transition (28a2–b2)

Socrates has now completed his formal defense against both the first and the present accusers. He calls his defense against Meletus "sufficient," the same word he used for his defense against the first accusers (24b4, 28a4). We have seen how far from sufficient his defenses were in fact. He goes on to say that

17. Hobbes, *Leviathan*, ch. 6, speaks of the connection between laughter and the opinion of one's superiority to another.

if he is convicted, he will be convicted not by Meletus or Anytus, but by the "prejudice and envy of the many." "This has convicted many others, and good men too, and I suppose it will also convict me." Although the substance of Socrates' defense against the two charges has failed, that is not the reason for his conviction. He would be acquitted if it were not for the prejudice and envy against him.

We have noticed that Socrates seems to go out of his way to boast about himself and to antagonize the jury. His treatment of Meletus as though he were an object of comic ridicule probably irritated the jurors. Although Socrates emphasizes how long the slanders against him have been spread about, he certainly adds to them through his "boasting" in the defense itself. Xenophon says he wrote his *Apology of Socrates to the Jury* to reveal that Socrates' boasting at his trial was intentional. In his summary Xenophon says, "Socrates, by exalting himself in the court, brought envy on himself and made the judges vote to condemn him."[18] Socrates was voted guilty as charged—but for the wrong reasons. It was the judges' envy, and not their understanding of Socrates' corruption of the young and impiety, which caused them to convict him. This fact, however, does not absolve Socrates from his injustice. Indeed, Socrates must accept responsibility for his judges' indulgence in envy, since they behave as they do as a direct consequence of his deliberately provocative (because truthful) manner of speech.

We have reached the low point of the *Apology*. Socrates' halfhearted attempt to refute the charges against him has failed. And that failure does not even matter, for the prejudice and envy of the judges will condemn him in any case. But the defense continues, and indeed is not much more than half completed. The rest of the speech presents a long digression in which Socrates raises and answers two possible objections to his way of life. In form the digression is an extended consideration of the fact that Socrates is about to be condemned to death. In substance, however, it continues the defense against the impiety and corruption charges. The two charges continue to be discussed in alternating sequence, beginning with impiety. The

18. *Apology* 1 and 32.

order of this part of Socrates' defense speech is far more difficult to discern than that of the part heretofore discussed. This apparent disorder may follow from Socrates' reluctance to admit explicitly the weakness of his defense so far. But the very fact that he does not end his speech at this point is an implicit recognition of the inadequacy of what has gone before.

At this juncture Socrates seems to be guilty beyond any doubt. How can his case be salvaged? In brief, he attempts to establish his innocence by the following plan: conceding in effect that he is guilty of impiety and corruption of the young as these activities are understood by the citizens of Athens, he redefines the meaning of impiety and corruption. Instead of being the only one in Athens who corrupts the young, as Meletus asserted, he will prove himself to be the only one who does *not* corrupt them, as he suggested to Meletus (25a12–b7). And piety, instead of being a belief in the city's gods, will be reinterpreted in terms of a new Socratic understanding of justice and nobility. Socrates himself will provide the new standard of education and piety, and the whole city of Athens will be judged guilty of corrupting the young and of impiety.[19]

19. Cf. Maximus of Tyre *Orationes* III.31a–b.

CHAPTER 4

Socrates as
Public Man (28b3-31c3)

Greater is the order of things that opens before me;
Greater is the work I begin.

—Vergil, *Aeneid*

The New Achilles (28b3-31c3)

Socrates voluntarily brings forward an objection that someone might raise: "Then are you not ashamed, Socrates, of having followed the sort of pursuit from which you now run the risk of dying?" The imaginary questioner believes that a way of life that cannot adequately defend itself is shameful or ugly. Socrates replies manfully with a "just speech" that criticizes that premise.

His response stands in sharp contrast to his answer to the objection raised earlier in the *Apology* (20c4–d1). There he had been asked to account for the slander against himself, while here he is being openly reproached. The earlier objector was politely reserved; the present one is rudely outspoken. Socrates called the earlier objection "just"; now he gives a "just" response to a statement he calls "not noble." Before the story of the oracle Socrates accepted the rebukes of others passively; now he does the criticizing. He is on the attack.

The argument he uses here seems quite sensible: a man should "consider this alone whenever he acts: whether his actions are just or unjust, and the deeds of a good man or a bad." The standards of the just and the good are raised to oppose a petty calculation of danger. However, Socrates' example of a just and good man, the hero Achilles, seems ill-chosen. As he is portrayed in Homer's *Iliad*, Achilles might well be considered unjust. His private anger against Agamemnon leads to great sufferings for his Greek friends and allies; his withdrawal from the fighting almost causes the destruction of their army.[1]

There are certain peculiarities in the way in which Socrates introduces his example. He refers to "the demigods who died at Troy, both the others and the son of Thetis." The "son of Thetis" was Achilles (Socrates never speaks of Achilles by name); Thetis, his mother, was a goddess (28c5), and the expression "demigod" or "half-god" acknowledges Achilles' mixed lineage as the son of a goddess and a mortal.[2] The word "hero" is the usual Homeric term for the noble warriors who fought at Troy; "demigod" occurs only once in Homer, in the phrase, "a race of men who were demigods."[3] By pointing so directly to Achilles' half-human and half-divine parentage, Socrates recalls the final argument that he used against Meletus. Daimons were said there to be "certain bastard children of gods, whether from nymphs or from certain others of whom it is also said they are born" (27d8–9). Thetis is a sea nymph. Socrates' argument about the generation of daimons employed this analogy: to disbelieve in gods would be as though "someone believed in children of horses or asses—mules—but did not believe that there are horses and asses" (27e1–3). (In Greek "ass" is *onos*, and "mule" is *hemionos*, "half-ass.") The analogy implies that daimons are the offspring of two different kinds of parents, namely, a god and a mortal, and that they are therefore "demigods" or "half-gods," *hemitheoi*. Those born of a nymph and a mortal—a female god and a male mortal—would be one kind of daimon. Those born of a god and "certain others"—a male god and a female human being—would be a second kind. Finally, Socrates argued that if he believes in daimonic and divine things, he must believe in daimons and gods *and heroes*. Some scholars have puzzled over the occurrence of the word "heroes" there, but the argument about the parents of daimons is equally valid for demigods like Achilles, who are also called

1. For a summary of Achilles' actions in the *Iliad*, see Translation n. 79.
2. Translation n. 76.
3. *Iliad* XII.23.

152

heroes.[4] What is the purpose of this subtle identification of daimons with heroes? I believe that it concerns Socrates' understanding of his notorious *daimonion*.

A complementary Socratic exposition on daimons occurs in Plato's *Cratylus*, a playful dialogue where, among other things, Socrates offers quite a few "etymologies" of Greek words. In the section of the *Cratylus* devoted to daimons and heroes, Socrates begins his discussion with a free interpretation of a passage from Hesiod's *Works and Days*, where the poet narrates the story of the five races of men. The first race was the golden, and when the men of this race died, they were called daimons. Hesiod did not mean that the men of this race were literally made of gold, says Socrates, but that they were "good and noble." A proof of this is that Hesiod called our own race iron, although we are not literally constituted by that metal. The good, of course, are none but the wise: they were called *daimones* because they were *daēmones*, "experienced" or "knowing." " So both he and many other poets speak beautifully who say that whenever someone good dies, he obtains a great fate and honor and becomes a daimon, which is the name he receives signifying prudence. In this way, then, I also deem that every knowledgeable (*daēmōn*) man who is good is daimonic, whether living or dead, and is rightly called a daimon."[5] In the *Apology* Socrates declares himself to be a wise and good man (20d6-9, 28a8-b2). He says that a divine and daimonic voice comes to him which opposes him when he is about to do something that is not good (31c8-d4, 40c2-3). Comparing himself explicitly to Achilles, the hero and demigod, Socrates presents himself more heroically in the *Apology* than in any other Platonic work. The *Apology* gives a "mythical" account of the meaning of the word daimon; the *Cratylus* describes the term prosaically. In the *Apology* Socrates traces his wisdom to an oracle or to an oracular daimonic sign ("my customary divination from the *daimonion*" [40a4]). The

---

4. John Burnet, ed., *Plato's Euthyphro, Apology of Socrates, and Crito* (Oxford, 1924), note on 27e6.

5. *Cratylus* 397d9-398c4; cf. Hesiod *Works and Days* 109-201. Significant parts of my arguments in this chapter were anticipated by Diskin Clay, "Socrates' Mulishness and Heroism," *Phronesis* 17 (1972), 53-60.

Cratylus, on the other hand, implicitly traces Socrates' daimonic epithet to his wisdom.

By comparing himself to Achilles, Socrates suggests that he is a hero or daimon, a suggestion we have seen confirmed playfully in the *Cratylus*. We recall that Socrates' task in the *Apology* is to demonstrate to the jury his nobility and justice.[6] He begins the second, positive portion of his defense with a comparison that identifies himself with the paradigm of nobility for the Greek imagination. The daimonic Socrates is to be seen as a demigod and a hero who stands on a par with the glorious Achilles. That Socrates should compare himself with Achilles is, of course, ludicrous. Before the judges stands an ugly old man of seventy who is about to be condemned by them to death. Achilles was the beautiful, strong youth whose courage and skill in battle had no equal. He was held in high repute by both men and gods, while the obscure Socrates is about to die a wretched death by drinking a cup of poison in jail.

If someone should object that Plato's *Cratylus* has little to do with the *Apology*, his doubts must surely be dispelled when he reads the section on heroes, which follows directly upon the discussion of daimons. Socrates begins there from the same premise as that established in the *Apology*: heroes are demigods, and "all of them have been born either from a god loving a mortal woman or a goddess loving a mortal man." This is precisely the description given in the *Apology* of the birth of daimons, heroes, and particularly of Achilles, the son of Thetis and Peleus. But Socrates' "etymology" of the word "hero" breaks the Achillean mold:

There is a small distortion of the name of love (*erōs*), from which the heroes (singular: *hērōs*) have been born, for the sake of a different name. And either this says what heroes are, or else it is because they were wise, and orators, and clever, and skilled in conversation, being competent at questioning (*erōtan*). For "to question" (*eirein*) is to speak. And as we were saying just now, ... heroes turn out to be certain orators and men skilled in questioning (*erōtētikoi*), so that the heroic tribe becomes a race of orators and sophists.[7]

6. See pp. 78–80 above.
7. *Cratylus* 398c6–e3.

By this account the erotic questioner Socrates replaces Achilles as the genuine hero. The true orator and expert in conversation becomes the first member of a new "heroic tribe." The half-god Achilles is brought in to support Socrates' cause—but he will come to light as inadequate in the glare of the new Socratic standards of action.

Let us see how the parallel between Socrates and Achilles is elaborated in the *Apology*. Socrates' quotation from the *Iliad* refers to Achilles' crucial decision to return to the battle from which he has held himself back for so long. By his choice Achilles accepts and embraces his fate, for he knows it will mean his own certain death. When Socrates retells the story, he changes somewhat the Homeric original.[8] Homer stresses Achilles' sorrow and despair over the death of Patroclus, of whom Achilles says, "I valued [him] above all my companions, the same as my own head." He desires to wreak a boundless vengeance on Hector and the other Trojans for the sake of his lost friend.[9] Socrates transforms Achilles' passion from the raging anger of revenge into a studied concern for justice. His Achilles is moved by a public-spirited sense of duty rather than by private grief. Hence he concentrates, as Socrates tells it, not upon Patroclus but upon Hector, the one to be punished for the "murder" of his companion. (Hector's name is mentioned three times within four lines in this passage of the *Apology*.) Moreover, Socrates' Achilles fears "to live as a bad man and not to avenge his friends" because he might become "ridiculous" or "laughable" in his shamefulness. Here again he takes liberties with the Homeric portrayal of the hero. Shame and ridicule do not enter into the account in the *Iliad*. Socrates makes Achilles use the expression, "inflict a penalty (*dikē*)[10] on the one doing injustice"—almost a legal formula for the punishment of a criminal.

Socrates' version of the story makes Achilles more just, but less noble and godlike. Care for justice and fear of the shame of injustice have replaced hybristic self-regard and unrestrained

8. The details of these changes are stated in Translation n. 79.
9. *Iliad* XVIII.81–82, 112–126.
10. On *dikē* see Translation n. 117.

pursuit of glory. In Socrates' revision Achilles has been domesticated: he is more civilized, less passionate, less splendid, more prosaic—on the whole, more Socratic. The comparison of Socrates to Achilles—at first blush so absurd—is rendered somewhat plausible by these changes. By ascribing quasi-legal language to Achilles, Socrates establishes a further similarity between Achilles' battlefield heroics and his own deeds in the courtroom contest with his accusers.

The accusers are the enemy with whom Socrates engages in mortal combat—mortal for Socrates, at least. Like Achilles, Socrates knows he will incur death as a consequence of choosing to meet their challenge openly rather than to escape by using clever rhetorical devices unworthy of him (38d3–e5). (Socrates later compares his conduct at the trial to that of a soldier who refuses to save his life by means of some shameless device such as throwing down his arms and begging the enemy for mercy [38e5–39a6].) Of course Socrates will not slay Meletus and Anytus as Achilles did Hector. His program of revenge—"to inflict a penalty on the one doing injustice"—will not be fulfilled until after he has died. Then the accusers will have to give an account of themselves to their new Socratic "judges" and "executioners," the young men he has hitherto held back. The accusers and hostile judges will be reproached for the injustice of having killed Socrates, a wise man (38c1–39d9). In this way Socrates will fight back against the politicians and citizens by whom he has been brought to trial. We have also seen that Meletus, as the accusing poet, stands for Aristophanes, who attacked Socrates so persuasively in the *Clouds*. Socrates also "avenges" himself on Aristophanes by affirming that philosophy is capable of both self-knowledge and self-defense, and that poetry is composed without knowledge, by "nature" or "inspiration." And beyond Aristophanes and the lesser poets looms the godlike figure of Homer, the author of the *Iliad* and of Achilles. Socrates means to challenge "the teacher of Greece"; he aspires to replace Homer as the authority to which future Greeks will turn in ordering their lives. Of course, Socrates does not undertake these polemical actions with full seriousness. Indeed, he allows his listeners to see how fruitless it would be for him to make a genuine effort to conquer Homer, the lesser poets, and the politicians within the confines of a single defense speech. Nevertheless, in the sequel Socrates will first lay down the principles of a new education (29b9–30c1); then he will attempt to establish his credentials as a poet by inventing the gadfly image, in order to capture the imagination of his listeners and persuade them of his superhuman heroic stature (30c2–31a7); finally he will describe his political deeds in service of the Athenians (31a7–c3). As educator, poet, and politician he will allow the outcome of his defense to depend upon the execution of this project. Its success would confirm the appropriateness of his boastful action. Even its failure could prove salutary for philosophy, since it would not prevent another man, such as Plato, from using the remains of the shattered venture as material for a fresh attempt to immortalize Socrates. In that case Plato would rightly assume the title of educator and poet, while Socrates, like Homer's Achilles, would be relegated to the lesser condition of hero in those Platonic dramas known as the Socratic dialogues.

Let us return to the comparison of Socrates to Achilles. We have noted a certain likeness between Achilles' enemy Hector and Socrates' accusers. Is there also a correspondence between Achilles' friend Patroclus and Socrates' beloved? What does Socrates love? Is it not philosophy above all else? In the following section of his speech Socrates will assert that philosophy exercises the greatest claim upon him, eliciting a devotion that exceeds even his love for the Athenians (29d2–5). And in the *Gorgias* he explicitly calls philosophy his beloved, comparing his erotic love for philosophy to that of a pederast for his boy.[11] Socrates has already interpreted the trial as a contest between philosophy—of which he happens to be the prime exemplar— and the traditional *ēthos* of Athens. The fact that Meletus cannot distinguish Socrates from the philosopher Anaxagoras supports Socrates' view that he is being prosecuted *as* philosopher (26d). By putting Socrates on trial, the accusers have attacked philosophy; Socrates comes to its aid and so tries to avenge this unjust treatment of his loved one.

The changes that Socrates introduces in his account of Achil-

11. *Gorgias* 481d1–4.

les make possible a tentative identification of the two "heroes." But in spite of those changes, the two men remain far apart in character. Achilles' element is war, while war for Socrates is only a necessary diversion from his true vocation, philosophy, which presupposes peace and leisure.[12] Socrates' life work was conducted through speech and conversation, at which he excelled all others,[13] while Achilles lived for and through the deeds of the warrior. (Socrates expresses his contempt for deeds later in his speech [32a4–5].) Perhaps the most significant difference between the two men lies in their respective attitudes toward public opinion. Achilles is guided by a fear of being laughed at and a strong sense of shame at doing anything publicly dishonorable. But Socrates, the butt of comedy in the *Clouds*, cares only about the truth of things, as he understands that truth from his conversations and calculations, and he persists in his allegiance to the truth even when by doing so he sets himself in opposition to respectable public opinion. Finally, the success of Achilles' revenge—the slaying of Hector—contrasts sharply with the failure of Socrates to make good his own threat of revenge. For that he must rely upon the work of others (39c4–d5).[14]

To understand better the purpose of the contrast between Achilles and Socrates, let us glance at the plot of the *Iliad*. After he is publicly insulted by Agamemnon, Achilles prays that Zeus honor him by making the Greeks suffer a near defeat. The poem tells the story of the working out of the plan that Zeus contrives in response to Achilles' petition. Achilles knows that many Greeks will die if Zeus grants him his prayer, but he is prepared to subordinate everyone and everything to his desire for honor. Whatever stands in the way of vindicating his nobility becomes an object of his wrath. Events seem to proceed in accordance with Achilles' desires as the Trojans drive the Greeks back to the sea and begin to burn their ships. Achilles apparently intends to rejoin the combatants at the crucial moment when disaster impends. But before he is ready to return to combat he allows his beloved friend and comrade Patroclus to precede him into bat-

---

12. *Charmides* 153a–d.
13. Xenophon *Memorabilia* I.2.14. Cf. Translation n. 79.
14. On Socrates and Achilles, cf. Allan Bloom, "Interpretive Essay," in *The Republic of Plato* (New York, 1968), pp. 353–358.

tle. He gives Patroclus his armor and sends him into the fray. Patroclus, foolishly emboldened by his initial successes, is drawn into combat with Hector, who kills Patroclus and strips him of his armor, the armor of Achilles. The death of Patroclus moves Achilles to deep grief—a striking response after his callous indifference to the deaths of so many of the other Greeks who perished in battle as a consequence of his prayer to Zeus.[15]

What does Patroclus mean to Achilles? Aristotle says that "the friend is another self."[16] When Patroclus asks Achilles for permission to wear his armor, he hopes to deceive the Trojans into thinking that he is Achilles, so that they will "desist from war." (When soldiers were wearing their armor, they could not be recognized by their faces; each hero had his own unique armor that distinguished him from the other warriors.) When Patroclus appears on the battlefield, the Trojans do indeed mistake him for Achilles at first. The last time Achilles sees Patroclus alive, it is as though he is looking at himself.[17] In Patroclus' death Achilles sees his own death for the first time. When he receives the news that Patroclus has been killed and stripped of his armor, he mourns with a sorrow hitherto unfelt. Achilles begins to know and to feel what it means to die young: it is his own fate as much as Patroclus' that he bewails.

What then is the ground of Achilles' friendship for Patroclus? Simply self-love, love of his own, without regard to whether the self that he loves is good. Achilles and Patroclus have grown up and shared a common life together as comrades in war.[18] Because Patroclus is "his own," Achilles loves and honors him as much as his own head. The nature of this love is imaged perfectly in Patroclus' farewell as Achilles' apparent double, dressed in his armor.

Socrates' attachment to philosophy, on the other hand, begins from the awareness that he longs for, but does not possess, adequate knowledge of the virtue of man and citizen, the virtue that would make him "noble and good." Precisely the sense of his own lack leads Socrates to a love that seeks completion be-

15. *Iliad* I, XVI, XVIII.1–126.
16. *Nicomachean Ethics* 1166a31–32.
17. *Iliad* XVI.40–42, 278–282.
18. *Iliad* XXIII.83–90.

yond complacent self-satisfaction or the empty applause of public honor. Paradoxically, Socrates' love of philosophy looks like self-love, since, as the paradigm of "human wisdom," Socrates is philosophy. Yet that love is not for himself as self, but for himself as one on the way to achieving the human good. He holds philosophy to be "the greatest good for a human being" because he hopes thereby to make the good his own. Only for that reason does philosophy become worthy of a love as strong as that of Achilles for Patroclus.

When Achilles chooses to avenge Patroclus, he does so knowing that after he kills Hector, he himself will soon die. This fact is emphasized in both Socrates' and Homer's versions of the story, since it is of central significance in both instances. When Achilles finally slays Hector in the *Iliad*, he cannot help being reminded of his own fate soon to follow, for Hector stands before him in Achilles' own armor, which he earlier stripped from the body of Patroclus. When Achilles kills his deadliest enemy, he simultaneously kills himself, both in image and in truth. Motivated by a desperate anger at the loss of Patroclus, Achilles is willing to choose death for the sake of his revenge, a choice that Homer presents as something close to suicide.[19]

Socrates too knows that if he fights against his accusers (rather than "retiring from the battle," as he considers at 29c ff.), he must soon die. Indeed, his condemnation to death takes place in the *Apology* itself. Socrates' avenging of the accusers' attack on philosophy also includes a willing acceptance of death. He, like Achilles, will achieve thereby a certain reputation and glory. But Socrates' glory will be the glory of a type, not of a man. His death will enable philosophy to live. Socrates' death and glory serve a higher end than the mere propagation of his own name. Philosophy will begin to acquire a good opinion in Athens; its work will continue in the quasi-legitimate institutions of Plato's Academy and Aristotle's Lyceum.

19. *Iliad* XXII.248–369. My understanding of the *Iliad* owes much to Harry Neumann (in conversation) and to Jacob Klein, "Plato's *Ion*," *Claremont Journal of Public Affairs* 2 (Spring 1973), 23–37. Also helpful were Seth Benardete, "Achilles and Hector: The Homeric Hero," Ph.D. dissertation, University of Chicago, 1955, and Benardete's articles on the *Iliad*: "Achilles and the *Iliad*," *Hermes* 91 (1963), 1–16; "The *Aristeia* of Diomedes and the Plot of the Iliad," *Agon* 2 (1968), 10–38.

In the passage of the *Cratylus* discussed earlier Socrates refers to Hesiod's five races of men in his analysis of daimons. Our age, in Hesiod's account, is the age of iron, which was preceded by a "divine race of heroes, who are called half-gods." This was the age of Homer's warriors who fought at Troy. But the first and best age was the golden: a man is "golden," Socrates says, if he is a good man who is wise. He holds out the hope of improving on the greatness even of Homer's world. For any man of today, if he becomes wise, can return, as it were, on an individual basis, to the golden age.[20] In this way he expresses "mythically" the boastful claim of philosophy.

Socrates' (or Plato's) contest with Homer is illustrated in a more substantial way by the very structure of the *Apology of Socrates*. The first part of the dialogue describes Socrates' "odyssey," his wandering and labors in the pursuit of wisdom (22a6–7). Like Homer's Odysseus, he learns "the mind of many human beings." Both Socrates and the "divine Odysseus" are acknowledged by the gods as the wisest of men: Socrates by the god in Delphi, and Odysseus by Zeus, who calls him "beyond mortals with regard to mind." At the end of his long wandering Socrates is sure of the oracle's meaning—that he should examine himself and others—and he begins to defend his way of life seriously. The defense of his "Odyssean" wisdom is the theme of the second or "Iliadic" part of the *Apology*. The wily, wandering Odysseus is transmogrified into the noble warrior Achilles, who fights and dies for the sake of his hard-won human wisdom.[21]

In his "correction" of Homer, Socrates reverses the order of his own "Iliad" and "Odyssey." In Homer the *Iliad* comes first: the Greeks are at war far away from home, seeking glory. The *Odyssey*, which describes the voyage and adventures of Odysseus as he returns home from Troy, follows the *Iliad*. The movement of the two poems as a whole is from war to peace, and from foreign and exotic lands to home. "One's own," aptly imaged by Odysseus' marriage bed, which is literally rooted in the earth, is the goal.[22] Socrates' odyssey, on the other hand,

20. Hesiod *Works and Days* 156–165, 109–126; *Cratylus* 397e5–398b1.
21. *Odyssey* I.3, 65–66.
22. *Odyssey* XXIII.173–232.

leads from ignorance to knowledge, and culminates in the discovery of the life that seeks the human good. The good has replaced home as the end. Socrates comes to know his ignorance about the greatest things, and he orders his life in accordance with his knowledge. When that life is threatened, he defends it: he becomes Achillean. In Homer's world the man of war (Achilles) and the man of peace (Odysseus) are two different human beings. When Socrates reshapes the myth to fit himself, he himself takes on the roles formerly divided between the two Homeric heroes. Socrates presents himself as a man who encompasses the nobility and beauty of the most honored Greek as well as the deep-sighted wisdom of the man of many devices. If Socrates' deeds match his boast, he will have overcome the dichotomy of beauty and truth outlined in the proem. However, the sequel will show why he cannot live up to his remarkable claim.

So far Socrates has only been clearing the ground for his educational task. He has attacked the leading hero of Homer, the most respected poet-educator of the tradition. This is the negative beginning that must precede the positive dispensation of his own novel doctrine. Socrates will now present the "theory" (28d6–29b9) and "practice" (29b9–30c1) of his "philosophic education" of the Athenians. The "theory" is articulated through a discussion of the principle that is to overturn the Homeric teaching and provide the foundation for his own.

Socrates begins his interpretation of Achilles' choice as follows: "Wherever someone stations himself, holding that it is best, or wherever he is stationed by a ruler, there he must remain and run the risk, as it seems to me, and not take into account death or anything else before what is shameful." Achilles chose to "station himself" in the battle against Hector; by comparing himself to Achilles, Socrates implies that he stations himself as a philosopher in the battle against the accusers. He lists three campaigns in which he participated during the war against Sparta, which recently ended in defeat. Of the three, two were clear defeats for Athens, and one was a costly victory. We recall by contrast that every engagement in which Achilles participates proves a conclusive victory for the Homeric warrior. Socrates' prowess as a "warrior-hero" does not bear comparison with Achilles' martial virtue. Indeed, he mentions his wartime experience only to dismiss it: he says he did nothing more nor less than anyone else.

Socrates is far more serious regarding the accusers' challenge to his way of life. He was commanded to live "philosophizing and examining myself and others" by the god, "as I supposed and assumed." He considers military virtue, the virtue of Achilles, a common thing, something that "anyone" can do. His divine mission has the authority of "the god" behind it. The analogy to Achilles implied that Socrates stationed himself because he believed that it was best, but now he traces his "order" to the god. Just as he did earlier in the section on the Delphic oracle, Socrates continues to obfuscate the question of whether he acts by his own choice or because he has been ordered by the god. (The fate of the god who stationed Socrates at his post is foreshadowed by a common feature of the three campaigns: on each occasion the Athenian general in command died during the battle.)[23]

Socrates now proposes a definition or example of impiety. The present section as a whole (28b3–29b9) deals quietly with the impiety charge. But Socrates is no longer giving a merely negative defense: he defends himself by redefining impiety. If he stopped philosophizing, he says, he would justly be charged with not believing in gods. His disbelief would be shown in his "disobeying the divination, and fearing death, and supposing that I am wise when I am not." Perhaps Socrates adopts Meletus' charge of complete atheism because Socrates' gods, unlike the city's local deities, are the gods of all human beings as such.

He proceeds to argue that "to fear death, men, is nothing other than to seem to be wise, but not to be so." His knowledge of ignorance about "the greatest things" (22d7) is specified here to be knowledge of ignorance about "the things in Hades"—the fate of the human soul after death. Socrates suspends his judgment about the traditional accounts of the life after death. But those accounts constitute part of the Athenian view of piety. Homer describes a visit of Odysseus to the underworld in the

23. See Translation n. 81.

Odyssey. There the shade of Achilles tells him, "I would choose to be a serf on earth and serve another, a man himself without portion whose livelihood is not great, rather than to be lord over all the dead who have perished."[24] Death is worse than slavery. Socrates says that men "fear it as though they knew well that it is the greatest of evils."

Socrates attacks the traditional beliefs about the "things in Hades" by calling such beliefs self-deceiving ignorance. Socrates' standard of wisdom condemns the traditional views because those views are based on faith and trust, not knowledge. Here we see why the apparently harmless declaration, "I know that I know nothing," implies a rejection of the beliefs of the city. If the "things in Hades" (under the earth) are questionable for Socrates, how can he believe in the stories about the "things on Olympus" (in the heavens), the city's gods? For Socrates, to believe in the city's gods would also be "supposing that one knows what one does not know"; such belief would therefore be equivalent to not believing in gods: "disobeying the divination, and fearing death, and supposing that I am wise when I am not." The piety of Socrates is the impiety of the city—and vice versa.

There are three elements in Socrates' characterization of impiety: (1) disobeying a divine authority (the oracle); (2) fearing death; and (3) ignorance (false belief in one's own wisdom). Socrates equates the second element with the third, since he says that the fear of death is the same as supposing that one knows what one does not. The fear of death is ignorance. This means that his description of impiety can be reduced to two elements: disobeying a god and ignorance. These two elements correspond to Socrates' two alternative and contradictory explanations for his staying at his station and philosophizing: what the god orders him to do, and what he thinks is best (on the basis of his own calculating knowledge of his ignorance). It is possible that Socrates equates "disobeying the divination" with "ignorance," just as earlier, in the analogue between the four sections and four groups, he seemed to align himself with the

24. *Odyssey* XI.489–491.

god. In that case, Socrates' definition of impiety would be: impiety is ignorance. This would imply that piety is knowledge.

Socrates also identifies leaving one's station because of the fear of death with ignorance. Staying at one's station to face the enemy is the most common understanding of what constitutes courage. Hence courage is wisdom.[25]

He says that someone would "justly" prosecute him for disbelief in gods if he supposed that he knew what he did not know. Ignorance, the false belief in one's wisdom, is injustice. Justice is wisdom.

Socrates tacitly redefines the virtues as the prelude to his philosophic education of Athens. But one of the virtues is missing: moderation (sōphrosynē).[26] The word moderation does not even occur in the Apology of Socrates. This is appropriate to the character of the work as a whole. Socrates' speech is full of immoderation and excess, not to say hybris. It would surely be unfitting for him to speak of moderation in such a setting. Besides, from a divine point of view, moderation is a questionable virtue at best, and Socrates almost claims to be a god in the Apology.[27]

The theme of this section is the conquest of the fear of death through knowledge. Achilles, driven by an uncalculating fear of shame and of public disapproval, is used by Socrates first as his heroic precursor, then implicitly as an example of a manner of life to be rejected. Not shame but knowledge of what is good and bad must guide the choice of when to keep one's station and when to abandon it. The ministration of Socratic knowledge of ignorance disperses the anger and despair felt by Achilles when he lost Patroclus. Socrates will not be particularly angry at his accusers and judges when he is condemned to death (41d6–7). Indeed, his attack on "Meletus" as "care for one's own" requires a new attitude toward death. He redirects the care of the human

25. Plato Laches 190e5–6, 194d1–5; cf. Protagoras 349d–350c.
26. Republic 427e6–11. Paul Friedländer, Plato, II (New York, 1964), 163, 166, sees that the unity of the virtues is "of crucial significance in the Apology." However, he fails to mark the absence of moderation.
27. Phaedo 82a11–b3. Cf. Socrates' praise of divine madness, the opposite of moderation, in Plato Phaedrus 244–257; also Leo Strauss, Socrates and Aristophanes (New York, 1966), pp. 281–282.

being away from mere self-preservation toward a care for virtue—that is, for wisdom. The redemption from the fear of death (care for one's own) will allow the full pursuit of philosophy (care for how the soul will be the best possible). When Achilles spoke to Odysseus in the underworld, he was literally nothing but "soul" (*psychē* in the sense of "shade" or "ghost").[28] He thoroughly despised himself and wished he were alive—as embodied soul—on earth. Socratic "care for the soul" is in some respects difficult to distinguish from the love of death.[29] At the end of the *Apology*, Socrates will outline an anti-Homeric myth describing an afterlife that is happier than life on earth (41c5–6).

Philosophic Education (29b9–30c1)

Socrates' "greater work" has begun. The principles of the best way of life, "learned" from a transformed Achilles, will now provide the foundation for his definitive teaching to the Athenians. The transition from "theory" to "practice" is so smooth that the beginning of a new section is barely noticeable. Since Socrates will give his philosophic teaching, the politician Anytus, who is more concerned with Socrates' corruption of the young, is the accuser mentioned here. In his speech before the judges Anytus said that Socrates should be put to death, arguing that if Socrates is acquitted, "soon your sons, pursuing what Socrates teaches, will all be completely corrupted." Just as Socrates defended himself against the impiety charge in the previous "theoretical" section, so here in the "practical" section he defends himself against the corruption charge. The defense will be made along the same lines as in the Achilles section: Socrates will redefine the traditional understanding of corruption of the young. The opposite of corruption is education (24d3–e5), and Socrates will show how he educates the youth and the city of Athens.

What would he do, Socrates now asks himself, if the Athenians offered him the alternative of acquittal, on the condition

28. *Odyssey* XI.467.
29. Cf. *Phaedo* 61b7–d5.

that he cease philosophizing, but that he will be put to death if he continues? He asserts most emphatically that, in such a case, "I will obey the god rather than you; and as long as I breathe and am able to, I will not stop philosophizing." He is prepared to disobey the laws of the city if they should interfere with his divinely ordered mission. Socrates directly opposes the city's laws; his own "laws," sanctioned by the god, replace them. This defiance of the city in the name of philosophy stands at the exact center of the *Apology*. His philosophic discourse which attempts to become politically effective is *the* defense against the charge, as it is simultaneously the very reason he is about to be condemned.[30] The life of philosophy, pursued not in private but as an alternative to the political teaching of Athens, forms the core of Socrates' new education.

Socrates shows how he teaches the Athenians by recounting a typical example of the speeches he makes to whomever he happens to meet. He begins his hypothetical exhortation by addressing his interlocutor thus: "Best of men, you who are an Athenian, from the city that is greatest and best-reputed for wisdom and strength...." Athens has just lost the war with Sparta, and her strength can no longer accurately be described as "great." Socrates casts doubt upon Athens' great wisdom by mentioning it together with her great strength. His "praise" of Athens recalls the glorious days of Themistocles and Pericles when the empire flourished and the great tragic poets were in their prime. Now all that has disappeared: Athens' reputation is utterly disproportionate to her greatness. Thus Socrates points to the disparity between the city's reputation or seeming (*doxa*) and the truth. A loyal Athenian should try to make his city be what it is reputed to be.

"Are you not ashamed," Socrates asks his nameless interlocutor, "that you care for having as much money as possible,

---

30. Maximus of Tyre, a commentator on Plato in late antiquity, wrote an essay entitled "Whether Socrates Acted Nobly in Making No Defense Speech." (He implies that the speech in the *Apology* is as good as no defense.) Maximus asks rhetorically whether Socrates should have made his defense "by saying that he philosophized." He answers, "But it was at this that they were angry" (*Orationes* III.29b).

and reputation, and honor, but that you neither care nor think about prudence, and truth, and how your soul will be the best possible?" The imaginary objector whose question began this part of the *Apology* asked Socrates, "are you not ashamed . . . ?" (28b3). Socrates turns this question back against the common opinion that considers death the most shameful thing. Since the opposite of what is shameful or base (*aischron*) is what is noble or beautiful (*kalon*), Socrates' pronouncement expresses negatively his new standard of nobility.

He lists three things which it is shameful to care about, and three things which it is shameful not to care about. The central item of the first list is reputation or opinion (*doxa*), and the central item of the second is truth. This antinomy, which was indicated in the remark about Athens' reputation and greatness, forms the axis of the Socratic understanding. Without truth, reputation is empty. The Greeks had been taught, through the example of Achilles, that the pursuit of *doxa*, reputation or glory, was man's proper aspiration. Now Socrates wants to shift the traditional care for opinion and honor toward a care for truth.

Socrates' frequent repetition of the word "care" in this section (29d9, e2, e3, 30b1) recalls his critique of Meletean care in the name of Socratic care. Socrates' care for wisdom was shown to be, from the point of view of the city's laws, the cause of his corrupting the youth's attachment to the city. The care for one's own is embodied in those laws: they defend property and lives through their enforcement of criminal justice, and they support the existence of the city through their praise of courage in war and their blame of cowardice. Socrates exhorts men to turn away from these "merely" bodily concerns to a dedication to "prudence, and truth, and how your soul will be the best possible." He speaks as though men had no bodies to worry about—as though the soul could survive perfectly well without a body. Any care at all for one's own body is condemned as shameful. Socrates may exaggerate his praise of care for the soul in order to bring out the contrast between philosophy and the city as clearly as possible. But that exaggeration leads to a view of life that is as false as the one it seeks to replace. Socrates' philosophic education, taken literally, is as utopian as the regime of the *Republic*. Like that regime, it abstracts from the limits imposed upon life by the body.[31]

Socrates exhorts the Athenians to care for prudence, truth, and the soul. He seems to suggest that the way to care for the soul is to care for prudence and truth. Prudence (*phronēsis*, good sense or practical wisdom) is an intellectual virtue. Socrates in effect calls upon men to become wise: care for prudence and truth and the soul is care for wisdom. From the point of view of action or practice, however, wisdom (*sophia*, 29d8) is primarily prudence (*phronēsis*). Although Socrates speaks here in practical language, his intent is to wean men away from political concerns so that they will nurture their souls on philosophic reflections.

Socrates says that if the person with whom he is speaking protests that he does care for these things, Socrates will continue to test and examine him. And if he does not seem to Socrates to possess virtue, he reproaches him, "saying that he regards the things worth the most as the least important, and the paltrier things as more important." Socrates might appear here to claim to know what virtue is. Yet he did not know in his conversation with Callias, which occurred just before the trial (20a3–5). Even if his interlocutor cares for virtue, Socrates will not be satisfied unless he possesses it. No one escapes the lash of Socratic exhortation except those who have achieved complete virtue. But even Socrates, the wisest of men, says he does not know what virtue is. Hence no one will be exempt from his caustic reproaches. Life consists in a ceaseless examination of oneself and others. The search for virtue must be pursued with diligence and persistence, however fruitless that search may appear to be in practice.

Socrates' program turns life upside down.[32] Confidence must give way to self-criticism, and the ordinary understanding of virtue must be discarded. Socrates' exhortations, if seriously followed, would turn the city into a chaotic mass of questioners who would have no time for the pursuits and activities whose

31. *Republic* 592a10–b6; Leo Strauss, *The City and Man* (Chicago, 1964), pp. 110–112, 127–128, 138.
32. *Gorgias* 481c1–4; Franz J. Weber, in his edition of *Platons Apologie des Sokrates* (Paderborn, 1971), p. 93, speaks of a Socratic "transvaluation of values" (a phrase he borrows from Nietzsche) at this point in the *Apology*.

products furnish the basic necessities of life. The city would become a sort of huge seminar where everyone, having been made aware of his lack of wisdom and virtue, would incessantly examine himself and others in what must appear to practical men a pointless exercise in comparative ignorance. The "ten-thousandfold poverty" of Socrates would be multiplied many times over as the citizens neglected their personal occupations, their families, and their city. The implications of Socrates' exhortations would make any kind of orderly, stable human life utterly impossible, and the ensuing confusion would necessarily also destroy the very condition—the leisure that comes from wealth (23c2-3)—which allows Socrates and his followers to philosophize. Money is the first item on Socrates' list of things that are shameful to care about (29d8), but money is the presupposition of the life and leisure without which there can be no thought. The attitude toward money which Socrates exhibits here is like that of Shakespeare's Brutus, who chides Cassius for his underhanded means of procuring money, while demanding of him that he furnish the money that he himself needs but cannot obtain honestly (cf. 36e1).[33]

These political implications are present in Socrates' speech. But his praise of the philosophic way of life, like much else in the *Apology*, is purposely exaggerated. As a serious political proposal, it is not to be even momentarily entertained. Socrates reveals here his incompetence at the educational art while implicitly boasting that he is competent to replace Homer's authority. Just as he admitted in the dialogue with Callias, he demonstrates here in deed that he does not understand the art of education or legislation. Socrates' greatest boast in the *Apology* depends upon his successful practice of that art of education. Yet the central section of the *Apology of Socrates* reveals his claim to be unwarranted. Socrates is too "theoretical" to know the "practice" of any art, and especially the educational art. His is the way of the seeker, who seems either unable or unwilling to codify his way of life and make it respectable. His critique of opinion is too severe to serve as a guide for establishing the

33. *Julius Caesar* IV.3.1–82.

good repute of philosophy in the eyes of the city, for every city must foster and sustain an array of shared opinions that support the life and concerns of the community. Since Socrates does not possess adequate knowledge of the virtue of a human being and a citizen, his boastful attempt at legislation must remain playful. The immoderation of the *Apology* will be corrected by the humility of the ensuing dialogue, the *Crito*. There, his defiance of the laws will be transmuted into a display of reverent respect in their august presence.

After his exhortation to virtue, which abstracted from the limitations of men's bodies, Socrates remarks incidentally that he spends more of his time speaking to his fellow townsmen than to foreigners, since "you are closer to me in kin (*genos*)." In other words, Socrates does recognize the needs and attractions of one's own, however much he may seem to depreciate such bonds in the greater part of his speech. His closeness to the Athenians derives from blood and family relations, which as such have nothing to do with prudence, truth, and the soul. Indeed, this kinship through bodily ties helps to account for Socrates' own willing "descent into the cave" of communal life and his concern for the political things. It is the compelling love of his own which turns the philosopher toward his city and induces him to educate its citizens.[34] Socrates denies the claim of the body in his playful educational exhortation, but the reason he attempts that education itself can be traced to his corporeally grounded connections to his own city.

He continues with the following remark: "Know well, then, that the god orders this. And I suppose that until now no greater good has arisen for you in the city than my service to the god." Socrates' boast that he is the greatest good in the city must seem absurd to the judges. His appearance is closer to the lowly beasts than to the noble gods. One is not likely to look to a ridiculous satyrlike figure for guidance in ordering one's life. Socrates' laughable attempt to educate Athens incongruously juxtaposes the serious tragic theme of educational legislation with the play-

34. Strauss, *City and Man*, p. 128.

fulness of comedy. This mocking mixture of tragedy and farce is precisely the character of the ancient satyr-plays.[35]

Socrates now repeats with a slight modification what he said prior to this digression, that he does nothing else except to "persuade you, both younger and older, not to care about bodies and money before you care just as vehemently about how your soul will be the best possible." The more extreme earlier statement was followed by the interlude just discussed, where Socrates alluded to the inevitable needs of the body. The reformulation of his exhortation here admits the legitimacy of those needs. The word "bodies," which has not yet occurred in the *Apology* (and will not occur again), now appears. He does not call the care for money shameful; he only says that one should care "just as vehemently" about the soul. This more moderate formulation represents the most practical of Socrates' educational suggestions. Suitably beautified and adorned, it could provide the basis for an actual legal order. However, such an order is outlined not by Socrates but by an Athenian stranger, who appears in Plato's *Laws* as a seemingly more practical and moderate version of Socrates.

Socrates concludes this section, the decisive defense against the corruption charge, with this ambiguous statement: "If, then, I corrupt the young by saying these things, they may be harmful." He does not assert that his speeches do not corrupt. He admits that there is room for doubt. Only if his proposed educational program were politically feasible and adopted by the Athenians would his speeches not be corrupting. In any regime except the philosophic utopia implied by Socrates' exhortation, his speeches must be judged corrupting in their tendencies, since they induce the young to despise the established laws, to disobey their parents, and to neglect their duties to the city. The "care for virtue" in the strict human sense undermines the care for vulgar or citizens' virtue. The survival of the city depends upon the virtues of justice, moderation, and battlefield courage,

35. A satyr-play was performed as the fourth and concluding drama, following three tragedies, in the Athenian festivals for the presentation of tragedy. Plato and Xenophon confirm that Socrates looked like a satyr: Plato *Symposium* 215b3–4; Xenophon *Symposium* 4.19. For legislation (education) as tragedy, see *Laws* 817b.

but Socrates' exhortatory speeches criticize those virtues from the perspective of wisdom. Socrates' conclusion, then, is rather a statement of the question than an assertion of his innocence: "If, then, I corrupt the young by saying these things, they may be harmful." Xenophon indicates his awareness of this same problem when he says, "How then could this sort of man [Socrates] corrupt the young? Unless, perhaps, the care for virtue is corruption."[36]

At the beginning of the *Apology* Socrates contrasted his own unpersuasive manner of speech with the persuasive diction of court oratory. Now Socrates talks of his "persuading" the Athenians to care for virtue (30a8; also 30e7 and 31b5). Through his persuasive speech Socrates becomes politically active. He thus enters the competition with others who try to persuade: the politicians, poets, sophists, and educators.[37] His philosophic speech, hitherto described as private conversation, must now be reckoned a public factor. The *Apology* is the outstanding example of Socrates' philosophical-political rhetoric.

Although Socrates' new manner of speech deliberately fails to reach its aspirations, it does define the central problem of political philosophy. It aims to be simultaneously persuasive and truthful, beautiful and ugly, just and unjust; it seeks to transcend and include the dichotomies of the two ways of speech introduced in the proem. The same conversation that investigates the truth of the beings must edify even as it defends its own enterprise. Socrates' philosophic education fails as a teaching for contemporary Athens; however, his speeches and deeds at the trial succeed in delineating the terms of every future attempt to achieve a rhetorical accommodation of philosophy and politics. Such was the heritage Socrates bequeathed to his successors, Plato, Xenophon, and Aristotle.

Socrates concludes the section by declaring that he will never stop philosophizing, not even if he is to die many times. This repeated and heightened defiance of the jury and the Athenian laws apparently provokes another loud clamor of protest from the judges (30c2–3). Such is the answer Socrates receives to the

---

36. *Memorabilia* I.2.8.
37. Weber, p. 93.

vital core of his defense. It is the last time in the *Apology* that he mentions any disturbances by the jury. Any further outbursts would be anticlimactic; the clarity with which the opposition between Socrates and Athens is here stated will not be surpassed. The judges now assume an ominous silence.

The Gadfly, or Gift of the God (30c2–31a7)

The first two sections of that part of Socrates' defense treated in this chapter presented the theory and practice of Socrates' political teaching to the Athenians. He derived his new understanding of piety and justice from a free interpretation of the example of Achilles from Homer's *Iliad*. He then showed how he teaches this virtue to the Athenians. The next two sections will illustrate Socrates' usefulness to Athens by concentrating on Socrates the man rather than on his piety or teaching. The first of these two latter sections shows that Socrates is a "gift of the god" (an answer to the impiety charge). The second describes Socrates' lack of care for his household that is due to his constant activity on behalf of the Athenians (an answer to the corruption charge). In these four sections taken together Socrates portrays himself as a political man, both as a heroic paradigm for the community and as a self-sacrificing public servant.

Socrates proceeds to enumerate his remarkable qualities to the jury. First, the Athenians will benefit by listening to him, so that if they kill him, they will not harm him more than themselves. This claim presupposes Socrates' value to the city, a value which will turn out to derive from his being a gift of the god. He continues: "For Meletus or Anytus would not harm me—he would not even be able to—since I do not suppose it is lawful for a better man to be harmed by a worse." Socrates speaks as though he has no body, or as though his body is not truly part of him. He assumes that the only evil a man can suffer is to be made a worse man—more unjust, cowardly, impious, or ignorant. Since the prosecutors threaten none of these things, they cannot harm him.[38]

38. Burnet's note on 30c9.

Socrates presupposes something like the immortality of the soul, for only if the soul lives on independently of the body will death fail to injure Socrates. If the soul dies with the body he will indeed lose his wisdom and other virtues, and thus be harmed. Socrates develops an argument for the soul's immortality in Plato's *Phaedo*, but his argument is not conclusive. When it becomes time for Socrates to die by drinking the poison, the proof that the soul lives forever after the body's death still suffers from unresolved difficulties. He acknowledges this fact by supplementing the arguments with a myth of the afterlife. But his myth does not pretend to be a reasoned argument, and the issue remains in doubt even as Socrates dies.[39] The same dubiety is anticipated in the *Apology*, where Socrates associates breath—that is, bodily life—with his continued ability to philosophize: "as long as I breathe and am able to, I will not stop philosophizing" (29d4–5).

A second explanation of Socrates' claim that Meletus and Anytus may not be able to harm him is that Socrates is divine. He suggests that he has something of the superhuman regenerative powers of the gods when he says that he will not stop philosophizing, even if he must "die many times" (30c1). As a "gift of the god" he does "not seem human" (31b1). He speaks as though he were free of the ordinary limitations of the mortal life. He even associates the word *themiton* (translated here as "lawful"), which has connotations of divine law and right, with himself. He formerly used the word in connection with the Delphic god (21b6).

Socrates retreats from this outlandish posture as he continues. He now admits that he can be killed or banished or dishonored, but denies that these things are great evils. (He does not deny that they are evils: death, therefore, *is* an evil, even if not the greatest evil.) Finally, he says that he regards "trying to kill a man unjustly" as a great evil. The effectiveness of this counteraccusation against the accusers depends upon the proof of his innocence. That proof rests upon his success in teaching the new piety to the Athenians (piety as wisdom), so that he can prove himself a just man. If his attempt to educate Athens fails,

---

39. Jacob Klein, "On Plato's *Phaedo*," *The College* 26 (January 1975), 1–10.

then he must be judged guilty and endure the punishment, since the judgment will be guided by the laws presently in force. Socrates admits this failure in the *Crito*, where the laws—the ancestral laws of the Athenian tradition—appear alive in all their awful majesty, showing dramatically that Socrates has not succeeded in overturning them. He admits this educational failure in deed by accepting the jury's verdict and drinking the fatal drug.

Socrates now hyperbolically asserts his boundless devotion to the Athenians, proclaiming that he is not speaking in his own defense, but "rather on your behalf, so that you do not make a mistake about the gift of the god to you, by voting to condemn me." He claims to be purely public-spirited. He presents himself as utterly indifferent to the outcome of the trial, as far as his own fate is concerned; his only care is for the Athenians. Socrates abstracts from his body when he boasts that no one can harm him; here he abstracts from both body and soul as he describes himself as a sort of selfless minister to the public weal. He "forgets" himself because of the intensity of his concern that the Athenians might harm themselves.

He illustrates through an image how he is a gift of the god. He says he has been "set upon the city by the god, as though upon a great and well-bred horse who is rather sluggish because of his size and needs to be awakened by some gadfly." As the gadfly (or horsefly) Socrates does not "stop settling down everywhere upon you the whole day." Socrates himself calls the image "rather ridiculous." As he "awakens and persuades and reproaches" the Athenians, his admonitions seem to them like the bites of an irritating insect. This ugly, ridiculous, paltry creature dares to accuse the entire city of injustice while claiming to be a gift of the god.

Socrates now modifies the image by comparing the city to men who are drowsy rather than to a horse. Socrates' sharp bites awaken them, and, angry at being disturbed in their rest, they slap and kill the insect. "Then you would spend the rest of your lives asleep, unless the god sends you someone else in his concern for you." Socrates expects to be killed as easily as a man smashes a mosquito that annoys him in his sleep.

What a gulf separates the two central images of the *Apology*!

From a man akin to the noble Achilles, Socrates is reduced to an insignificant insect who will be brushed aside by the flick of a wrist. In the first instance he compared himself to a heroic half-god; now he likens himself to a subhuman gadfly. As a manly warrior, Socrates could stand his ground against his enemies; as a gadfly, he is at their mercy. How can the Gadfly and the New Achilles be the same man? Between the Achilles comparison and the gadfly image Socrates attempted to execute his "philosophic education." The hostile reaction of the judges indicated his failure to inculcate in them a respect for his pursuit of wisdom. His success in assuming the role of Achilles depended upon the success of his endeavor to impose his standards on the city through persuasive speech. When that project failed, his self-presentation as a man of strength also failed. He is revealed to be an ignoble failure, an insect about to be killed with a slap. The gadfly comparison thus appropriately supplements and corrects the earlier heroic boast.

The oxymoronic combination of the irritating gadfly with the Achillean hero makes up the total Socrates of the *Apology*. He is a gadfly who boastingly presents himself as Achilles—a sort of sheep in wolf's clothing. He is unable to lay down the foundations of a new order. His philosophy tries and fails to become politically effective. When it comes to the test, not Achilles but the gadfly most accurately depicts the truth about Socrates' engagement in politics. But although he failed in life, he succeeded after his death. It is one of the remarkable events of Western history that later generations saw in Socrates the Achilles of philosophy, while at the time of his death he appeared hardly more significant than an insect.

The gadfly image presents a further, unattractive aspect. When the horsefly bites a horse, it does not do so for the horse's benefit; it sucks the blood of the beast for its own nourishment. Socrates' image subtly draws attention to the parasitical character of his own life. His contribution to the well-being of the city may well be only an unintended by-product of his primary concern, his own private pursuit of the human good. He is supported by those with the most leisure, the sons of the rich, whose wealth also makes possible the preservation of the body politic. Socrates' comparisons of himself to Achilles and the gadfly divert attention from the benefits he derives from his activities. He leaves the impression that he does everything out of a painful acceptance of an unpleasant duty. Whether as heroic warrior or monitory insect, Socrates has been stationed by the god where he must live dangerously. His own happiness is forgotten in the hard service to the god and the community. Recollection of the gadfly's blood-sucking properly qualifies Socrates' posturing as a man moved wholly by public-spiritedness.

Socrates' Service to Athens (31a7–c3)

Here begins the fourth and final section of that part of the *Apology* treated in the present chapter. Socrates shows himself through all four of these sections as a man whose primary activity is in public life. He now sums up his public services. Indeed, he exaggerates them, as is usual in this part of the *Apology*. This exaggeration will be corrected to a certain extent in the succeeding part, where his way of life will be re-presented from a more private point of view.

As evidence that he is a gift of the god, Socrates says "it does not seem human" for him to mind the affairs of his fellow citizens at the expense of his own affairs. The theme of "care," again associated with teaching, indicates that Socrates is dealing with the corruption charge. Socrates mentions twice that he does not care for his own things (31b2, b3); he minds the Athenians' business, and he persuades them to care for virtue (31b5). How can these claims be understood in light of Socrates' critique of care in the conversation with Meletus?

The primary conflict is between the care for one's own— ultimately one's own body—and care for the good of the soul. One's own, as we saw in the case of Meletus, can be one's own body, family, or city. When Socrates says he lacks care for his *oikeia*, he means these things, and especially his household and family.[40] He does not say that he cares for the Athenians; he says that he persuades them to care—for virtue. Through his conversational philosophy, which he conducts with other Athe-

40. See Translation n. 53.

nians (and foreigners), Socrates cares for his own wisdom while exhorting others to care for wisdom. By caring for how his own soul will be the best possible, Socrates leads his listeners to care for their souls. One might say that his service to Athens is based ultimately upon a selfish pursuit of his own good. The gadfly bites the horse in order to suck blood for the insect's own nurture. But the horse benefits from the bites by being awakened from its lethargy. The self-interested activity of the gadfly who is Socrates promotes the welfare of Athens.

Socrates calls his philosophy, "minding your business"—literally, "practicing your thing." In the first sentence of the next section he calls himself a "busybody" (31c5). In the *Republic* justice is defined as "minding one's own business and not being a busybody." In the *Gorgias* a pious life is said to be that of "a philosopher who minds his own business and is not a busybody."[41] It seems, then, that in the *Apology* Socrates characterizes his life as unjust and impious. This should not be surprising, considering that he is clearly guilty of disbelief in the city's gods and corrupting the young—as these things are understood by the Athenians. However, a little later in his speech Socrates says that anyone who wishes may listen to him "minding my own business" (33a6-7). For Socrates, "minding my own business" is conversing about virtue and examining himself and others (38a3-5). Yet this is the very activity that persuades the Athenians to care for virtue. In other words, for Socrates, "minding my own business" is the same as "minding your business"—it is his admonitory conversational philosophy.

The basis for justice in the *Republic* is the practice of one's own art and no one else's. "Minding one's own business" means primarily doing one's own art well.[42] The art of conversation, dialectics, is Socrates' art—the "heroic" art of the *Cratylus*.[43] But conversation cannot be practiced alone: its "business" necessarily involves the participation of others. It is the one practice that seems to be simultaneously just and unjust as well as pious and impious. It is just and pious because a human being's proper

41. *Republic* 433a8-9, *Gorgias* 526c1-5.
42. *Republic* 369e-370c.
43. See p. 154 above.

"business" is to search out his appropriate virtue in order that he may pursue it. Yet it is unjust and impious because conversational inquiry invariably brings into question the generally accepted views of virtue and the gods. In his paradoxical manner of life Socrates is both a busybody and one who minds his own business. In order to transcend this contradiction, dialectics must achieve its goal—knowledge of virtue—and transform itself into the art of education. Otherwise, Socratic dialectics will undermine the established order of the arts and other pursuits without providing a suitable practical alternative. From the perspective of political life, Socrates' philosophy is therefore unjust and impious.

But in this part of the *Apology*, where Socrates portrays himself as a political man and his boasting reaches its height, he speaks as though he does possess the art of education—precisely the art he said he did not understand in the earlier, parallel conversation with Callias (20a–c). At that time Socrates compared the art of education to the art of horse-training. The comparison was restated in the conversation with Meletus (25a9–c1). Now Socrates the gadfly appears to be able to train the horse which is Athens through his monitory exhortations. Yet the very image reveals Socrates' limitation: his irritating bites can wake up the horse, but he gives the horse no guidance once it is awake. Socrates is unsurpassed at exhorting men to virtue, but he cannot show them what virtue is.[44] He cannot show them because he does not know the greatest good for a human being. As a philosopher (*philo-sophos*, a lover of wisdom) rather than a wise man (*sophos*), Socrates is at best only on the way to an adequate understanding of human excellence. Hence his attempt to practice the art of education within the *Apology of Socrates* is neither successful nor seriously intended. Only when Socrates is transfigured and resurrected by the art of Plato does he appear to obtain the forcefulness and confidence of one who knows. But this appearance is deceptive: Plato lets us see the true Socrates, who is uncertain about the educational art and the best way of life, behind Plato's own rhetorical Socrates "made young and beautiful," who became the new teacher of Greece and eventually of the Western world.

44. Plato's *Cleitophon* portrays a former follower of Socrates, now disaffected, making this very complaint.

CHAPTER 5

Socrates as
Private Man (31c4–34b5)

The *Daimonion* (31c4–33a1)

The beginning of a new argument is indicated by the words, "Perhaps, then, . . ." (*isōs an oun*), the same words used when Socrates brought up the objection earlier which led to his comparison of himself with Achilles (28b3). The objection raised here, however, remains an unspoken opinion: "Perhaps, then, it might seem to be strange that I go around counseling these things and being a busybody in private, but that in public I do not dare to go up before your multitude to counsel the city."

The two parts of the *Apology* beginning with "Perhaps, then" (the subjects of the preceding and the present chapters) are devoted to a defense of the Socratic way of life; that life is viewed first from the public and then from the private perspective. The first account began with an objection in speech (speech is heard by others), while the second begins with an objection in thought (thought is silent). In the preceding part Socrates dwelt on his service to the public; in this part he will show himself as a private man who retreats from public life. He will correct the mistaken impression someone might have gotten that he cares more for his fatherland than for his own soul. The preceding part of his speech culminated in a section where Socrates talked as though his whole life were lived in service to Athens. But now Socrates says he is not politically active at all. He particularly avoids politics in the ordinary meaning of that term: he does not speak in the Assembly of the people.

The hypothetical silent objector seems to doubt Socrates' courage. Socrates conjectures that someone might charge that Socrates does not "dare" to speak before the Assembly. Socrates answers by tracing his lack of political activity to "something divine and daimonic" which comes to him, ·"a voice," which opposes his involvement in politics. Yet he goes on to argue that the opposition of the daimonic sign is "altogether fine" (*pankalōs*). For he would have perished long ago if he had supported justice in a public capacity. The beauty or nobility of the daimonic voice is vindicated by the consideration that practicing politics justly is dangerous. Socrates would have been of no use either to the city or to himself if he had practiced politics and as a consequence been killed.

This argument appears to contradict the argument Socrates used when he compared himself to Achilles. There he maintained that a man should not take death or danger into account when he acts; he should look only to the question of the justice and goodness of his deeds (28b5–9). At that point he came close to calling his own philosophizing an act of courage, likening it to remaining at one's post in battle. A divine order seemed to be the cause of his philosophic activity in the public arena. Now, however, he says a divine and daimonic voice *opposes* his practicing politics because it is too dangerous. How can these two accounts be reconciled?

The comparison to Achilles was part of a Socratic boast which reached its peak in his tacit effort to replace Homer as a new kind of educator. The failure of that boast, shown by the jury's hostile reaction to his claim, required a second image to correct the misleading impression left by the first. The manly and powerful Achilles was replaced by the tiny, defenseless, and exasperating horsefly. Socrates' brief venture into politics—his present defense speech—seems to reach exactly the end "predicted" by the *daimonion*: he will be condemned to death. He lived his life prior to the trial in accordance with the "fine" (noble) dictates of the daimonic voice, which kept him in a private station. But now that he is seventy years old, the voice does not obstruct his political action. Socrates later calls it "amazing" that the *daimonion* did not oppose the way he made his defense speech (40a3). It is amazing because the daimonic sign seems to permit what it earlier forbade, Socrates' risking of his life "fighting for justice" in public. Socrates' old age may help to account for the change: no matter what happens, he cannot now be far from death (38c5–7). Socrates' manliness in public, then, is only a recently acquired virtue at best. Through most of life he avoided acting "as one ought" with respect to ordinary public activity (32e4). He did not aid justice, because his *daimonion*, agreeing with his own calculations of death and danger, opposed him. If it is unjust not to promote justice, then Socrates did injustice by shirking political action.

Socrates' "divine and daimonic" sign is mentioned here only incidentally, to account for his refraining from entering politics. The bulk of the section is a narration of Socrates' quarrels with the governments under which he has lived. He tells two stories of his conflicts with the democracy and the recently deposed oligarchy in Athens. But we must resist the temptation to follow Socrates' lead in rushing past the question of the *daimonion*. In the context the strongest reason to linger is his casual but nonetheless jolting admission that his daimonic voice was the main target of the impiety charge: he says Meletus "made a comedy" over it in the indictment.[1]

We have already seen that Socrates equates daimons, demigods, and heroes in the *Apology* (27d4–28a1, 28c). His comparison to Achilles, and the parallel passage from the *Cratylus* on daimons and heroes, suggested that Socrates, the daimonic man who possesses "human wisdom," is a demigod and hero.[2] This equation, having been formally delineated, stands in need of explanation and interpretation. When Socrates discussed the difference between his own wisdom and the pretended wisdom of the sophists earlier in his defense, he called his wisdom "human," and theirs "greater than human, or else I cannot say what it is" (20d6–e2). This greater-than-human wisdom is the understanding of the virtue of human being and citizen, and how to teach it. It is identical to the art of education. Such wisdom is simply not accessible to human beings, Socrates implies. It is only possessed by gods. On the other extreme Socrates found many who suppose themselves to be wise, but who are in fact not wise at all. Theirs is an unredeemed ignorance. Between this

1. See ch. 3, n. 11 above; also Georg W. F. Hegel, *Vorlesungen über die Geschichte der Philosophie* (Frankfurt a. M., 1971), I, 498.
2. See pp. 153–154 above.

divine wisdom and human ignorance stands the human wisdom of Socrates. He is neither wise nor ignorant, for he knows that he knows nothing and seeks to replace his ignorance with wisdom. Philosophy, the love of wisdom, is the pursuit undertaken by those who are aware of their ignorance and long to overcome it. This is the serious meaning of Socrates' calling himself, or comparing himself to, a daimon or half-god. He participates in humanity through his ignorance, but he achieves something of divinity through his wisdom, limited though it may be. As a daimonic man possessing human wisdom, he is midway between the foolish complacency of human ignorance and the perfection of divine wisdom. It is just this human wisdom which is, and causes, his philosophizing.

In Plato's *Symposium* Socrates gives a speech on love to an intimate audience. The most intelligent poets and thinkers of Athens are present at the banquet. In that speech Socrates reveals the mysteries of love and the daimonic. His revelation there agrees in every decisive respect with the treatment given to daimons and the *daimonion* in the *Apology*. Eros, or love, says Socrates, which most men believe to be a great god, is in fact a great daimon. Everything daimonic is between god and mortal. And whoever is wise with respect to *daimonia* is said to be a daimonic man. As a daimon, Eros is between wisdom, which only the gods possess, and ignorance. Neither the gods nor the ignorant philosophize or desire to become wise, for the gods are wise already, while the ignorant seem to themselves to be "noble and good, and prudent," but are not. Thus they do not desire what they do not suppose they need—wisdom. But the daimon Eros, aware of his lack of wisdom, is a philosopher. If this description were not enough to remind the reader of Socrates himself, he includes the following in his portrait of Eros. "He is always poor, and is far from soft or beautiful"; he is "tough and squalid and shoeless and homeless," always "weaving certain stratagems." Moreover, Eros, like the "heroes" of the *Cratylus*, is a "clever sophist."[3]

---

3. *Symposium* 201d–204a. Socrates was famous for his bare feet (174a3–5). Eros is also called a "great daimon" by Xenophon's Socrates (*Symposium* 8.1). Cf. Diskin Clay, "Socrates' Mulishness and Heroism," *Phronesis* 17 (1972), 58. For objections to the view that Socrates is Eros, see Stanley Rosen, *Plato's "Symposium"* (New Haven, 1968), pp. 233 ff.

Socrates stays out of politics because of his daimonic voice. It is the voice of his eros, his love of wisdom. Philosophy demands leisure for thought and conversation. The time and effort called for by a public career in the service of justice would inhibit full devotion to the pursuit of wisdom. Heraclitus said, "Character is a man's daimon."[4] Socrates' character, formed by an erotic nature whose chief hallmark is the love of wisdom, vouchsafes to him its daimonic signs when he is about to do something that would interfere with that love. His *daimonion* is his prescient instinct or nature which opposes whatever hinders his growth in wisdom.[5]

The examples of the daimonic sign given in other works of Plato support this analysis. In the *Theaetetus* Socrates discusses his association with young men. With some of them, he says, the *daimonion* prevents the association, but with others it allows it, and these progress in wisdom. The *daimonion* thereby leads him into fruitful conversations with intelligent young men, while it discourages associations which will be of no profit to Socrates and his associates in regard to learning. In the *Euthydemus* and *Phaedrus* the occurrence of the sign prevents Socrates from missing important philosophic discussions.[6]

In the *Apology* Socrates presents his *daimonion* as something negative which rightly opposes his practicing politics. In the *Symposium*, on the other hand, the daimonic is represented by Eros, the positive desire for wisdom. The different portrayals of the two dialogues are functions of the different intentions of the two works. The *Apology* is a most compulsory dialogue, for as Socrates says, he speaks only because he is compelled by the law (18e5–19a7). The *Symposium* is Socrates' most voluntary dialogue: he goes so far as to dress up and put on shoes for the banquet. In the *Apology* Socrates speaks more publicly, before more people, than anywhere else. The unique privacy of the

4. Fr. 119, in Hermann Diels, ed., *Die Fragmente der Vorsokratiker*, 16th ed. (Zurich, 1972), I, 177. Cf. Eva Brann, "The Music of the *Republic*," *Agon* 1 (April 1967), 47.

5. Seth Benardete, "The Daimonion of Socrates: A Study of Plato's *Theages*," M.A. thesis, University of Chicago, 1953; Leo Strauss, "On Plato's *Apology of Socrates* and *Crito*," in *Essays in Honor of Jacob Klein* (Annapolis, Md., 1976), pp. 159–160. On the authenticity of the *Theages*, see also Paul Friedländer, *Plato*, II (New York, 1964), 147–154.

6. *Theaetetus* 151a3–5, *Euthydemus* 272e1–273a2, *Phaedrus* 242b8–c3.

Symposium is emphasized by the long chain of narrators it had to traverse before it could reach the light of day. Indeed, Socrates' speech there is the revelation of a mystery. By revealing the mysteries of the daimonic and the divine, Socrates commits an apparent act of impiety, while he claims to be the very model of piety in the *Apology*. In general the *Apology* presents Socrates from the harsh, compulsory perspective of convention and law, while the *Symposium* exhibits the free play of his natural inclinations. The word eros and its derivatives do not occur anywhere in the *Apology*: Socrates seems to be harsh, graceless, and unerotic; in the *Symposium* he excels in the urbanity for which he was justly famous.[7]

The *Apology of Socrates,* like the daimonic sign itself (which, "whenever it comes, always turns me away from whatever I am about to do, but never urges me forward") concentrates on the repulsive necessities that hinder the philosophic life. The greatest enemy of philosophy is the multitude when it is gathered together in the Assembly.[8] Its principal teaching is care for one's own. If this kind of care becomes too strong, philosophy becomes impossible. Socrates' strident attack in the *Apology* on care and the city is the reverse side of the erotic and pleasurable attractions of philosophy. The care for how the soul will be the best possible is consonant in the best case with the natural inclinations of the philosopher.

In a passage of the *Republic* where Socrates discusses the various kinds of "natures" of human beings, he considers the reasons why a man might pursue philosophy in spite of the competing objects of care offered by his body and the city. He gives two examples of such reasons. His companion Theages was constrained to abandon politics for philosophy because of a sickly body, while Socrates himself owes his philosophizing to his daimonic sign. In Theages' case the negative limitations imposed by his defective bodily nature provided the ground. In the context of the discussion of human "natures," Socrates' *daimonion* would seem to be the voice of his nature. Hence, like those

7. *Symposium* 172a–174a, 209e5–210a2. For the interpretation, see Leo Strauss, "Plato's *Symposium*," mimeographed transcript of a course given at the University of Chicago, 1959.

8. *Republic* 492a1–d1.

who justly despise their own petty arts and abandon them for philosophy, Socrates possesses a "good nature."[9] The *daimonion* would be a "mythical" equivalent of human nature's best inclination, the love of wisdom.

The part of the *Apology* treated in this chapter lets us see Socrates from the natural or daimonic perspective. It forms a parallel to the earlier "autobiography," where he traced his political philosophizing to an attempt to refute the Delphic oracle. Since then we have heard nothing about the oracle, although gods and "the god" have been mentioned often. Now Socrates brings up a new kind of "oracle," a private substitute for the Delphic. As we followed the use of the word "god" in the *Apology*, it became doubtful whether "the god" is Apollo. Now the divine and daimonic sign replaces the authority of the Delphic oracle—and ultimately of the Olympian gods altogether—in Socrates' new understanding of the human condition, articulated in "mythical" form. Near the end of the *Apology* Socrates refers to "my customary divination (*mantikē*) from the *daimonion*" (40a4). The oracle of Apollo yields to the daimonic oracle of Socrates. But Socrates' oracle is his *mantikē*, his art of divination, which in turn has its source in his daimonic, erotic love of wisdom. Just as Hegel maintained, Socrates was "the hero who, in the place of the Delphic god, established the principle that man knows in himself what is true."[10]

Socrates now gives "great proofs" that the opposition of the *daimonion*, preventing him entering politics, was "altogether fine" (31d6), that is, sensible in light of the danger such a career would have had for him. His proofs are "not speeches, but what *you* honor, deeds." Unlike the many, Socrates himself considers speech to be more important than deeds.[11] Hence he probably

---

9. *Republic* 494d–496e.

10. Hegel, I, 502–503; Friedländer (II, 153–154) speaks of Socrates' "private oracle." Strauss ("On Plato's *Apology*," p. 159) points out a conflict between the Delphic oracle, whose command made Socrates hated and thus brought him into mortal danger, and the commands of the *daimonion*, which preserved him by keeping him back from political activity. "The digression which begins with voicing utter contempt for concern with self-preservation [sc. 28b3–5] culminates in a vindication of self-preservation—of self-preservation that is in the service of the highest good."

11. *Republic* 473a, *Phaedo* 100a1–3.

does not greatly honor these proofs of the good sense of the *daimonion*. The missing "speech" that would provide a sufficient proof would argue the question from the point of view of the respective merits and demerits of the political and the private, philosophic ways of life (as is done in the *Republic* and *Gorgias*). However, such a discussion would take too long for the present occasion (cf. 37a6–b2).

The deeds he recounts are two incidents concerning men unjustly condemned to death by the Athenian government. Therefore they remind one of the case of Socrates. The first was a matter which arose when Athens was governed by the democracy, and the second occurred under the rule of the thirty oligarchs.

In recounting the illegal trial of the ten naval generals by the democracy,[12] Socrates stresses the difference between himself and the popular Assembly. He pointedly identifies the members of the jury with the democracy, using the word "you" (plural) five times in referring to the Assembly which unjustly condemned the generals. "You" were doing injustice, while Socrates, as he somewhat fastidiously maintains, refused to side with "you." Socrates praises his own righteousness while attacking the injustice of the democracy. By doing so he turns a common rhetorical device—the recitation of one's honorable deeds—into an insult. Instead of encouraging sympathy for himself, he tactlessly accuses the jury of injustice.

Next Socrates tells the jurors about his conflict with the oligarchy. When he and four others were ordered to arrest Leon of Salamis, he refused, for he knew that Leon was to be killed without a trial.[13] He declares that his refusal to arrest Leon showed "that I do not care about death in any way at all—if it is not too crude to say so—but that my only care is to commit no unjust or impious deed." He probably exaggerates his personal danger. One of the leading members of the Thirty was Critias, a former associate of Socrates. He seems to have maintained some friendliness toward Socrates even during his rule. In the *Memorabilia* Xenophon reports that the oligarchs forbade Soc-

12. See Translation n. 93 for a summary of the incident.
13. See Translation n. 95.

rates to teach "the art of speeches," but they did nothing about it when he did not obey their order.[14] Nor should we forget that Socrates' narration of these two conflicts between himself and the Athenian governments occurs in the context of a discussion of his daimonic voice. Apparently the voice did not oppose his conduct at the trial of the generals or when failing to arrest Leon. Perhaps the *daimonion* divined that Socrates was not in any real danger. In other words, Socrates may have correctly gauged how far he could oppose the injustices of the political authorities without bringing death upon himself.

Both incidents imply a tacit Socratic equation of the legal with the just. In the two cases men were executed without benefit of a judicial trial. Socrates tells the stories in a way that suggests that all would have been well if the accused men had been given trials in accordance with established custom. Yet he prefaced his narration with the statement that a man fighting on behalf of justice in public life cannot survive. Politics as such is corrupt, and Socrates seems to present the legal murders of Leon and the generals as characteristic of the abiding conflict between political life and justice. The examples exhibit the two typical excesses of politics. In the trial of the generals the democratic Assembly erred in its public-spirited but thoughtless belief that the generals were guilty of selfish neglect of their duty. Inflamed by their passion for justice, the people failed to take into account the particular circumstances (the storm and post-battle confusion) which prevented the generals from picking up the survivors and the dead after the naval battle. The Assembly's error exaggerates one characteristic of law as such, for legal enactments lay down general rules that are inherently incapable of anticipating all the relevant particulars of every possible case.[15] The defect of democracy is its well-meaning but unjust tendency to act without seeing things in their concrete complexity. The oligarchy of the Thirty, on the other hand, executed all men of importance who appeared to be potential opponents of the regime; others were killed simply for their wealth. We do not know the specific reason why Leon of Salamis was killed, but we can safely say that

14. *Memorabilia* I.2.31–38 (Charicles, not Critias, does most of the talking).
15. Plato *Statesman* 294e8–295b2.

he was hardly condemned because the oligarchs were pursuing justice with thoughtless zeal. The oligarchy, unlike the democracy, acted with dispassionate calculation and with a basely selfish intention. They judged with intelligence but without public spirit; the democracy judged with sincere but simpleminded passion.

The two examples of injustice suggest that political practice typically moves between the two poles of clever oligarchic self-interest and foolishly harmful democratic good will. Later in the *Apology* Socrates proposes that the Athenians adopt a law requiring the passage of many days before a verdict is reached in capital cases (37a7–b1). His recommendation would moderate the tendency of democracy to arrive at its judgments without due deliberation. But it would not change the nature of politics. Because political action is inevitably bound up with self-interest and immoderate passion for justice, ordinary law and justice will never be perfectly "lawful" or "just." Law intends to find out the truth of things and to order human beings accordingly, but it always fails to achieve its intention.[16] Therefore law is always unjust and hence in the court of reason "unlawful" to some extent. Socrates' account provides no way out for a just man: if he attempts to be politically active, he will expose himself to death; but if he lives as a private man, he must abandon any attempt to affect public policy for the better. Since the just man cannot safely or effectively exercise political responsibility, politics will be forever conducted by villains or zealots. Socrates leaves no middle ground for a prudent statesmanship; the true political art can only be practiced in private, where it must remain unconsequential.[17] Therefore Socrates can do nothing to preserve himself or other just men if the established government should turn against him or them.

Socrates was unable to save either the generals or Leon when they were being unjustly killed. Their cases parallel his own in this respect as well, since Socrates will prove unable to save

---

16. Plato *Minos* 315a2–b2.

17. *Gorgias* 521c9–522b2. Socrates declares that he is the only Athenian who attempts to practice the true political art; hence if he is ever brought to trial, he will be in the defenseless position of a doctor tried before a jury of children on a charge, brought by a pastry cook, that he poisons the young.

even himself. This weakness casts doubt upon his justice, since justice seems to require more than the mere avoidance of injustice.[18] Indeed, Socrates concludes the discussion here by saying that he would have perished long ago if he had practiced politics "in a way worthy of a good man" and aided justice as one ought. That is, he did *not* aid justice as he should have; he is deficient in performing his political duty to save the just, whether they are other men or himself. Socrates' critique of politics does not solve the problem of the danger to men who are good. The only way for them to be saved is for them to become politically potent, but a man must practice injustice in order to achieve that power. Yet a way of life that is nonpolitical is not a satisfactory alternative: one remains at the mercy of those by whom one is ruled.[19] The failure of Socrates' philosophic education leads to the consequence that Socrates is unable to protect himself and other philosophers from the injustices of established political orders.

Socrates and His Companions (33a1–c4)

The transition to a new section is unemphatic, and indeed, it is not until one has read two or three sentences of the section that it becomes clear that Socrates is raising a new subject: his relationship to those who are called his students. After the discussion of the *daimonion*, in response to the impiety charge, Socrates turns again to the corruption charge.

He begins by asserting that he has always acted the same in private and in public. "In public" refers to his political actions, while his dealings with those who listen to him conversing are "private." But later in the section he says, "If someone asserts that he ever learned anything from me or heard privately what everyone else did not, know well that he does not speak the truth." Here he distinguishes between a private or secret teaching and a public teaching accessible to anyone who listens to him. He shifts the meaning of "the public" from "the political"

18. Cf. Xenophon *Memorabilia* IV.4.10–11. In the passage of the *Republic* where Socrates mentions his *daimonion*, he claims to do no more than to remain pure of injustice and of impious deeds (496d9–c1).
19. *Republic* 347b–d; *Memorabilia* II.1.11–13, 18.

to "that which is in the open." After arguing that he avoids public activity because of his daimonic sign, he now denies, in effect, any important difference between the public and the private. His own most private activity, his conversation, is accessible to everyone equally. For Socrates, "minding my own business" (33a6–7) is the same as "minding your business" (31b3): his conversational philosophy is both private and public.

This section provides a moderating correction to the divergent tendencies of the two preceding sections. When he discussed his service to Athens, he talked as though his existence were entirely public, that is, dedicated to the good of the city at the expense of his own good. In the section on the *daimonion* he argued nearly the opposite: he has always lived privately and not publicly (32a2–3) in order to avoid being killed while helping justice. The apparent contradiction between the two sections is resolved by a Socratic paradox. His unique way of life combines—and transcends—the public and private lives as they are ordinarily understood. His speech, audible to anyone who cares to listen, is purely public. Its privacy lies in its subtle interior order which is accessible in principle to everyone but understood by few. Socrates is "always in the open," so to speak, but even in his openness or publicity he maintains his private thoughts.[20]

If there is no essential difference between the private and the public or political, then all of Socrates' private activity—his conversation with others—is in a sense political. This consideration becomes a problem with a view to Socrates' two most famous former associates, Critias and Alcibiades. It would be inappropriate for Socrates to mention these names in his own speech, which assumes such lofty pretentions and disdain for vulgar facts. For they were the two most notorious figures of the oligarchy and the democracy. Indeed, Critias was one of the Thirty responsible for the arrest and execution of Leon of Salamis, the incident that Socrates has just narrated. According to Xenophon, Socrates' accuser said that "Critias became the most avaricious and violent and murderous of all those in the oligarchy, and Alcibiades became the most unrestrained and insolent

20. Cf. pp. 92–95 above.

and violent of all those in the democracy." In the present section Socrates only alludes to these former associates by saying that he never conceded "anything to anyone contrary to justice—neither to anyone else nor to any of those who my slanderers declare to be my students." Socrates, like Xenophon, will not defend Critias and Alcibiades if they did any evil to the city; he merely denies that he permitted any injustice when they were with him "in private."[21] Again he implicitly admits his inability or unwillingness to prevent injustice in public.

Socrates repeats here his earlier remark that the young "enjoy hearing men examined who suppose they are wise, but are not." But he also adds something: "For it is not unpleasant." This is the first occurrence of the word "pleasure" or its cognates in the *Apology*. The interest of the young in Socrates' conversations now becomes fully intelligible: it is pleasant to watch the humiliation of the authorities. In the *Republic* Socrates describes more thoroughly the experience of the young when they first become acquainted with dialectic: "They themselves, imitating the men who refute them, refute others, for they enjoy it as though they were puppies pulling and tearing in speech those who are nearby." Socrates goes on to recommend that in the best political order the young not be permitted to study dialectic. He admits, in other words, that philosophic conversation has a corrupting effect on the young even in the best regime. The enjoyment they obtain in refuting their elders and authorities in arguments about nobility and justice fosters in them a contempt for the law and the ancestral traditions of the community. Winning easy successes in their arguments against the traditions, they turn not to serious thought but to the most powerful and evident alternative to the ancestral law and customs, pleasure.[22]

In the *Apology*, Socrates generally understates the intrinsic attractiveness of philosophy. Especially in the earlier "autobiography" section, he seemed to imply that it was a painful duty imposed on him by the god. It gave him pain, he said, when he perceived that he was becoming hateful to the men he examined (21e4). His service to the god causes him to live in "ten-

21. *Memorabilia* I.2.12–13.
22. *Republic* 537e1–539d6.

thousandfold poverty" (23c1). But now he alludes with careful restraint to the fact that his life is not all harshness and pain: "it is not unpleasant," not only for his youthful listeners, but also for himself. The present section—the most private part of Socrates' most public dialogue—reveals as much as can be revealed in such a setting about the truth of Socrates' private way of life.

How Socrates Receives Divine Orders (33c4–8)

Immediately after he speaks of pleasure, Socrates mentions again, suddenly and briefly, the divine authority for his philosophizing. Of all the sections in the first speech of the *Apology* dealing with the impiety or corruption charge, this is by far the shortest. It is quoted here in full:

I have been ordered to practice this, as I affirm, by the god, through divinations, and through dreams, and in every way that any divine allotment ever ordered a human being to practice anything at all. These things, men of Athens, are both true and easy to test.

Socrates laconically reveals the core of his divine authority. Not merely the single divination of the oracle at Delphi, but "divinations" direct him to philosophize. Socrates has not mentioned any divinations except that of the Delphic oracle—unless his *daimonion* provides "divinations."[23] The word "divination" (*manteia*), sometimes restricted to oracles alone, can also be used more loosely to mean "conjecture."[24] The divinations of the daimonic man finally replace Chaerephon's oracle, whose authority has been gradually undermined through the *Apology* until it is more clearly depreciated in the present passage.

Socrates claims to have received his divine orders also through dreams. Nothing has been said of dreams in the *Apology* so far. In the *Phaedo* Socrates discusses certain dreams of his which he had often during his life. The dreams always said, "Socrates, make music and work at it." Socrates thought that the dreams were exhorting him to do what he was already doing, "since philosophy is the greatest music." But while he was

23. After the trial is over, Socrates explicitly speaks of his "divination from the *daimonion*" (40a4).
24. Plato *Philebus* 66b5, for example.

in jail before his death, he decided to "make music" in the ordinary sense by composing a hymn to Apollo and writing some poems based upon the myths of Aesop, in case he had earlier misinterpreted the dreams.[25] Could these ambiguous dreams, whose meaning Socrates himself did not clearly understand, be the "dreams" Socrates refers to in the *Apology* which order him to practice philosophy? If so, the clarity of their "order" is no better than the "order" Socrates professed to discover in the Delphic oracle that said that no one is wiser than Socrates. Dreams and oracles in themselves do not show clearly what must be done. They need to be supplemented by the divinations of Socrates' own daimonic love of wisdom.

Besides dreams and oracles, Socrates receives his orders "in every way that any divine allotment ever ordered a human being to practice anything at all." In the *Theages* he says his *daimonion* is in him "by divine allotment."[26] The oracle of the god is superseded by divinely allotted daimonic dreams and signs.[27] Only once more in the *Apology* does Socrates allude to his divine orders: he says that his listeners suppose he is "being ironic" when he says that if he stopped philosophizing, he would be disobeying the god (37e5–38a1). Socrates' ironic claim that he is ordered by the god to philosophize—his "public" account—is corrected by the tacit but not imperceptible "private" indications in his speech that his divine authority is nothing more than his love of wisdom.

He concludes the section with the statement, "This is both true and easy to test (*euelenkta*)." The word for "easy to test" can also mean "easy to refute."[28] Can Socrates' assertions about his divine orders be both true and easily refuted? This is precisely the character of Socratic speech that was outlined in our discussion of the first accusers' charge that Socrates "makes the weaker speech the stronger." The single speech that Socrates

---

25. *Phaedo* 60d8–61b7. For the only other example of a Socratic dream, see *Crito* 44a5–b4. The dream recounted there is as ambiguous as the dream of the *Phaedo*.

26. *Theages* 128d2–3.

27. Cf. *Crito* 44b5, where Crito calls Socrates "daimonic" just after his report of the dream. On "divine allotment," cf. Jacob Klein, *A Commentary on Plato's Meno* (Chapel Hill, N.C., 1965), pp. 255–256.

28. Plato *Theaetetus* 157b8.

makes in the *Apology* has dual significance. The "public" meaning of Socrates' divine mission—Apollo's order to philosophize—is easy to refute, but its "private" meaning is true. Socrates has told the whole truth (33c1–2)—while hiding it. Adapting the language of old-fashioned piety, Socrates subtly replaces the old gods and becomes the paradigm for the new. In the place of the Olympian Apollo stands the daimonic Socrates, the man in search of wisdom. In accordance with the first example of piety offered in the *Euthyphro,* Socrates' piety consists in an imitation of the gods.[29]

The Relatives of Socrates' Companions (33c8–34b5)

Socrates passes smoothly into this section without a break from his statement on divine orders. The word "now" or "for" (*gar,* 33c8), with which he begins, seems to indicate that his next argument will show the truth (or easy refutability) of his claim to receive orders from the god. However, he returns to the theme of corruption. This is his final attempt to prove himself innocent of that charge. He argues that if the men whom he has supposedly corrupted and their families are truly angry at him for the harm he did them, they should come up before the court and accuse him. At least their relatives should presumably be glad to avail themselves of this opportunity to avenge themselves on Socrates. He names seven of his associates, living or dead, who have seven older relatives present at the trial.[30] Out of these and the many others Socrates could name, can Meletus not produce a single witness who will charge him with corrupting the young? Socrates offers Meletus the chance to offer such a witness, if he forgot earlier. He takes it as his final vindication that none of the relatives steps up to accuse him.

This curious argument suffers from a fundamental defect. Socrates speaks as though "corruption" were an evil of the same

29. *Euthyphro* 5d8–6a5.

30. What we know about the seven listed associates of Socrates suggests that they would have been little admired by ordinary Athenians, to say the least (see Translation n. 99). This includes Plato, some of whose relations were connected with the harsh rule of the Thirty (*Seventh Letter* 324c1–d2).

sort as theft or assault, where the one corrupted would be as eager as the one assaulted to testify against the wrongdoer. The premise is the same as that of his earlier discussion with Meletus, that an evil done to someone close to oneself is perceived and returned, if possible, by the recipient of the evil (25c–e). If someone is assaulted, he will fight back, if necessary by a prosecution in court. But the "corruption" with which Socrates is charged does not fit this description. Socrates even admits here, in three different places, that those who are corrupted are not likely to accuse him of corrupting them (33d4–5, e5–6, 34b1–2). Indeed, the reason for their reluctance is obvious. They would be accusing themselves of being corrupt, that is, evil. An assailant harms one's body, but a corrupter ruins one's soul. A man who attacked Socrates as a corrupter would be questioning his own worth as a man. He would have to say something like this: "Men of Athens, you see how contemptible I am; Socrates has made me a pitiable wretch, and I urge you to convict him of his crime." He would probably not want to admit even to himself that he was "corrupted"; he would certainly not be likely to make such statements before a public jury.

But Socrates argues that the relatives of his corrupted companions, at least, would not hesitate to accuse him. He seems to mean that although the corrupted ones might be reluctant to admit it, their older relatives, indignant at the evil Socrates has done, would eagerly speak out against it. Again Socrates "forgets" that a father or older brother would not enjoy calling attention to a son's or brother's defects. Even the older brother of the deceased Theodotus would be unlikely to sully his brother's memory by questioning his character (33e5–6).

The common thread in Socrates' argument is the abstraction from the love of one's own. Most men love themselves and their nearest relatives not because they are good, but because they are their own. Only if Socrates' "philosophic education" were adopted and freely accepted would the relatives of the corrupted associates of Socrates become willing to charge their sons and brothers with a lack of virtue. If a person were truly convinced that such self-accusation is beneficial, then he would first accuse himself in order to be redirected as quickly as possible toward a better way of life. (Socrates persuades his interlocutor Polus of the truth of this proposition in the *Gorgias*.)[31] Socrates' argument about the relatives would be correct only if he had already persuaded them of their duty to accuse themselves and their own families of wrongdoing in order for them to be corrected if they are evil. In other words, they would accuse their sons and brothers only if they were already "corrupted" by Socrates' novel doctrine replacing care for one's own with care for the good. But in that case, since Socrates' associates have themselves been "corrupted" by this very doctrine, they would not appear corrupted to their relatives, but educated. Socrates' argument fails, either because of the relatives' love of their own sons and brothers, or because of his success in corrupting or educating his companions and their relatives.

This does not prevent Socrates from construing the silence of the fathers and brothers in a way most flattering to himself. He maintains that they would even be willing to come to his aid. "What other reason would they have to come to my aid except the correct and just one, that they know that Meletus speaks falsely, and that I am being truthful?" (The "other reason," not stated by Socrates, would be that because of their love of their sons and brothers, they would defend Socrates as a friend of their own rather than as a truth-teller.) The word translated "come to my aid" (*boēthein*) occurs three times in this section (34a7, b2, b4). Both his companions and their relatives are ready to "come to the aid" of Socrates. In Socrates' opinion it is correct and just to come to the aid of one who tells the truth. In other words, justice is aiding and defending the wise man, the only one who knows the truth and speaks it. Socrates continues his "corruption" of the Athenians even while he defends himself, for his defense depends upon changing their perception of what constitutes corruption. He tries to teach them to revere himself, the paradigm of the wise man, in preference to caring for their own.

When Socrates quoted the formal charge against him in his defense against Meletus, he changed it from "bringing in new *daimonia*" to "believing in new *daimonia*." He interpreted the corruption charge to mean that he teaches the young to believe

31. *Gorgias* 480a1–e4.

in new *daimonia* (26b2–5). In the first place the charge refers to Socrates' *daimonion*, his monitory voice. But the more serious meaning of Socrates' reformulation of the charge is this: he corrupts by teaching the Athenians to believe in himself, the daimonic lover of wisdom, in the place of the city's gods.[32] He teaches his followers to "come to his aid" as though he were divine, just as Socrates earlier "came to the aid" of the god (23b7). In this final defense of himself against the corruption charge, Socrates shows how he truly corrupts the young in Athens. His earlier combination of the charges of impiety and corruption (26b) agrees with the truth of the matter as he reveals it here.

At the end of the group of four sections discussed in the last chapter, which presented Socrates from the point of view of his usefulness to Athens, he appeared to devote himself entirely to the service to the city and to neglect his own family and household (*ta oikeia*, 31b2). The present group of four sections, showing Socrates as the daimonic and private man, culminates in a complete reversal of that appearance. The Athenians who are his companions and their relatives are ready to neglect their families (*hoi oikeioi*, 34a8) and come to the aid and service of Socrates, the just and daimonic and wise man who tells the truth.

The preceding four sections constituted a group that presented Socrates in his role as a public educator. That part of his speech paralleled the Callias section, whose subject was the art of education. We have seen Socrates try and fail to practice that art. Earlier we saw a similar parallel between Socrates' conversation with the poet Meletus and his attempt to refute the impiety part (stated by Aristophanes) of the charge of the first accusers. There was a further parallel between Socrates' account of the origin of the present charge from the Athenian politicians' anger at their cross-examinations by the young, and the prothesis, which showed Socrates from the popular-political perspective. Now the four sections discussed in the present chapter make up a group that portrays Socrates as a private man. This group parallels the earlier section describing the Delphic oracle and the origins of

32. Aristodemus, a companion of Socrates, believes in the gods only to the extent that he believes in Socrates' *daimonion* (Xenophon *Memorabilia* I.4.15).

Socrates' philosophy. We have been shown in practice the meaning of Socrates' previous assumption of the role of the Delphic god. Thus the bulk of the first speech of the *Apology of Socrates* contains four pairs of parallel sections. Each of the four pairs corresponds to one of the four groups that Socrates examined when he tried to refute the Delphic oracle. The first four sections show Socrates from the perspectives of the political men, poets, would-be educators, and god; in the last four Socrates tries to replace the authority of the politicians, poet, educator, and god.[33] This coherent plan of the speech confirms the centrality of the themes we have stressed in our analysis of the dialogue thus far. Moreover, the formal correspondences in the structure encourage the interpreter to consider the similarities and differences we have noted between the parallel sections.

33. See Appendix for the analytical outline.

CHAPTER 6

The Epilogue

(34b6–35d8)

The substance of Socrates' defense is now complete: "These, and perhaps other such things, are about all I would have to say in my defense." He concludes his speech with a few final remarks to the judges. This was the usual occasion for the defendant to bring forward his wife and children to arouse the pity of the jury. Rejecting pathos, Socrates prefers to criticize the customary supplication from the standpoint of his own novel standards of justice and nobility.

The epilogue recalls the difficulty posed by the proem—that Socrates undermines the city's view of human excellence without providing an adequate alternative—and shows how he attempts to resolve that difficulty with a new teaching on human virtue. He will sum up the case for his own nobility and justice in order to remove the impression created at the beginning of the speech that he lacks nobility and grace while being insufficiently just. Thus the proem and epilogue share not only their unique positions at the beginning and end of the speech, surrounding the four pairs of sections we have discussed; they parallel each other also with respect to their themes. Socrates devotes his conclusion to an indictment of the custom of supplicating the jury, arguing that such behavior is shameful and base (*aischron*) as well as unjust.

Socrates' Humanity (34b6–d8)

First Socrates must remove a doubt which may have arisen. For some time he has been speaking of himself as though he were divine, or at least daimonic. Socrates now reassures the judges that he, like the rest of them, is a human being, that he is born of human parents. He proceeds here on the droll assumption that he has been so successful in persuading his listeners of his superhuman status that he must make an argument to prove his mere humanity. He specifically mentions his three sons in support of his claim to be human. Socrates says that he too has "grown up" from human beings.[1] The Greek word he uses, *pephyka*, contains the root *phy-*, which is also the root of the work *physis* or nature. The Olympian Apollo was earlier replaced by the demigod or daimonic Socrates; now Socrates admits and asserts that he is entirely natural, a human being. What appeared to be divine or daimonic turns out to be merely natural. However, Socrates' nature can still be thought daimonic in a nonmythical sense, insofar as it surpasses other natures through its love of wisdom. Socrates' transcendence is grounded not in a divine lineage but in his superior nature. Here, at the end of his defense, he is brought from the heavens down again to earth. The "myth" of the *Apology* portrayed a divine and daimonic Socrates superseding the old gods. But now the full arrogance of that myth comes out. Nature—or rather the highest aspiration of human nature, wisdom—is asserted to be more worthy of reverence than the old gods. From this point in the *Apology* Socrates will base his self-praise upon his human wisdom; in the second speech the gods will disappear entirely.[2]

Socratic piety, then, is a piety toward nature. It can be said to consist in behavior that duly respects the natural end of man—of which Socrates himself happens to be the preeminent exemplar. In the present context he shows his piety through his refusal to appeal to the jurors' pity by bringing forward his disconsolate family. Socrates thereby denies the love of one's own as a

---

1. The expression "from an oak or a rock," which Socrates quotes here from Homer, is used once by Odysseus and once by Hector (Translation n. 101). Socrates may be indicating the distance between himself and the demigod Achilles by aligning himself with Achilles' victim Hector and with the Homeric alternative to Achilles, Odysseus, the man whose excellence is free from dependence upon reputation.

2. Socrates does mention "the god" at 37e6, but only to admit that everyone believes that he is "being ironic" when he speaks of obeying the god's orders.

legitimate principle of conduct. He said earlier that his lack of care for his own family and household "does not seem human" (31b1–3). He will now argue that *human* virtue depends precisely upon the rejection of the love of one's own, especially of one's own life, as the guide for right action. The ancestral gods of the Greeks stood for the defense and glory of one's own city, family, and body. Socrates turns this understanding on its head by calling the mere concern for survival—whether of the city, the family, or the individual—unjust and ignoble. Socratic piety is indifferent to mere preservation. The common court practice of bringing in relatives and friends appeals to the judges' compassion for the threatened injury to or loss of one's own. For Socrates, such care for one's own implies a lack of care for virtue and wisdom, the only sufficient standard of human conduct.

Socrates' Nobility (34d8–35b8)

Socrates uses the following argument to prove his nobility. It does not seem to him to be noble for anyone with a reputation for virtue to beg for his life. Such men behave as though they think they will be immortal if they are acquitted. They bring shame on the city, and those who do such things do not seem to be any better than women. They deserve to be condemned for making the city ridiculous, whereas he who keeps quiet ought to be acquitted.

The ordinary Greek understanding identifies nobility with reputation. The noblest warrior is the one reputed to be the best, and the noblest statesman is the one chosen to lead the city. Socrates implicitly criticizes the view which refuses to distinguish between "seeming to be" and "being" noble. On the contrary, he argues that for one who "seems" or "is reputed" to be virtuous, the proper task is to *be* virtuous. Opinion by itself is indifferent to truth and falsehood (34e5). Not reputed but true virtue is the fitting light in which to examine claims to nobility. This is the first step of Socrates' argument.

His next step is a critique of the common view of *andreia,* manliness or courage. The Athenians hold that manliness consists in the ability to defend oneself and preserve one's life, whether in war or in a court of law. In the *Gorgias* Socrates is ridiculed by Callicles for his overattention to philosophy and neglect of forensic rhetoric. Callicles predicts that Socrates' shameful lack of manliness will culminate in a condemnation to death if he should ever be brought to trial.[3] Now Socrates reverses the Calliclean view. He suggests that *he* is manly or courageous because he is willing to face death calmly, while the man who pleads and begs the court for mercy, playing on his fellow citizens' sympathy for his fate, is no better than a woman. He alone is truly manly, while the citizens and politicians are effeminate and worthy of blame (34e1–2, 35b2–3). What is truly shameful and ridiculous is precisely the excessive love of one's own which leads to the unmanly compulsion to save one's life at the expense of one's honor.

In the end Socrates traces the "effeminacy" of the Athenians with good reputations, as one might expect, to their lack of wisdom. They act as though they will be deathless if they obtain an acquittal in court. They are ignorant about death. They are like those mentioned earlier who, although they do not know whether death does not happen to be the greatest good for a human being, "fear it as though they knew well that it is the greatest of evils" (29a6–b1). Socrates, on the other hand, seems to have a manly attitude toward death because of his knowledge of his ignorance about it. Especially for a man of his age, it would be unreasonable to make too much of it, since, as he points out later, he is bound to die soon in any case (38c5–7). Socrates names two of the four cardinal virtues, wisdom and manliness, in the context of this proof of his nobility. But his manliness or courage is only the external face of his wisdom. Socrates' nobility rest upon his apparently ugly but truly profound conversational philosophy. He is the only Athenian with a reputation who is truly noble, because he is the only one who is truly manly or, rather, wise. Thus manliness, formerly the virtue tied most closely to the defense of oneself and one's own, now becomes paradoxically associated with Socratic indifference to one's own death.

3. *Gorgias* 482c–486d.

Socrates' Justice (35b9–d8)

Now that he has established his nobility, Socrates attempts to prove his justice. It does not seem to him to be just, he says, "to beg the judge, nor to be acquitted by begging; one should rather teach and persuade." The judge "has not sworn to favor whoever he pleases, but to give judgment according to the laws." Therefore the defendant should not accustom the jurors to swear falsely, nor should the jurors become accustomed to it.

What is justice? For the accusers, it is to obey the laws of the city. Socrates' philosophic conversation is unjust because it questions those laws, which seem to be based upon nothing more solid than opinion (*doxa*), in the name of truth. But now Socrates contrasts the laws with what "pleases" the judges, what seems good (*dokei*) to them. The laws point to a higher standard than the opinions of the judges. Justice also requires not begging but teaching and persuading, the appeal to the rational faculties of the judges rather than to their self-indulgent pity. To beg the jurors for mercy is to tempt them to break their oaths. For begging is an attempt to distract the minds of the judges from the truth of the case by arousing their thoughtless compassion. The habitual supplication of defendants is not in accord with law. What the law wants, Socrates implies, is the truth, brought forth in an atmosphere free from passion and interest.

Socrates' new understanding of justice depends upon a new understanding of law. He looks at the laws from the point of view of their highest tendency, the achievement of a just and fair judgment of a human being through the exercise of human thought. He defines law not as what is customary and accepted, but as what the law intends. Justice for the defendant can only be achieved if he "teaches and persuades" the judges with arguments, maintaining as great an indifference as possible to his own fate. The just and the legal, properly understood, require one to speak the truth and, if necessary, to deny the love of one's own.

In the proof of his own justice and nobility Socrates begins from assumptions implicit in the common opinions about nobility and justice, but reaches conclusions antithetical to the ordinary understanding. He wants to transform the traditional views of nobility and justice by teaching a view that finds its ultimate justification in the recognition of wisdom as the standard of human excellence. Socrates, having discovered the best way of life, finds that the existing political order is hostile to it. In order to reconcile the political order with his way of life, that order must be changed.[4] This requires a change in the opinions of the Athenians regarding the gods. The Olympians stand for the protection of one's own through the city's justice and through the nobility of the warrior-hero. Socrates' gods defend and protect the way of life of the philosopher by removing the terrors of death and sanctioning the virtue of wisdom.

Hence Socrates concludes the epilogue with a brief discussion of the gods. He swears by Zeus, the principal god of the old order, to affirm that begging for acquittal is "neither noble nor just nor pious." This appeal to Zeus masks the difference between his gods and the gods of the Athenians. "Clearly," he says, "if I should persuade you and force you by begging, after you have sworn an oath, I would be teaching you to hold that there are no gods, and in making my defense speech I would simply be accusing myself of not believing in gods." Like the old gods, Socrates' gods require a man to tell the truth and to judge truly. But unlike the old gods, they make no allowance for the preservation of the individual. In any case of conflict between one's own and the truth, the preservation of one's own must yield. Socrates turns it over "to you and to the god" to judge him; he is confident that the judgment of the truth will vindicate him, just as he is convinced that the jury will convict him. The jury's standards and gods are not the same as those Socrates reveres. In a defiant affirmation, repeated on many subsequent occasions, great and small, down through the ages, Socrates declares, "For I believe, men of Athens, as none of my accusers does." For the moment, the gods of the accusers prevail: Socrates is voted guilty. But the judgment of posterity condemns

---

4. Muhsin Mahdi, ed. and trans., *Alfarabi's "Philosophy of Plato and Aristotle,"* rev. ed. (Ithaca, N.Y., 1969), pp. 64–67.

the accusers and their gods with more conviction and faith than the Athenian judges felt in condemning Socrates. The noble and avenging gods of the Greeks were replaced by the Socratic God of Reason, who continues to be worshipped up to the present day.[5]

5. Cf. Homais' declaration of faith in Gustave Flaubert, *Madame Bovary*, part 2, chapter 1 near the end; Martin Heidegger, ''The Word of Nietzsche: 'God Is Dead,''' in *The Question Concerning Technology and Other Essays* (New York, 1977), p. 112 (final sentence of the essay).

CHAPTER 7

Second Speech: The Counterproposal (35e1–38b9)

Two things have happened since the end of Socrates' defense speech proper: he has been voted guilty as charged, and Meletus has spoken and proposed the penalty of death. According to the law, Socrates must now offer an alternative penalty to the judges, whereupon they will choose between the penalties proposed by accuser and accused. The convicted defendant customarily proposed a penalty lighter than the one proposed by the accuser, but severe enough to be acceptable to the jury. Socrates refuses to follow this custom.

Socrates has been voted guilty, but he says he is not vexed. He says there are a number of reasons for this non-Achillean attitude, although the only one explicitly named is that the vote was "not unexpected" (*ouk anelpiston*, 36a2). Does Socrates mean that he does not mind being voted guilty because he was able to foresee the outcome? Does foreknowledge necessarily imply equanimity? When one knows that an evil is approaching, the evil does not always become less vexing. Perhaps *ouk anelpiston* should be translated according to its more basic signification, "not unhoped for." If this interpretation is correct, Socrates preferred to be voted guilty. This may seem strange, but there were many indications throughout his defense that he intentionally antagonized the jury by exalting himself before the court. In this second speech Socrates' audacity and defiance of the Athenians will reach even greater heights than before.

He professes surprise at the number of judges who voted for his acquittal. A change in thirty votes would have acquitted him (36a3–6). Apparently he is surprised because his speech turned out to be more persuasive than he expected. Not only Socrates, but also other philosophers, sophists, poets, and politicians have contributed to the decline of traditional piety and patriotism. The typical juryman is perhaps more tolerant of the philosopher than he ought to be. If the city were healthier, it would have reacted more vigorously against the one attacking its ancestral manner of life.

Therefore, says Socrates, he has been acquitted as far as Meletus is concerned. Although Socrates defiantly challenges the authority of the city's laws and gods, only a small majority can be persuaded to convict him of disbelief in the city's gods, of introducing new *daimonia*, and of corrupting the young. Already disbelief in the city's gods has spread even among the citizens, and the young are becoming devoted followers of philosophers and sophists (19e4–20a2, 23c2–5). Socrates mentions Meletus in particular as the accuser who is disappointed in the vote; Anytus and Lycon, as we have seen, care more about taking vengeance on the one responsible for the young men's contempt for their elders (23c2 ff.).

Socrates concludes his discussion of the outcome of the vote with the assertion that Meletus would not have gotten even one-fifth of the votes if Anytus (and Lycon) had not joined in the prosecution. Socrates seems to pretend to believe that each of the three accusers is responsible for exactly one-third of the votes against him.[1] Socrates speaks of the judges as merely passive, almost mechanical followers of the men of influence, accepting uncritically whatever the prominent men persuade them to. Far from there being a universal prejudice against Socrates and philosophy, as had been maintained earlier, the trial's outcome hinged, according to Socrates, on the personal effect of the three prosecutors. The conflict between Socrates and Athens exists more in principle than in practice, for the citizens' attach-

1. See Translation n. 106.

ment to ancestral tradition is weak. They ignore this unique opportunity to reaffirm the old ways.

In his introductory remarks on the meaning of the vote to convict him, he disparages the interpretation that he is guilty: from Meletus' point of view he has been acquitted. In the discussion of his counterproposal, which he now begins, he talks as though the court has not found him guilty at all: he simply ignores their verdict. Therefore Socrates first presents a restatement on his way of life as a whole. Not the decision of the court, but his own judgment will guide his choice of an appropriate counterproposal.

We saw that Socrates structured his first speech in accordance with the impiety and corruption charges against him. His self-presentation was therefore affected and perhaps distorted by the compulsory perspective of the charges. In particular, he tried to prove his piety by drawing a connection between his philosophic activity and a divine or daimonic authority. In the second speech, on the other hand, Socrates is free from the encumbrance of responding to the particular indictments. He presents himself here in a simply human manner, without regard to any superhuman authority. This makes the second speech more frank than the first. It also helps to account for its more arrogant tone. Socrates' superiority to other men is based upon nothing more solid than his own goodness—judged by a standard of good and bad which, as he himself points out, the jurors are inclined to recognize even less than his claim to receive divine orders (37e5–38a6).

Socrates names seven things for which most men care, but of which he is careless (36b6–9). All of them concern body, family, or city. Socrates' philosophizing is opposed to these practices which are concerned with "one's own." He offensively asserts that he considered himself "really too decent" to survive if he went into such activities. In the first speech he stated that the daimonic voice forbade his entering politics (31c4–d5), but now he says that his private way of life was a result of choice. He would have been "of no help either to you or to myself" in public life. Socrates' political uselessness became apparent in his earlier narration of his conflicts with the democracy and the oligarchy. In neither case was he able to help the men suffering injustice.

Instead of going into politics, Socrates says, he "went to each of you privately," trying to "persuade each of you" to care for "himself, how he will be the best and most prudent possible." He is paraphrasing his exhortation given in the "philosophic education" section earlier (29d7–e3). But here he adds that he urges his listeners not to care for the things of the city until they care for "the city itself." Socrates thereby draws a parallel between man and the city. "The city itself," the true essence or soul of the city, may be said to be its *politeia* or regime.[2] Before one cares for the "things of the city"—its freedom and empire—one must care for the regime of the city, how it will be the best possible. The city's political order, whether it be a democracy, oligarchy, or monarchy, must submit to the same kind of Socratic examination that investigates the order of the soul. The *Republic* shows how Socrates cares for "the city itself" by investigating the various kinds of regimes and considering their merits and demerits. In effect, Socrates exhorts his listeners to become dialecticians and political philosophers. Such is his benefaction to the citizens.

Socrates accordingly offers a shocking counterproposal which is the very opposite of a penalty. (In ordinary speech the Greek court term for "propose [as one's punishment]" means simply "estimate [one's] worth." Socrates takes advantage of this verbal ambiguity when he proposes a reward for himself instead of a penalty.)[3] He proposes "to be given my meals in the prytaneum." In order to appreciate the impious arrogance of this claim, it must be understood that the prytaneum was the ancient common hearth of the city, the vital symbol of its sacred center. The honor of taking one's meals there was granted to victors at the Olympian games, distinguished generals, and the descendants of certain families that had performed noble public services. Socrates' outlandish gesture is the fitting culmination of his attack on the ancestral piety of the city and the perfect

2. Leo Strauss, *What Is Political Philosophy?* (New York, 1959), pp. 33–34.
3. Translation n. 107.

climax of his own revolutionary education. The common meals at the city's hearth affirmed the ancient unity of the city and its gods, and Socrates' philosophy, liberated from the authority of both, seeks to replace them as the central care of human life.[4]

He claims to deserve maintenance in the prytaneum more than any victor in the Olympian games. "For," Socrates says, "he makes you seem to be happy, while I make you be happy; and he is not in need of sustenance, while I am in need of it." For the first time in the *Apology* the final end and justification of Socrates' way of life comes to sight: happiness. The Olympian victor brings honor and reputation (*doxa*) to the city, which makes the city seem or be reputed (*dokei*) to be happy. But opinion or seeming (*doxa*) is not being: only the practice of that activity which is the "greatest good" for man (38a2) truly leads to happiness. Socrates' claim, of course, is an empty boast: his human wisdom, aware of its own ignorance about the end of human life, cannot make men happy because it does not know what happiness consists in. Moreover, the intrinsic difficulty of philosophic dialectic, not to mention the obligations of life's elementary necessities, excludes most men from any substantial degree of participation in Socrates' pleasant conversations.

Socrates stubbornly ignores the sacred character of the prytaneum in making his counterproposal. The Olympian games were held in honor of Zeus, and its victors reflected glory on the gods as well as the city.[5] The honor of a seat in the prytaneum had nothing to do with food as mere sustenance, as Socrates seems to suggest. It was an honor corresponding to the honor the Olympian victors brought to the city and its gods. Socrates treats the sanctified hearth of the city as a kind of free eating place for the deserving poor. Fustel de Coulanges, in his book on the ancient city, sees the gradual decline in the sacred status of the prytaneum, already far advanced at the time of Socrates' trial, as an egregious symptom of the philosophic transformation of the city and its gods.[6]

4. Fustel de Coulanges, *The Ancient City* (Garden City, N.Y., n.d.), pp. 25–33, 155–158, 354; cf. *Protagoras* 337d5–e2.

5. Pindar's *Olympian Odes* bring together the themes of Olympian victors and the gods.

6. *Ancient City*, pp. 354–357.

Second Speech

Rejected Alternatives (37a2–e2)

Socrates brings up two possible objections to his counterproposal, one an unspoken thought, and the other a spoken question.[7] The silent thought of the first objection is that Socrates is acting "quite stubbornly," just as he did in his refusal to beg the jury for mercy. Socrates' answer to the objection is that he voluntarily does injustice to no one, and he is certainly not about to injure himself. All possible counterproposals that might be acceptable to the jury are unjust because they are bad for him; hence he will not propose any of them.

Socrates answers the first objection with an explanation of why he rejects the other possible counterproposals. He will not do himself an injustice by saying that he deserves slavery or a fine or exile. He speaks negatively here, as he did throughout his defense. (There are frequent cross-references between this section and various parts of the first speech.)[8] When he answers the second objection, on the other hand, he will state concisely and positively the life he chooses for himself, suggesting that it is "the greatest good for a human being."

Because Socrates and the jury have only "conversed" together for a short time, he says, they are unpersuaded of his unwillingness to do anyone, including himself, an injustice. Then, asking himself seven rhetorical questions, he discusses the alternative counterproposals of jail, paying a fine, and living in exile. He rejects jail because it is equivalent to slavery to those who are in authority there. His knowledge that slavery is bad probably derives from his knowing that to refuse to obey one's better, whether man or god, is bad (29b6–7). He knows that he is better than the jailers; it would therefore be bad for him to obey a worse man. What is true of the jailers is of course also true of the people of Athens as a whole: Socrates knows that the principle of democratic (and oligarchic) rule is wrong because it is bad, and it is bad because in each case the better (one who knows that he does not know) is compelled to obey the worse (the ignorant).

7. *Apology* 32a2–4, e3–4 (both sections begin with the words *isōs oun,* "perhaps, then"); cf. 28b3–5, 31c4–7, and p. 181 above.

8. Almost every major section of the first speech is recalled in 37a2–e2 (see Appendix): I.B, II.D, III.A, IV.A, V.A. V.B, V.D, VI.

The alternative of a fine, with imprisonment until he pays, is rejected because "this is the same as what I just now said, for I have no money to pay." He seems to mean that he would languish in prison indefinitely as a debtor.[9] But, as Plato and the others demonstrate at the end of the speech, he has friends who are eager to help him pay (38b6-8).[10] Does Socrates mean that he would fall into their debt and be obliged to obey them if he accepted their money? Does Socrates think he is better than Plato? But he has accepted gifts from Crito and others throughout his life, and indeed accepts their offer of money at the end of this speech. Why, then, does he refuse to propose a fine as his counterproposal? Socrates' procedure has the appearance of a deliberate choice to die. He encourages this appearance by reaffirming that death is something "about which I declare that I do not know whether it is good or bad."

Finally, he turns to a consideration of exile. He is not so hasty in dismissing this as the other alternatives: half of his answer to the first objection to the counterproposal is devoted to the question of exile (37c4–e2). He is aware that the jury would probably vote for exile if he proposed it. It is the most likely counterproposal, and Socrates must explain here clearly why he rejects it.

He says that he would certainly be possessed by "excessive love of life" if he were not able to reckon that his questioning will be as intolerable to foreigners as it is to the Athenians. He implies that his choice between exile and death depends upon the relative strength of his "love of life" (*philopsychia*) and of his reckoning ability (*logizesthai*). The word *philopsychia*, whose literal meaning is "love of soul," is ordinarily used in Greek as a synonym for cowardice. The opposite of *philopsychia* in this sense is *andreia* or manliness.[11] Socrates, however, does not say that his choice for death is manly or courageous; he chooses it because of a reasoned consideration. It should be no surprise that reckoning would replace manliness as the proper attitude in

9. John Burnet, ed., *Plato's Euthyphro, Apology of Socrates, and Crito* (Oxford, 1924), notes on 37c2, c3.
10. Cf. also *Crito* 45b.
11. Cf. Translation n. 112.

the face of danger: courage was already implicitly redefined as wisdom earlier in the *Apology*.[12]

Socrates "reckons" that if his ways of spending time and his speeches are hard for the Athenians to bear, they will be even harder for others: "Fine, indeed, would life be for me, a human being of my age, to go into exile and to live exchanging one city for another, always being driven out." Socrates seems to use the word fine (noble, beautiful) sarcastically, meaning that life would not be fine under such conditions. And yet—is it not noble to live a life of hardship and labors? He earlier compared himself to Heracles by saying that he was "performing certain labors" (22a6–8). Now he renounces a life of heroic toil in favor of an easy death.[13] Here is a typical example of Socrates' peculiar way of speech: he says exactly what he means—that he chooses not to live nobly—but the listener tends to believe that Socrates must mean the opposite of what he says. On the only occasion where the word "noble" is used in the second speech, it is rejected by Socrates as a standard, because it is contrary to his reckoning of what is good for himself.

Students of the *Apology* have noticed that in his second speech Socrates adopts phrases and expressions used by characters in Greek tragedy. This fact has been construed to mean that Plato is attempting to situate Socrates within the tradition of Greek heroism.[14] However, Socratic heroism, as we have seen, has little in common with the traditional form. By using the language of a heroic past which he now seeks to replace with a different understanding of heroism, Plato's Socrates appeals to deeply rooted imaginative associations in the memories of his readers. He creates a formal affinity between himself and the heroes whose virtues will be subjected to Socrates' dialectical

12. Cf. the denigration of "reckoning" (a man should not "take into account [*logizesthai*] the danger of living or dying") in Socrates' first speech (28b, d).
13. Cf. Xenophon *Apology* 32.
14. Erwin Wolff, *Platos Apologie* (Berlin, 1929), pp. 60–62, hears resonances of Euripides' Polyxena (*Hecabe* 342 ff.), Andromache (*Andromache* 384 ff.), and Heracles (*Heracles* 1255 ff.), among others, in Socrates' second speech. Bernard M. W. Knox, *The Heroic Temper* (Berkeley, 1964), pp. 45–47, 50–52, 67 traces the heroic background of the language of stubbornness in Aeschylus' *Prometheus Bound*, the *Iliad*, and Sophocles' *Antigone*. (Socrates uses such language at 34d9 and 37a4.)

examinations if he should go to Hades after his death (41b–c). But Socrates' excellence exhibits itself in conversation and argument, not in the noble deeds of the warrior or statesman. His choice for death over exile appears tragic, yet he acts upon a reasoned calculation of what is good for him (38a2, 40a–41d) and not upon the traditional view of manly nobility. Plato indeed allows his Socrates to portray himself heroically, but his is the novel heroism of the daimonic man.[15] The lofty figure of Socrates calmly facing his own death will supersede the heroes of Greek epic and tragedy in the post-Platonic world. Justice, manliness, and nobility are recast in a new mold. In Xenophon's words:

> Showing clearly the strength of his soul, he won glory by speaking at his trial the truest and most just things of any human being, and by bearing the sentence of death with the most ease and manliness of anyone. For it is agreed that, of the human beings who are remembered, no one ever bore death more nobly.[16]

The Socratic Life (37e3–38a8)

Socrates' dismissal of unsatisfactory alternative counterproposals, accompanied by his subtle adaptation of the trappings of tragedy, prepares the way for a positive statement that appropriately distinguishes the ground of Socrates' manner of life from the traditional standards of human conduct. He makes his statement in response to a second objection to his counterproposal of maintenance in the prytaneum: "Perhaps, then, someone might say, 'By being silent and keeping quiet, Socrates, will you not be able to live in exile for us?' It is of all things the hardest to persuade some of you about this." The listeners who have no respect for philosophy cannot understand the importance that Socrates ascribes to talking. They honor deeds above speeches (32a4–5), but Socrates knows that speeches are more significant and more potent than deeds.

With a view to this common opinion, Socrates spoke in the first speech as though his conversational philosophy were a

---

15. Cf. Hans-Georg Gadamer, review of *Platos Apologie*, by Erwin Wolff, *Göttingische Gelehrte Anzeigen* 5 (1931), 196–199.
16. *Memorabilia* IV.8.1–2.

god-ordered mission. It is easier to persuade the many that philosophy has a divine authority behind it than to persuade them
that it is the greatest good for a human being: they believe the
latter even less than the former. But here in the second speech,
which removes the mythical veil from Socrates' way of life, he
admits that his claim to receive divine orders is looked upon as
ironic. He does not deny that his claim is ironic; indeed, he goes
on to offer an alternative account of his philosophizing:

> But again, if I say that this does happen to be the greatest good for a
> human being, to make speeches every day about virtue and the other
> things about which you hear me conversing and examining both myself
> and others, and that the unexamined life is not worth living for a
> human being, you will believe me even less when I say these things.

Socrates gives the jury two alternatives: either he practices
philosophy because he is ordered to do so by the god, or he does
it because he believes or knows that it is the greatest good for a
human being. The judges clearly disbelieve that the god gives
orders to Socrates, for they proceed to condemn him to death.
The argument of Socrates' first speech also suggested that the
attribution of his way of life to a divine authority was ironic:
there the "authority" of his "divine and daimonic" voice replaced that of the Delphic god. Can there be any doubt that Socrates philosophizes only because he believes that it is the greatest good for a human being?

This statement is Socrates' most lucid recapitulation in the
Apology, and indeed anywhere in the Platonic dialogues, of his
own way of life. It shows that he sees the core of his activity in
"making speeches." He admits that he speaks not only about
virtue, but also about "other things" that remain nameless here.
Socrates' philosophic activity covers a broader area than he has
so far admitted. It probably includes the study of nature.[17] It
certainly limits itself to conversation. (This is true even if his
self-examination is silent, for such examination is nothing more
than the soul's conversation with itself.)[18] It concerns itself prin-

---

17. Cf. *Memorabilia* IV.6.1: "Therefore he never ceased considering together
with his companions what each of the beings is." For the translation and a
discussion, see Leo Strauss, *Xenophon's Socrates* (Ithaca, N.Y., 1972), pp. 116–
120; cf. also *Memorabilia* IV.7.
18. Plato *Theaetetus* 189e–190a.

cipally with the examination of oneself and others; it is a critical thoughtfulness applied to the various aspects of the question concerning the best way of life. The answer to that question, whether attainable or not, remains unattained for Socrates: the only livable life for a human being is one of constant self-examination. A human being who became wise would be a god, for he would no longer engage in the characteristic human activity of questioning.

From the point of view of the fully human life, even the heroic or manly life appears imperfectly human—or even subhuman. Hence Socrates looks like a god among men. But the limitations imposed on him by his imperfect wisdom, which remains critical and tentative, hinder him from achieving the status of divinity. The peak of humanity is to know that one does not know—to be a lover of wisdom, a philosopher. He is a true human being among imperfect human beings, or, metaphorically, a demigod among men. He penetrates the illusory attractions of the heroic life of tragedy and treats it with the satyric playfulness it deserves. But he cannot rise above his daimonic, in-between position on the border between the divine and the human. Like Eros in the *Symposium*, he is poor and tough, always scheming to gain the wealth and beauty of the gods, but destined never to succeed in achieving what he longs for.[19]

Plato and Socrates (38a8–b9)

Finally, Socrates unexpectedly changes his counterproposal. Contrary to what he said before (37c), he now says that he would be willing to pay a fine, "for that would not harm me." Since he would not regard a fine as a penalty, he off-handedly proposes to pay about one mina of silver.

But there is an interruption here, led by Plato himself. (Plato's name is mentioned first and is emphatically set off in the text from the other three names.) Plato and the others bid Socrates to offer a fine of thirty minae, and they offer to stand surety for the money. The verb *keleuein* means "bid," "order," "urge," or "call upon." It has occurred twice before in the *Apology*, once con-

19. *Symposium* 203c–204a.

cerning the god ordering Socrates to practice philosophy (30a5), and once concerning the Assembly which ordered Socrates to yield to its desire to try the accused generals as a group (32b9). Socrates obeyed the order of the god and disobeyed the order of the Assembly. He accepts the authority of the divine, but rejects that of the imperfectly human. In the present case Socrates does not hesitate to obey the "order" of Plato and the others.

Plato and those who offer to pay are wealthy. Their willingness to help Socrates exhibits their friendly generosity at a time when he is in need. It goes without saying that their superiority to Socrates in wealth does not imply a superiority in any other respect. Socrates always argued that money, being a merely external good associated with the body, has nothing to do with a man's worth. But this must also be considered: Plato allows his name to be mentioned only three times (outside the letters) in the whole of his written works. Of the three, two are in the *Apology of Socrates* and one is in the *Phaedo* (where he is said to have been absent on the day of Socrates' death, probably because of sickness).[20] The central occurrence of the three is Plato's order (or bid) that Socrates pay a fine of thirty minae.

Plato ironically depreciates his helpfulness at the trial of Socrates. His offer of mere money cannot save Socrates from being condemned to death. But by writing the *Apology of Socrates* and the other Socratic dialogues, Plato achieves what Socrates failed to achieve at the trial itself: he provides Socrates with a successful defense.

There is an ambiguity in the title of the *Apology of Socrates* which we have hitherto not had occasion to consider. the "apology" (defense speech) proper is completed with the first speech. If "apology of Socrates" means "Socrates' own defense speech," then a disproportion between the title and the work as a whole cannot be denied, since Plato saw fit to include all three speeches under this title. But "of Socrates" can be an "objective" as well as a "subjective" genitive. In other words, the correct understanding of "Plato's apology of Socrates" may be "Plato's speech in defense of Socrates." Grammatically, the title does not tell us whether it is Plato or Socrates who is making the

20. *Phaedo* 59b10.

defense. But if we take it to mean "*Plato's* defense of Socrates," then the inappropriateness of the title for the work as a whole disappears. The latter two speeches would be a fitting part of Plato's defense, for they help persuade his readers of the justice of Socrates' cause.

The *Apology of Socrates* contains Socrates' greatest boast: he implicitly claims to know the art of education or legislation. That claim was shown to be false in the section where he attempted to teach the Athenians his "philosophic education." In the end, Socrates cannot be an educator because he does not know what virtue is. His wisdom takes the negative and necessarily amorphous form of exhorting men to virtue without explaining what virtue is, and of examining himself and others. This daimonic or human wisdom cannot with consistency transform itself into a positive teaching unless that teaching remains satyrically self-mocking and playfully serious. The *Apology* is Socrates' first and only attempt at public speaking. The outcome of the trial shows that Socrates' defense fails with its immediate audience, the Athenian jury. But when the speech is brought back to life and recast by the art of Plato, it achieves a posthumous success greater than its immediate failure. Plato defends Socrates by making him "young and noble" (or "new and beautiful").[21] It is Plato's defense of Socrates, and not Socrates' defense of himself, that has exercised such a powerful and lasting influence on subsequent Western history and thought. And it is Plato, not Socrates, who successfully practices the divine art of education.[22]

Plato's remarkable literary powers enabled him to present his Socrates from three simultaneous and contradictory perspectives. In his role as a tragic hero, Socrates replaces Achilles and becomes the new paradigm for noble action. As a demigod who playfully mocks the heroic life, Socrates turns his own tragedy into a satyr-play. And as a would-be teacher of new modes and orders he reaches toward godhood. But of these three faces of

21. Plato *Second Letter* 314c4.
22. The distinction between Socrates as daimonic philosopher and Plato as divine educator may correspond to Heidegger's distinction between Socrates as the West's "purest" thinker and Plato as a "great" thinker. For Heidegger, Socrates' purity is connected to the fact that he did not write. (Martin Heidegger, *What Is Called Thinking?* [New York, 1968], pp. 17, 26.)

Socrates, only one—the satyrical half-god or "daimonic" man—truly describes the man himself. Whatever divinity shines forth from the Socratic persona emanates from the rhetorical transfiguration effected by Plato. He begins from the droll satyr-play that makes up the core of Socrates' defense and places it into a rhetorically edifying tragic frame. Plato employs these three persons of Socrates as aspects of a dramatic whole that educates his readers, whatever their abilities, by telling the truth while hiding it.

CHAPTER 8

Third Speech: Parting
Words to the Jury (38c1–42a5)

After Socrates makes his counterproposal, a second vote is taken, and he is condemned to death. Diogenes Laertius reports that the vote for the death penalty was considerably larger than the vote to convict.[1] Whether the story is correct or not, such a reaction would be likely in response to Socrates' heightened arrogance and antagonism in the second speech as compared with the first. This attitude, as well as the jury's perception of it, seemed to follow from Socrates' deliberate abandonment of the gods and the *daimonion* as the justification of his manner of life, for, as he said, the judges believe him even less when he refers to the good rather than to the god for his authority (38a6). The second speech is the least mythical part of the *Apology:* Socrates discards therein the noble and divine pretensions that formed the basis of his defense in the first speech.

In the third speech Socrates reintroduces mythical elements, although in a way quite different from the first speech. The myth of the first speech was primarily a "countermyth," a weapon whose purpose was to bring down the remnants of the Homeric tradition. It faced the past and strove to overcome it. Socrates seemed to draw his divine authority from one of the old gods, Apollo, but he used that authority, interpreted philosophically, to replace those gods. The nonmythical import

1. Diogenes Laertius II.42.

of that attack was the critique of the love of one's own—a love supported by the noble and just Olympian gods—in the name of "care for the soul," or philosophy. This negative attack was a purification, a catharsis, so to speak, of the old gods.

The second speech was devoid of myth. Socrates referred there but once to his divine authority, only to dismiss it in favor of "the greatest good for a human being." The myth that Socrates receives orders from the god was discarded once it had served its purpose. The old gods are removed from the stage. The "piteous dramas" (35b7) of the typical defendant trying to save his own life are replaced by Socrates' satyr-play with its peculiar combination of the seriousness of tragedy (Socrates' impending fate) with the comic mockery of the heroic through his seemingly ludicrous speech and appearance. The noble actions of gods and heroes yield to the earnest buffoonery of the daimonic and satyric but emphatically human Socrates. If the first speech, with its combative and negative spirit, necessarily looked to the *past*, the second speech looked to the *present*, the culminating and most significant deed in Socrates' long and rich life—his open-eyed and deliberate decision to die. That choice was the theme of the central speech of the *Apology*, and the tendrils of its ramifications penetrate to the limits of the Platonic corpus. In his confrontation with death—the ineluctable term of the human condition—Socrates, stripped entirely of his "tragic gear," comes clearly to sight as the *human* being he is. In his decision to die Socrates shows himself more truthfully than anywhere else in the *Apology*.

After the jury votes to condemn Socrates, his impending death and its meaning become the burden of the remaining speech. Accordingly, the third speech is directed toward the *future*. Socrates tentatively projects a new, positive myth into the void left by the mutual consumption of the thesis of the old myth and the antithesis of his countermyth in the first speech. This new myth will confirm the cosmic and divine support for a human being who, like Socrates, lives well by caring for his soul, and dies well by being moderate in the love of the body. This myth will become the framework of a new teaching on human life elaborated by some of the younger friends and companions of Socrates, notably Plato and Xenophon. After the gods were purged in the first speech, they now return as the sublime but nonvengeful guardians of good men (41d1–2).

At the beginning of the *Apology*, when Socrates first spoke of the charge of the older accusers, he said that he was accused of being a "wise man" (18b7). But now Socrates affirms that after he is dead, the Athenians will be reproached, by those wishing to abuse the city, with the charge that "you killed Socrates, a wise man" (38c3). The name of wisdom was a term of slander and reproach in the mouths of the first accusers, but in the order of things as judged by Socrates, the killing of a wise man is a great injustice.

Socrates thus reveals his intention at the beginning of his third speech to become the "first accuser" of those who voted to condemn him to death (just as Aristophanes was the first of Socrates' first accusers). The seeds are planted that will eventually grow into a reversal of the Athenian attitude toward Socrates. His accusers, according to accounts stemming from antiquity, will later be punished, either by exile or by the death penalty itself.[2] By indulging themselves in the luxury of condemning him to death—an indulgence which, as Socrates suggests, amounts to stupidity in view of his old age and death soon to come in any case[3]—the Athenians themselves bring on the very thing they wish to prevent, namely, the final corruption of the old regime. The image of the noble Socrates fearlessly facing death did more for the good reputation of philosophy than any quantity of impeccable arguments and refutations could have accomplished, for the many honor deeds far more than speeches (32a4–5).

Socrates now divides the jurors into two groups: those who voted to condemn him to death, and those who voted to have him pay the thirty mina fine (38d1–2). For some reason he considers this division more significant than the division between those who voted him guilty or innocent of the original charge of impiety and corruption of the young. I believe the explanation is

2. See ch. 2, n. 75 above, and Georg W. F. Hegel. *Vorlesungen über die Geschichte der Philosophie* (Frankfurt a. M., 1971), I, 513.

3. Werner Jaekel and Siegfried Erasmus, *Lehrerkommentar zu Platons Apologie* (Stuttgart, n.d.), p. 100.

this: Socrates knew that he was guilty of the specific charge and therefore silently agreed with the judgment of guilty. But through his second speech, he took the opportunity offered by the need to make a counterproposal to state in the broadest terms the trans-political worth of his life as a human being. The true counterproposal was maintenance in the prytaneum, for this stated the alternative in its clearest form. But even the proposal of a fine was not appreciably different, for Socrates made it clear that paying a fine would not harm him, and that he would consider a vote for the fine an approval of his own way of life. Precisely because he was guilty of impiety (toward the traditional gods) and corruption of the young (from the point of view of the city's laws), Socrates judged himself worthy of the greatest honor that the city could offer. The very philosophic activity that is impious and corrupting in Athens happens to be the greatest good for a human being.

Socrates says the jury would have been most pleased to hear from him the kind of defense they are accustomed to hear from others—the wailing and lamenting of a defendant begging for his life. Socrates calls such behavior daring, shameless, unworthy of him, and slavish (38d–e). He compares such self-loving conduct to throwing away one's weapons in war and begging one's pursuers for mercy (39a). Thus Socrates again presents himself as a manly warrior, although, unlike such a warrior, he cannot defend himself against his enemies. His fight can only lead to defeat, just as the man fighting for justice will always be killed if he is politically active (32a).

Socrates complements his earlier accusation of Meletus and the other prosecutors with an account of the outcome of *their* trial by *him* (39a–b). Socrates has been found guilty "by you" (the ignorant jury) and sentenced to death, but they (the accusers) have been found guilty "by the truth" of villainy and injustice. The truth is personified here as a judge of justice and injustice. It takes the place of the punitive gods—and that is precisely its defect. Socrates is condemned to death, while the accusers are convicted of injustice, a crime for which the truth can exact no penalty. Since truth is weak, it needs the aid of human beings to enforce its judgments. Socrates therefore goes on to describe the human executors of truth's judgment.

He proceeds to "deliver oracles" to his condemners, just as the Homeric warriors Patroclus and Hector forecast the deaths of their respective slayers in the *Iliad*.[4] In order to emphasize the harshness of the punishment in store for his condemners, Socrates swears by Zeus, the avenging god of the tradition. But Socrates' vengeance will be executed by human beings, who will continue the way of life he has discovered and who will carry forward the examinations and refutations of the Athenians and others. However, there will be this difference after Socrates is dead: his followers will be harsher than Socrates himself because they are younger. Socrates admits, then, a certain gentleness in himself, a gentleness that might be construed as weakness. It could be said that Socrates is unable to execute his will—in both senses. The superior manliness of Plato (and Xenophon) will be the means by which Socrates gains the political power over his enemies which he needs to enforce the "judicial decisions" of the truth.

As he concludes his oracle and divination to those who condemned him to death, he uses the word "noble" (fine, beautiful) three times in succession (39d5–6). This is the last appearance of the word *kalon* in the *Apology*. In each of the three places where it is used, it could be replaced by "good" or "prudent." For his condemners, the noblest alternative is "to equip oneself to be the best possible." In other words, they should care for how they will be the best and most prudent possible: they should philosophize. In its last occurrence the word "noble" is connected with "easy," rather than with the harshness of the old heroic virtues. Socrates' world is a softer place, a world of peace and leisure, where philosophic investigations can proceed unimpeded by the ungracious intrusions of necessity.

Socrates turns now with pleasure to those who voted for the fine (39e). He first says that he and they will converse (*dialegesthai*) with each other, but quickly corrects himself, saying that they will "tell tales (*diamythologein*) to one another." Socrates thereby warns his listeners not to take the rest of his speech too seriously. As usual in Plato, the distinction between myth and *logos* is fundamental. A myth is a tale that edifies but is probably

4. See Translation n. 121.

untrue.[5] The *Apology* concludes with a myth concerning the goodness of death and divine care for the wise man.

It appears that Socrates speaks more truthfully to those who voted against him than to those who voted for him. In order to understand Socrates, it is necessary to contradict him; those who accept what Socrates says without question will never learn the truth.[6] Perhaps the Athenians who condemned him to death understand him better than those who voted for him.

Nevertheless, Socrates addresses those who voted for him as "judges" (40a2)—the customary court address, avoided by him until now in the *Apology,* for the members of the jury as a whole.[7] In the present context only those can be judges who dispense Socratic justice, which has nothing to do with the city's justice. After Socrates reaccepts the laws' authority in the *Crito,* he will not hesitate (in the *Phaedo*) to refer to the members of his jury as judges.[8]

The bulk of Socrates' *mythologia* discusses the significance of the fact that the daimonic sign did not oppose the way he made his defense speech. "The sign of the god" always opposed him in the past if he were going to do something "incorrectly" (40a2–b6). "Incorrect" means "not good" here, for "there is no way that the accustomed sign would not have opposed me, if I were not about to do something good" (c2–3).

He proceeds to a consideration that shows "how great a hope there is that [death] is good" (40c4–5). It should be remembered that the silence of the *daimonion* indicates only that Socrates' death in particular, at this time, is something good; however, Socrates changes the focus to the more general question of whether death as such is good. This change will remain significant to the extent that his arguments for the goodness of death in itself fail. In that case the grounds for Socrates' choice to die would be inseparable from his own peculiar circumstances.

5. *Gorgias* 523a1–3; cf. *Phaedo* 61d10–e3, 114d.

6. Xenophon says Socrates' conversations with those who contradicted him led to *truth,* but when he explained something by himself in speech, he proceeded through generally accepted opinions and secured the greatest *agreement* from his listeners (*Memorabilia* IV.6.13–15).

7. Cf. 26d4.

8. *Phaedo* 63b5.

Plato's Defense of Socrates

Death, says Socrates, must be one of two things. Either it is such as to be nothing, or it is a change of location for the soul from here to another place, "in accordance with the things that are said" (40c5-9).[9] If it is nothing, it is no different from a dreamless sleep. Now if someone were to consider how many nights and days of his own life he passed better and more pleasantly than a night of dreamless sleep, "I would suppose, not that some private man, but that the Great King himself" would discover that few of them surpassed that night (d2–e2). The key to Socrates' argument might be the hint that a man in a private station (in contrast to the Persian king) would be able to name many days which were "better and more pleasant" than a night of dreamless sleep. The reason why the Persian king would prefer to be asleep than awake might follow from his faulty way of life. He is a paradigm of someone who cares for money and his body instead of how his soul will become the best and most prudent possible.[10] Socrates intimates that the king leads an unhappy life during the day and that at night he is tormented by unpleasant dreams. His political life necessarily partakes of injustices and self-neglect, and he must pay the penalty of unhappiness.[11] For such a man death, or sleep without dreams, might well be better than life. But for a private man, especially a Socrates (who says he has always lived "privately" [32a2]), it is far better to be awake than asleep. Sleep is even a term of reproach for Socrates:[12] he is the gadfly who wakes up the sleepy horse that is Athens. The greatest good for a human being, the life of philosophy, requires the wide-awake possession of all one's faculties. Hence death would only be something good if the alternative of living were worse than a night of dreamless sleep. One such circumstance is the life of a tyrant; another, as Xenophon's Socrates suggests, is the life of someone too limited or too old to live the fully human life.[13]

Socrates then considers the other alternative: if death is a

9. Cf. Translation n. 124.
10. See Translation n. 125.
11. Cf. *Theaetetus* 176e3–177a8, *Republic* 330e6–331a1, 571c3–572b9.
12. In *Republic* 476a9–d7 political men are compared to men dreaming and philosophers to men who are awake.
13. Xenophon *Apology* 1–9, *Memorabilia* IV.8.1–8.

228

change of abode of the soul from here to another place, it would be a great good (40e4–7). Socrates describes a Hades peopled by figures from Homeric and other poetry, but now transformed by his own presence (40e7–41c7).[14] In his version of the underworld, life continues exactly as on earth, with the exceptions that those who are judges there are truly just, and that everyone in Hades is "immortal" (since everyone is already dead, no one can die a second time). Socrates playfully portrays himself going from one dead hero to another, examining them and refuting them if they think they are wise, but are not. Those who are in Hades are "happier" than those who are alive, says Socrates. He reverses the judgment of Achilles, who would have preferred to be a slave on earth than lord over all the dead in Hades.[15] The earthly, embodied life offers Socrates no pleasure worth mentioning besides that of conversation, and in Hades he can converse forever. As usual in the *Apology*, Socrates abstracts from the body and its role in providing happiness. He says that to converse and to associate with the heroes and the countless others, both men and women, who might be mentioned, would be "inconceivable" happiness.[16] Is it "inconceivable" because it is impossible? The word translated "inconceivable" is *amēchanon*, literally, "unable to be devised." Can the soul exist independent of the body? We have already spoken of Socrates' doubts about this possibility.[17] Indeed, he emphasizes his reservations about his own tale of Hades by repeating three times that his remarks are based upon "the things that are said" (40c7, e5–6, 41c6–7)—which means above all the poetic tradition. Earlier in the *Apology* he made it clear that he does not believe the things that are said about the life after death (29b5–6). It is unlikely that he has changed his mind since then.

The two alternative accounts of death were meant to show that death is a good thing. About the first possibility, that death is nothing, Socrates' argument established that death is good for

14. See Translation nn. 126–129 and cf. *Odyssey* XI. For a useful discussion of the named men who populate Socrates' Hades, see George Anastaplo, "Human Being and Citizen: A Beginning to the Study of Plato's *Apology of Socrates*," in *Human Being and Citizen* (Chicago, 1975), pp. 20–24.
15. *Odyssey* XI.489–491.
16. See Translation n. 130.
17. P. 175 above.

someone whose life while awake is unhappy. The second possibility depends upon the truth of a transformed Homeric Hades which Socrates himself does not believe in. This life after death, in turn, depends upon the ability of the individual soul to survive and live without the body; Socrates cannòt prove that the soul has that ability. It seems that the goodness of death cannot be demonstrated.

Accordingly, when Socrates turns to his concluding remarks, he tells the men who voted for him that they should think that "there is nothing bad for a good man, whether living or dead, and that the gods are not without care for his troubles" (41c8–d2). He exhorts them to such beliefs as a matter of duty (*chrē*, 41c8) rather than argument, for they cannot be proved. The thought that the gods protect good men remains on the level of opinion, for there is no available knowledge about such things.

But Socrates is much more certain about his own particular case. He says, "Nor have my present troubles arisen of their own accord, but it is clear to me that it was now better for me to be dead and to have left troubles behind" (41d3–5). If his troubles did not arise by themselves, how did they come about? Did Socrates cause them himself? He may imply that he intentionally brought about his own condemnation because he thought "it was now better for me to be dead and to have left troubles behind." He does not say what "troubles" he is leaving behind.

According to Xenophon's account, Socrates' old age was the most important consideration in his decision to die. He thereby escaped the most burdensome part of life, when one becomes less capable of thought and the senses gradually grow weaker. A man who is seventy years old must look forward to the eventual decline of his faculties as he grows older. Socrates' statement in Plato's *Apology* about the troubles he is leaving behind may refer to these approaching hardships of old age.[18]

Socrates declares that he is not very vexed with his accusers, although they deserve blame for intending to harm him (41d6–e1). He asks them to treat his sons just as he treated the Athe-

18. See n. 16 above; *Crito* 43b10–11; Leo Strauss, "On Plato's *Apology of Socrates* and *Crito*," in *Essays in Honor of Jacob Klein* (Annapolis, Md., 1976), pp. 162–164; James Riddell, ed., *The Apology of Plato* (1877; repr. New York, 1973), p. 107.

nians: to examine them, and to reproach them if "they are reputed to be something when they are nothing." Apparently, for the purpose of raising his sons, he expects the citizens hostile to philosophy to be better suited than his imitators and admirers. He thereby tacitly indicates his practical agreement with his accusers about the proper education for the young—or at least for most of the young, those of less than outstanding capacity. Socrates mentions his sons just after he speaks of "leaving troubles behind." Raising children is an onerous task which he gladly escapes.[19] Finally, after reaffirming his knowledge of ignorance, Socrates takes his leave of his listeners: only the god knows whether life or death is a better thing. The tales of his third speech furnish no secure ground for the philosophic questioner who refuses to be satisfied with opinions without knowledge.

Socrates' life is now complete. He has stated the decisive questions about human excellence and happiness and has investigated them as far as he is able. Death at such a time cannot properly be called tragic, nor, perhaps, even sad. It would seem more properly viewed as a fitting end to a career that has reached its natural conclusion. Within the limits of what he was, Socrates has lived a perfect life. It remains to climax that life with an appropriate death. Moreover, Socrates knows that those who come after him will remember him as a just and wise man (38c).[20] His posthumous reputation will in some way coincide with his true worth, and the life-long disparity between his appearance and the truth will finally be overcome. As the newly admired paradigm of philosophy, the image of the dying Socrates will now, after death, become able to inspire men to respect the philosophic life.[21]

Socrates does establish a kind of unity in his life by accepting in deed, for his body, what he denies in speech for his soul, the authority of the city's laws. He shows this by his refusal to escape from prison and by his calm imbibing of the deadly drug when it is time for him to die. But he does not succeed in making his life a harmonious whole because he cannot reconcile soul

19. *Crito* 45c8–d6.
20. *Phaedo* end; Xenophon *Memorabilia* IV.8.10, *Apology* 7.
21. *Phaedo* passim; Nietzsche, *Birth of Tragedy*, section 13 end.

and body, philosophy and citizenship. They are left in unresolved tension because he must pursue the good by philosophizing, yet he must also bow to the city's rule over his body as long as he cannot change the Athenians' opinions and political order through his philosophic education. Socrates neither flees into a life of the mind that remains oblivious to its political context, nor does he embrace a preference for his fatherland over his own soul. His life's end comprises a profound gesture of obedience to each of the two great authorities over him, but he does not and cannot finally choose one over the other or pay consistent homage to both. Being neither entirely of this world nor beyond it, he achieves a singly-principled existence only after the death of his body, in the works of Plato, where, as a character in the dialogues, Socrates lives on as a disembodied image whose being consists in pure speech.

Analytical Outline of
the *Apology of Socrates*

The outline shows the structure of the *Apology* in three ways. The main outline gives the broad divisions of the *Apology* as a whole. At the left margin are shown the four pairs of sections that correspond to the four groups of human beings examined by Socrates in his attempt to refute the Delphic oracle (21c3–22e5). On the right are listed the fifteen sections which, in alternating sequence, deal with the "impiety" and "corruption of the young" parts of the charge against Socrates.

Appendix

Bibliography

Adkins, Arthur W. H. *Merit and Responsibility.* Oxford: Clarendon Press, 1960.

Anastaplo, George. "Human Being and Citizen: A Beginning to the Study of the *Apology of Socrates.*" In *Human Being and Citizen: Essays on Virtue, Freedom, and the Common Good.* Chicago: Swallow Press, 1975. Pp. 8–29, 233–246.

Bernadete, Seth. "Achilles and Hector: The Homeric Hero." Ph.D. dissertation, University of Chicago, 1955.

――. "Achilles and the Iliad." *Hermes* 91 (1963), 1–16.

――. "The *Aristeia* of Diomedes and the Plot of the Iliad." *Agon* 2 (1968), 10–38.

――. "The Daimonion of Socrates: A Study of Plato's *Theages.*" M.A. thesis, University of Chicago, 1953.

――. "Some Misquotations of Homer in Plato." *Phronesis* 8 (1963), 173–178.

Benveniste, Emile. *Indo-European Language and Society.* Trans. Elizabeth Palmer. Coral Gables, Fla.: University of Miami Press, 1973.

Bloom, Allan. "An Interpretation of Plato's *Ion.*" *Interpretation* 1 (Summer 1970), 43–62.

――, trans. and ed. *The Republic of Plato.* New York: Basic Books, 1968.

Brann, Eva. "The Music of the *Republic.*" *Agon* 1 (April 1967), 1–117.

――. "The Offense of Socrates: A Re-reading of Plato's *Apology.*" *Interpretation* 7 (May 1978), 1–21.

Burnet, John, ed. *Plato's Euthyphro, Apology of Socrates, and Crito.* Oxford: Clarendon Press, 1924.

Clay, Diskin. "Socrates' Mulishness and Heroism." *Phronesis* 17 (1972), 53–60.

Croiset, Maurice, ed. *Platon: Oeuvres Complètes.* Vol. 1. Paris: Société d'Edition "Les Belles Lettres," 1920.

Cropsey, Joseph. "Political Life and a Natural Order." In *Political Phi-*

Bibliography

losophy and the Issues of Politics. Chicago: University of Chicago Press, 1977. Pp. 221–230.

Derenne, Eudore. *Les procès d'impiété intentés aux philosophes à Athènes au Vme et au IVme siècles avant J.-C.* 1930; repr. New York: Arno, 1976.

Diels, Hermann, ed. *Die Fragmente der Vorsokratiker.* 3 vols. 16th ed. Zurich: Weidmann, 1972.

Dodds, E. R., ed. *Plato: Gorgias: A Revised Text with Introduction and Commentary.* Oxford: Clarendon Press, 1959.

Dover, K. J., ed. *Aristophanes: Clouds.* Oxford: Clarendon Press, 1968.

Friedländer, Paul. *Plato.* 3 vols. New York: Pantheon, 1958–1969. Vol. 2, *The Dialogues: First Period.*

Fustel de Coulanges, Numa Denis. *The Ancient City: A Study on the Religion, Laws, and Institutions of Greece and Rome.* Garden City, N.Y.: Doubleday Anchor, n.d.

Gadamer, Hans-Georg. Review of *Platos Apologie,* by Erwin Wolff. *Göttingische Gelehrte Anzeigen* 5 (1931), 193–199.

Guardini, Romano. *The Death of Socrates: An Interpretation of the Platonic Dialogues: Euthyphro, Apology, Crito, and Phaedo.* Trans. Basil Wrighton. Cleveland and New York: World Publishing Co., Meridian Books, 1962.

Guthrie, W. K. C. *Socrates.* Cambridge: Cambridge University Press, 1971.

Hackforth, Reginald. *The Composition of Plato's "Apology."* Cambridge: Cambridge University Press, 1933.

Havelock, Eric A. "The Socratic Self as It Is Parodied in Aristophanes' *Clouds.*" *Yale Classical Studies* 22: *Studies in Fifth-Century Thought and Literature.* Ed. Adam Parry. Cambridge: Cambridge University Press, 1972. Pp. 1–18.

————. "Why Was Socrates Tried?" In *Studies in Honour of Gilbert Norwood.* Ed. Mary E. White. *Phoenix* suppl. vol. 1. Toronto: University of Toronto Press, 1952. Pp. 95–109.

Hegel, Georg W. F. *Werke.* 20 vols. Frankfurt a. M.: Suhrkamp, 1971. Vols. 18–20, *Vorlesungen über die Geschichte der Philosophie,* I–III.

Heidegger, Martin. *An Introduction to Metaphysics.* Trans. Ralph Manheim. Garden City, N.Y.: Doubleday Anchor, 1961.

————. *Nietzsche.* 2 vols. 2d ed. Pfullingen: Neske, 1961.

————. *What Is Called Thinking?* Trans. J. Glenn Gray and F. Wieck. New York: Harper & Row, 1968.

————. "The Word of Nietzsche: 'God Is Dead.'" In *The Question Concerning Technology and Other Essays.* New York: Harper Colophon, 1977. Pp. 53–112.

Hildebrandt, Kurt. *Platon: Logos und Mythos.* 2d ed. Berlin: Walter de Gruyter, 1959.

Jaeger, Werner. *Paideia: The Ideals of Greek Culture.* Trans. Gilbert Highet. Vol. 1, *Archaic Greece; The Mind of Athens.* 2d ed. Vol. 2, *In Search of the Divine Center.* New York: Oxford University Press, 1943–1945.

Jaekel, Werner, and Siegfried Erasmus. *Lehrerkommentar zu Platons Apologie*. Stuttgart: Klett, n.d.

Jebb, R. C. *The Attic Orators from Antiphon to Isaeos*. 2 vols. 2d ed. London: Macmillan, 1893.

Kendall, Willmoore. "The People versus Socrates Revisited." In *Willmoore Kendall Contra Mundum*. New Rochelle, N.Y.: Arlington House, 1971. Pp. 149–167.

Kirk, G. S., and J. E. Raven. *The Presocratic Philosophers: A Critical History with a Selection of Texts*. Cambridge: Cambridge University Press, 1957.

Klein, Jacob. *A Commentary on Plato's Meno*. Chapel Hill, N.C.: University of North Carolina Press, 1965.

———. "On Plato's *Phaedo*." *The College* [alumni magazine published by St. John's College, Annapolis, Md.] 26 (January 1975), 1–10.

———. "Plato's *Ion*." *Claremont Journal of Public Affairs* 2 (Spring 1973), 23–37.

Knox, Bernard M. W. *The Heroic Temper: Studies in Sophoclean Tragedy*. Berkeley: University of California Press, 1964.

Krüger, Gerhard. *Einsicht und Leidenschaft: Das Wesen des platonischen Denkens*. 4th ed. Frankfurt a. M.: Klostermann, 1973.

MacDowell, Douglas, ed. *Andokides: On the Mysteries*. Oxford: Clarendon Press, 1962.

Mahdi, Muhsin, ed. and trans. *Alfarabi's "Philosophy of Plato and Aristotle."* Rev. ed. Ithaca, N.Y.: Cornell University Press, Agora Paperback Editions, 1969.

Mansfield, Harvey C., Jr. "Liberal Democracy as a Mixed Regime." *The Alternative: An American Spectator* 8 (June/July 1975), 8–12.

Marrou, H. I. *A History of Education in Antiquity*. Trans. George Lamb. New York: Sheed and Ward, 1956.

Maximus of Tyre. *Orationes*. Ed. H. Hobein. Leipzig: Teubner, 1910.

Meyer, Thomas. *Platons Apologie*. Stuttgart: Kohlhammer, 1962.

Nauck, August, ed. *Tragicorum Graecorum Fragmenta*. 2d ed. Leipzig: Teubner, 1889.

Neumann, Harry. "Plato's *Defense of Socrates*: An Interpretation of Ancient and Modern Sophistry." *Liberal Education* 56 (October 1970), 458–475.

The Oxford Classical Dictionary. Ed. N. G. L. Hammond and H. H. Scullard. 2d ed. Oxford: Clarendon Press, 1970.

Plato. *Opera Omnia*. Ed. John Burnet. 5 vols. Oxford: Clarendon Press, 1900–1907.

Razi, Muhammed b. Zakariyya al-. *The Book on the Way of the Philosopher*. Trans. Edward J. Erler. Mimeographed typescript. Translated from Paul Kraus, "Raziana I," *Orientalia* 4 (1935), 300–334.

Redfield, James. "A Lecture on Plato's *Apology*." *Journal of General Education* 15 (July 1963), 93–108.

Riddell, James, ed. *The Apology of Plato*. 1877; repr. New York: Arno, 1973.

Bibliography

Rosen, Stanley. *Plato's "Symposium."* New Haven: Yale University Press, 1968.

Sallis, John. *Being and Logos: The Way of Platonic Dialogue.* Pittsburgh: Duquesne University Press, 1975.

Scholia Platonica. Ed. William Chase Greene. Haverford, Pa.: American Philological Association, 1938.

Sesonske, Alexander. "To Make the Weaker Argument Defeat the Stronger." *Journal of the History of Philosophy* 6 (July 1968), 217–231.

Sinaiko, Herman L. *Love, Knowledge, and Discourse in Plato: Dialogue and Dialectic in "Phaedrus," "Republic," "Parmenides."* Chicago: University of Chicago Press, 1965.

Strauss, Leo. *The City and Man.* Chicago: Rand McNally, 1964.

——. "On Plato's *Apology of Socrates* and *Crito.*" In *Essays in Honor of Jacob Klein.* Annapolis, Md.: St. John's College Press, 1976. Pp. 155–170.

——. "Plato" and "Niccolo Machiavelli." In *History of Political Philosophy.* Ed. Leo Strauss and Joseph Cropsey. 2d ed. Chicago: Rand McNally, 1972. Pp. 7–63, 271–292.

——. "Plato's *Symposium.*" Mimeographed transcript of a course given at the University of Chicago, 1959.

——. *Socrates and Aristophanes.* New York: Basic Books, 1966.

——. *What Is Political Philosophy? and Other Studies.* New York: Free Press, 1959.

——. *Xenophon's Socrates.* Ithaca, N.Y.: Cornell University Press, 1972.

——. *Xenophon's Socratic Discourse: An Interpretation of the "Oeconomicus."* Ithaca, N.Y.: Cornell University Press, 1970.

Taylor, A. E. *Plato: The Man and His Work.* 7th ed. London: Methuen, 1960.

——. *Socrates: The Man and His Thought.* Garden City, N.Y.: Doubleday Anchor, 1953.

Vlastos, Gregory, ed. *The Philosophy of Socrates: A Collection of Critical Essays.* Garden City, N.Y.: Doubleday Anchor, 1971.

Vogel, C. J. de. "The Present State of the Socratic Problem." *Phronesis* 1 (November 1955), 26–35.

Weber, Franz J., ed. *Platons Apologie des Sokrates.* Paderborn: Schoeningh, 1971.

West, M. L., ed. *Iambi et Elegi Graeci ante Alexandrum Cantati.* 2 vols. Oxford: Clarendon Press, 1971–1972.

West, Thomas G. "Phenomenological Psychology and Aristotelian Politics." Revision of a paper delivered at the 1976 Annual Meeting of the American Political Science Association. Mimeographed.

Wolff, Erwin. *Platos Apologie.* Berlin: Weidmann, 1929.

Zeller, Eduard. *Die Philosophie der Griechen in ihrer geschichtlichen Entwicklung.* 5th ed., 1922; repr. Darmstadt: Wissenschaftliche Buchgesellschaft, 1963. Part 2, vol. 1, *Sokrates und die Sokratiker; Plato und die alte Akademie.*

Index of Authors

Index of Authors

Shakespeare, William, 170
Sinaiko, Herman L., 120n
Sophocles, 67n, 74n, 215n
Strauss, Leo, 19, 54n, 67n, 71n, 83n,
   87n, 88n, 90n, 103n, 104n, 111n,
   124n, 145n, 146n, 165n, 169n,
   171n, 185n, 186n, 187n, 211n,
   217n, 230n

Taylor, A. E., 71n
Thucydides, 17n, 60n, 66n

Vergil, 151
Vlastos, Gregory, 88n
Vogel, C. J. de, 88n

Weber, Franz J., 169n, 173n
West, M. L., 54n
West, Thomas G., 116n
White, Mary E., 98n
Wolff, Erwin, 71n, 129n, 215n

Xenophanes, 74n
Xenophon, 17n, 19, 51n, 52n, 54n,
   57n, 61–66n, 79n, 87–89, 92–95,
   98n, 104n, 107n, 115n, 124, 126n,
   132, 137, 144n, 149, 158n, 172n,
   173, 184n, 188, 191n, 192–193,
   199n, 215n, 216, 217n, 224, 226–
   228, 230, 231n

Zeller, Eduard, 99n, 124n

Plato's *Apology of Socrates*

Designed by Richard E. Rosenbaum.
Composed by The Composing Room of Michigan, Inc.
in 10 point VIP Palatino, 2 points leaded,
with display lines in Palatino.
Printed offset by Thomson/Shore, Inc.
on Warren's Number 66 Text, 50 pound basis
Bound by John H. Dekker & Sons, Inc.
in Holliston Book Cloth
and stamped in All Purpose foil.

Library of Congress Cataloging in Publication Data
(For library cataloging purposes only)

West, Thomas G   1945–
   Plato's "Apology of Socrates."

   Bibliography: p.
   Includes index.
   1. Plato. Apologia.   2.   Socrates.   I.   Plato.
Apologia. English. 1979.   II.   Title.
B365.W47   184   78-11532
ISBN 0-8014-1127-0